Christian Glo

HYLA DOC

HYLA DOC

Surgeon in China
Through War and Revolution
1924-1949

Edited by Elsie H. Landstrom

Q.E.D. Press
Fort Bragg, California

Published by Q.E.D. Press
155 Cypress Street
Fort Bragg, California 95437

Publicist: Elizabeth S. Allen
520 Old Post Road
Tolland, Connecticut 06084

Typeset in ITC Garamond by CompType, Inc., Fort Bragg, CA

Printed in the U.S.A.

Library of Congress Cataloging in Publications Data
Hyla Doc.
   Hyla Doc: Surgeon in China Through War and Revolution, 1924–1949,
 / edited by Elsie H. Landstrom.—1st ed.
     p. cm.
  Letters and memoirs of Hyla S. Watters.
  ISBN: 0-936609-19-2
  1. Hyla Doc.   2. Surgeons—United States—Biography.   3.Surgeons—
China—Biography. 4. China—History—Republic, 1912–1949.
I. Landstrom, Elsie H.   II. Title.
RD27.35.H95A3   1990
951.04′092 -dc20
  [B]   90-40637
                                         CIP

To the memory of my husband
Norman Landstrom
who made this book possible

Hyla Doc, 1930s, with a patient who had a large piece of diseased bone removed from her shin, then returned to loading iron ore on ships at the bund. *(Howard A. Smith)*

CONTENTS

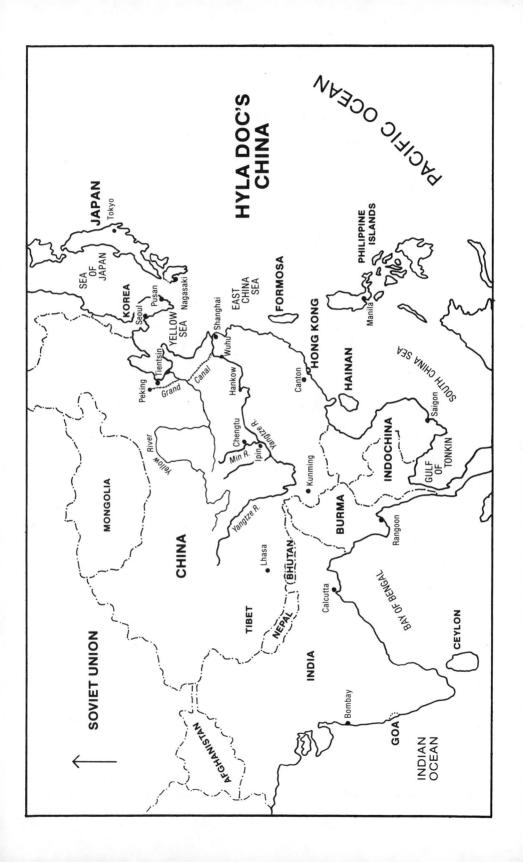

HYLA DOC'S CHINA

PACIFIC OCEAN

SOVIET UNION

JAPAN
Tokyo

SEA
OF
JAPAN

KOREA
Seoul
Pusan
Nagasaki

YELLOW
SEA

Shanghai
Wuhu

EAST
CHINA
SEA

FORMOSA

HONG KONG

PHILIPPINE
ISLANDS

Manila

Peking
Tientsin
Grand Canal

Hankow

Canton

HAINAN

SOUTH CHINA SEA

Yellow River

Chengtu
Min R.
Ipin
Yangtze R.

Kunming

Saigon

INDOCHINA

GULF
OF
TONKIN

MONGOLIA

CHINA

Yangtze R.

Lhasa

BHUTAN

BURMA

Rangoon

TIBET

NEPAL

Calcutta

AFGHANISTAN

INDIA

Bombay

BAY OF BENGAL

GOA

CEYLON

INDIAN
OCEAN

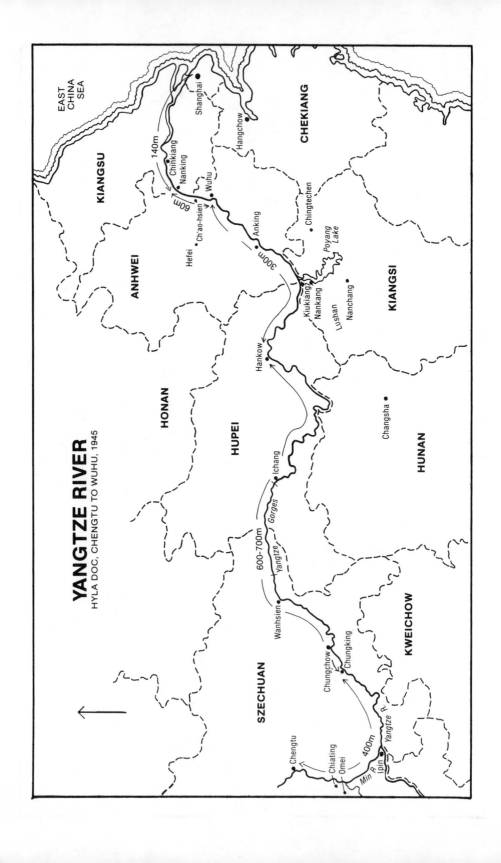

YANGTZE RIVER

HYLA DOC, CHENGTU TO WUHU, 1945

EAST CHINA SEA

KIANGSU

ANHWEI

HONAN

HUPEI

SZECHUAN

KWEICHOW

HUNAN

KIANGSI

CHEKIANG

Shanghai

Hangchow

Chinkiang
Nanking

Wuhu

Ch'ao-hsien

Hefei

Anking

Chingtechen

Poyang Lake

Kiukiang
Nankang

Lushan

Nanchang

Hankow

Changsha

Ichang

Yangtze Gorges

600-700m

Wanhsien

Chungchow

Chungking

Chengtu

Chiating

Omei

Ipin

Min R.

Yangtze R.

400m

140m

60m

300m

Foreword

Hyla S. Watters, known as "Hyla Doc" to distinguish the surgeon from other Hylas in her family, sat at the big table that centered the main room of Birchwood, her cottage on the edge of the woods above the Raquette River in Tupper Lake, New York. It was 1985 and Hyla Doc was ninety-two years old, but with considerable gusto she helped me to sort out a pile of letters we had unearthed from cartons stored under Birchwood beds.

Written to her family whenever she could snatch a free moment, these letters told the story of her years as Chief Surgeon at Wuhu Hospital in Anhwei Province in China, 1925 through 1949, years of war and revolution that she chronicled vividly and with good humor.

Hyla Doc and I had been friends since 1925 when she came to live with my family in Wuhu. I was two years old. My father was an administrator of the Methodist Episcopal Central China Conference, primarily as Secretary/Treasurer, and sometimes stood in as superintendent of the hospital. My mother taught English to the nurses at the School of Nursing, who had no texts in Chinese. She also worked with women's and orphans' groups and ran our large home as a way-station for Yangtze travelers, both those from various missions and foreign businesses.

Until I was twelve, Hyla Doc was our neighbor and friend. As I grew old enough to be a likely candidate for the attentions of a born teacher, she took time out of her busy days to help me name the birds and plants and stars, how to signal the British and U.S.

warships on the Yangtze. She turned the hospital into my playground and classroom, had me hold x-rays while she explained what she did during surgery. Her exuberant welcome of whatever life brought, her sense of fairness, her joy, colored my world and struck a responsive chord in me that has echoed all my life.

Old in years (although it was unthinkable to regard anyone so youthful in spirit as elderly), Hyla Doc became a gracious lady, undemanding, slow to judge. But she was not always so. In her youth and exuberance and delight in work well done, she was impatient with minds slower than her own, tart with sloppy performance, demanding of those who trained under her. Some of the Chinese nurses feared her; some of the foreign children too, although this side of her I never experienced.

Because large gaps were left in her letters when she was unable to take time from the demands of surgery to write, or was on some perilous journey, and because there were none of the stories of her childhood that I remembered her telling, I had a tape recorder going as she pushed herself up to her full four feet eight, and walked over to the stone fireplace to add a log to the fire with shaking hands.

"It's not at all certain I was born," Hyla Doc chuckled. "When I needed a passport to go to the London School of Tropical Medicine in 1923, I could find no record of my birth. But my brother, Philip, swore before a notary that he remembered the day—and that the doctor who delivered me had to forego the international yacht races to which he had tickets. I always felt I owed that doctor an apology."

On 13 October 1893, her older brother and sister, Philip and Florence, were packed off to dig to China among the tomatoes. When they dashed back into the kitchen of the parsonage in Dobbs Ferry, New York, to report an unsuccessful dig, they had a new sister. No one suspected this squally baby would be the one to reach China, then chalk up a distinguished career as Chief Surgeon at the Wuhu Hospital.

After graduating from Smith College in 1915 with a major in philosophy, Hyla Doc taught for a year at Atlanta University at the urging of her father. A Methodist pastor, Philip Watters was then president of Gammon Theological Seminary in Atlanta. He was skeptical of her plan to go to China and knew she had an irregular heartbeat. But since childhood Hyla Doc had gathered up and mended birds with broken wings, dogs and cats with broken legs. She knew she wanted to be a surgeon. Her interest in China dated from the age of eight when she read a story about a Chinese child that made a deep impression on her. This early interest was strengthened by the tales of returned missionaries from China, who spoke in her father's churches, and by family values placed on service to others. China looked like a place of great adventure and a place where she could be of service.

To be a surgeon and to go to China combined in firm resolve, and in 1921 Hyla Doc earned her M.D. from Cornell Medical School (with her father's blessing), one of six women in the class of thirty-six. She interned at Bellevue Hospital in New York and took a second year at Morristown Hospital in New Jersey. On completing the course at the London School of Tropical Medicine, Hyla Doc was in 1924 conjointly awarded the Diploma in Tropical Medicine and Hygiene by the Royal College of Surgeons of England and the Royal College of Physicians of London.

Hyla Doc's medical work in China continued a tradition begun in 1834 when Peter Parker, sent by the Congregationalists, opened Canton's first eye clinic. The Methodist Church bought land at Wuhu in 1881 on a promontory above the Yangtze called I-chi-shan, but it was not until 1 October 1889 that the first small, wooden, smoky, fly-ridden hospital opened its doors to patients.

When Hyla Doc arrived in Wuhu, a modern hospital was in the making. The first small hospital, where families camped at bedsides, tied chickens to bedposts and insisted on being present en masse during surgery, had burned down in 1923 while the surgeon was operating. All the patients were safely evacuated. The burned bricks were carefully cleaned and set aside in the hope of a new building, but for four years two men's wards, the examining room and surgery, were housed in primitive buildings thrown up at the foot of the hill. The Women's Annex had partially survived the fire and was affectionately called "The Ark" by the newcomer on the scene, Hyla Doc, who found its roof leaking so badly that she had to employ a servant to hold an umbrella over her and her patients. The Ark's halls were often filled with smoke from the kitchen on its first floor, which also provided its heat, and her surgical patients were carried by stretcher down the hill in all sorts of weather to the surgery near the gatehouse.

Mission files are jammed with reports of controversies surrounding the construction of the new hospital in which two strong-willed men were involved. Frank P. Gaunt was superintendent when Robert E. Brown arrived, and it was Gaunt's vision and initiative that brought the new hospital into focus. He is remembered as a brave, able, intelligent and dedicated man, well-liked by his patients and those who did not have to work under his direction. But those who did found it impossible to work cohesively, and it became clear to the presiding bishop that he must be returned to America and Robert Brown assigned the responsibility to bring the building plans to fruition.

Designed by McKim, Mead & White, leading architects in the United States known for their plans of the Pennsylvania Railroad Station and Columbia University in New York, and the Boston Public Library, the new plant was underwritten half by the China Medical Board of the Rockefeller Foundation and half by the Methodist Church. When it opened 8 December 1927, without a day of construction missed despite occupation by southern soldiers on Chiang's Northern Expedition, Wuhu General Hospital easily ranked with the finest facilities in the United States.

This is the hospital that stands on the banks of the Yangtze at Wuhu today. Damaged almost to destruction by occupying Japanese troops during the Sino-Japanese War (1937-1945), and again during the Cultural Revolution after 1966, Wuhu I-chi-shan Hospital has now grown to seven hundred beds. It is today the teaching hospital for Wannan Medical College, the leading Anhwei provincial medical school.

Hyla Doc's quarter century in China coincided with a time of great confusion; few, either Chinese or Westerner, understood the forces at work. When she arrived in October 1924, for her year at Nanking Language School before plunging into the grueling schedule at Wuhu, China was well into the years of the warlords, soon followed by uneasy and partial unification under Chiang Kai-shek in 1928. Bandits (China's most visible form of unemployment), warlords and Nationalist Party (Kuomintang) armies moved about in bewildering directions made even more confusing when Chiang expelled the Communists from the Kuomintang in 1927. Chinese villagers in the countryside, with no central authority to protect them, suffered the most. Foreigners, who had taken advantage of chaos (in the nineteenth century as China's last dynasty came to an end) to claim privileges for themselves, in turn became easy targets for Chinese frustrations. The years of Hyla Doc's career in China all fell within this turbulent transitional period between the downfall of the Ch'ing dynasty in 1912, and the founding of the People's Republic of China in 1949.

In 1926 Chiang launched the Northern Expedition envisioned by Sun Yat-sen to reunify China, and brought enough stability to undertake modernization programs in transportation and communication, industrialization, health and education. Because of their long experience in China in many such programs, Western missionaries took part at Chiang's invitation. But what might have been a promising start toward modernizing and unifying the country, disintegrated under natural disasters on a grand scale, official corruption and short-sightedness, war with Japan and civil war with the Communists. By 1949 the missionaries, indistinguishable to the triumphant Communists from cultural imperialists, and far too closely linked to Chiang's programs to be trusted, became a danger to their Chinese friends and began to leave the country. Over the next several years Christian missions in China came to an end.

Throughout the years that Hyla Doc worked in China, ancient Chinese culture was undergoing immense change under the impact of its opening to the West. Hyla Doc was alert to both differences and similarities between China and the West, and spelled them out in her letters as she encountered them in everyday life. She admired the Chinese people, their fortitude and good humor in the midst of enormous suffering. She was deeply attracted to the beauty of their land and to their temples where she found priests who spoke of eternal verities with which she could identify. She sympathized with China's promising, patriotic and idealistic young people who tried to seize the new opportunities opening to them, to voice their nation's heart-desire to be a free people. She recorded her role in presenting such opportunities to which China's young people responded with enthusiasm, unaware she played such a role or that again and again, even to the present time, their demonstrations would burst out only to be silenced once more.

Hyla Doc put her role of healer ahead of personal comfort or safety. In 1927, after the Nanking Incident only sixty miles away, in which six foreigners were killed, others injured and evacuated under protective fire from warships on the Yangtze as Southern troops moved into the city on Chiang's Northern Expedition, she operated until the last possible moment before being evacuated. In 1928, before Western women were allowed upriver, she returned to her hospital by stowing away on a British steamer.

During the relatively peaceful years of flood, famine and epidemic that followed, she involved in the work of the hospital the medical officers of both the British and United States navies patrolling the Yangtze. They were glad of a chance to practice their skills, and the hospital benefitted from their assistance. Hyla Doc learned how to signal in Morse Code to keep them posted with operating schedules; and the navy signalmen passed on through her to the foreign community news that would otherwise have arrived days later. During the first years of the war between Japan and China, assistance given Wuhu Hospital by ships of both U.S. and British navies in large part kept the hospital from closing down.

After Pearl Harbor in 1941, Hyla Doc had to send home all her patients, well or dying, so that the hospital could be turned over to the Japanese Army. She was confined to the Episcopal Sisters' compound in Wuhu until interned in Shanghai in July 1942. Repatriated to America in October 1943 on the Swedish liner, *Gripsholm*, she soon wangled a place aboard an enormous U.S. Army troop ship heading back across the Pacific. Under Army orders she reached West China from India over The Hump, as the Himalayas were known. She was on Mt. Omei, in Szechuan Province, in 1945 when news of Hiroshima reached her. With a huge document supplied by the Chinese National Health Service that authorized her to take back Wuhu Hospital from the Japanese, Hyla Doc made her way by sampan and steamer the 1500 turbulent Yangtze miles downriver to Wuhu. There she rebuilt the services that had been destroyed by the Japanese. In December 1949, Communist forces were only a mile away across the Yangtze. Chinese friends urged her departure, and when she understood that her presence endangered them she caught the first train out, ending her career in China.

But her work as a medical missionary continued in the small jungle village of Ganta, Liberia, where she was assigned in 1950. There in West Africa she spent the next eleven years learning a new language, exploring a new culture and establishing a much needed medical service in the bush. Her zest for adventure and grace under stress never deserted her. At the age of sixty-seven, when she reluctantly accepted the decision of the Methodist Board of Foreign Missions not to reappoint her to Liberia, she took that decision as an opportunity to set out on foot, with one companion, to cross Africa. By hitching rides on bush-hopping planes, trucks and busses traveling desert stretches, she explored Tombouctou and Khartoum, floated down the Nile to Luxor and Cairo, and fulfilled a lifetime dream touring Israel. A small Israeli freighter, rounding the Mediterranean and crossing the Atlantic, delivered her safely to Montreal three months after she left Ganta.

Born into a Methodist parsonage family during the days when pastors were moved frequently, Hyla Doc was happiest at the family Tupper Lake summer camp, the only home she knew. Back in Tupper Lake from Africa, Hyla Doc worked at the Sunmount Veterans Administration Hospital. In 1967, when it switched from serving veterans to caring for the retarded, she stayed on for a short time, then retired to private practice. That year she was named "Woman Of The Year" by the Women's Medical Society of New York, and in 1969, "Woman Of All The Years" by the Business and Professional Women of Tupper Lake. In 1950 Smith College had conferred on her the honorary degree, Doctor of Science.

In 1980, when Hyla Doc was eighty-seven years old, colleagues urged her to consider her age and the hazards of remaining in practice as lawsuits became more popular. This moment of decision coincided with the easing of restrictions on travel to China, so she sold her car and used the money to return to China to renew old friendships and lecture to students at the new medical college connected with Wuhu Hospital.

Until the last year of her life, Hyla Doc continued to speak to American audiences about both China and Liberia, her messages always those that touched the spirit. In recognition of this spoken ministry, in 1953 she had been ordained at the 120th Annual Conference of the Methodist Episcopal Church of the Republic of Liberia.

Toward the end of her life Hyla Doc needed a cane, two hearing aids so uncomfortable she seldom wore them, a pacemaker, and to read her voluminous mail two magnifying glasses taped together. She had one bypass operation and two minor heart attacks, but the will that propelled her through nearly a century of adventures remained strong. In July 1987, when I reached her in intensive care, she seized pencil and paper and scribbled directives about the book we were engaged in editing together.

That will seems to have been the outstanding characteristic of the many colorful characters that grew on her family tree. Talent, initiative, intelligence and imagination converged in Hyla Doc through a long line of vigorous and able ancestors from both sides of her family. Generally law-abiding, they rode over opposition, particularly bureaucratic, but always on the side of principle and for the good of the individual as they saw it. In Hyla Doc this took the form of the missionary impulse. A special ability, running through the generations of these several families from England, Ireland, France and Germany, flowered in Hyla Doc. She was a born storyteller.

Foreword

This gift came to the service of her deepest love, her family, in a stream of letters that reflect her eager interest in people, how they lived and worked and dressed, what they ate, their hopes and sorrows, and what they believed. The letters disclose her fascination with how mechanical things work, her exuberant love of the sea and ships, of dogs, big dogs, of flowers and trees, insects, birds and stars. She was at home anywhere in the world life took her, voluble about what she saw and learned, always ready to alter her opinions in the face of new understandings. She struck up conversations with everyone she met, through sign language if necessary, entered their names in the fat address book that went everywhere with her, and became a part of their lives.

Full of stories and jokes, always the ready teacher, Hyla Doc was silent about her personal life, tongue-tied when it came to sorrow. There is no record in her spoken or written words of the death of her father; only one letter, written months after the event, of the death of her mother; nothing at all about two young missionaries, whose baby she had delivered, killed by the Communists.

Hyla Doc was equally comfortable with men and women and had many friends of both sexes. There was never a whisper of romance, and she merely smiled silently when asked about that part of her life. She had a delight in food and an intellectual interest in recipes, which she collected, but the height of her homemaking abilities found expression in peanut butter sandwiches. Single-minded in her role as surgeon, she gave an unqualified "No!" when asked whether she regretted not having children. She had had quite enough children among her nieces and nephews, she said, and the waifs and strays that were always a part of her household. Indeed, as some of us children noticed in relation to her, she was impatient with infants and small children and took an interest only when we were old enough to be taught. She saw potential doctors and nurses everywhere, and her role was to teach them what she knew.

Hyla Doc never had a problem being a woman in her profession. If any of the men around her were put off by her drive, she was either unaware of how they felt or ignored it, and soon won them over into professional admirers and eager colleagues, or good pals on some lark.

Hyla Doc was thoroughly at ease with who she was and wasted no time or energy wishing she were someone other. Above all, she showed that life for a woman can be meaningful and fulfilled and joyful in other than a conventional role. Hers was an upbeat world; her favorite word was "joy."

When Hyla Doc read the collected materials used as a base for this book, she wanted to make substantive changes, to correct the vision of the young Hyla she saw to have been something of a fool. Fortunately for us, there was no time left for her to edit away the young Hyla's fresh impressions of China, nor to dilute her record of the interaction of Western and Chinese culture. China was in a period of vast and crucial change; Hyla Doc was young and eager to understand, with an eye quick to note and a hand to record.

When I said to Hyla Doc that it was an impressive story, she responded slowly, "What impresses me about it is that it is the story of the goodness of God." Never one to foist her religious beliefs on others but to learn what it was they believed, Hyla Doc did not hesitate to speak of her own convictions. God was very real to her. Through all the griefs and hardships and challenges of her life, she voiced a constant thanks to God for the loveliness of the world and the goodness of people, for the countless times in which a way opened before her to do what she felt called to do.

On 3 August 1987 Hyla Doc's heart gave out. When she died, the remnant of her letters was left in my hands. As I gathered them together I could see her exuberant figure seated at her typewriter, "Chatty" Remington, propped on her knees or handy on a suitcase or upended trunk on docks, ocean liners, Yangtze steamers, on trains crossing Europe and India, Japan and Korea, wherever she lit even briefly in the African bush. Torn and creased, some pages missing, many of them carbons or on flimsy paper "liberated" from a building owned by the railroad when the order was given to destroy Wuhu as the Japanese approached in 1937, the letters were falling apart.

Foreword

Shel Horowitz, of *Accurate Writing and More* in Northampton, undertook the enormous job of retyping these letters. Fortunately, to fill in gaps, Elizabeth Allen (Hyla Doc's niece) and her husband Daniel and I had taped many stories. But there remained pages of questions to ask Hyla Doc. Many remain mysteries, but some answers were found and spliced into her story from letters from her mother, Ada Stowell Watters, and from other members of the I-chi-shan community: Robert E. Brown and Mae Willis Brown, Frances Culley, Florence Sayles, Loren Morgan and Ruth Morgan, and from my father, Paul G. Hayes. For the loan of the Morgan Papers, which covered the Japanese occupation of Wuhu while Hyla Doc stewed in Manila aching to be there, I am indebted to their son, Carrel Morgan; for early history of Wuhu hospital, I thank the General Commission on Archives and History of the United Methodist Church, and archivist William C. Beal; and my gratitude to Smith College Archives for use of a manuscript Hyla Doc wrote about her early years and the impact of Smith on her. For the story of John and Betty Stam's deaths at the hands of the Communists in 1934, I had four sources: my father's account written for the *Shanghai Evening Post and Gazette*, "The Triumph of John and Betty Stam," by Mrs. Howard Taylor and published by the China Inland Mission, an unsigned letter among the Morgan Papers that I would attribute to George Birch of the China Inland Mission, and my own memories.

Hyla Doc passed through the magnificent Yangtze Gorges at the end of the war with Japan, with no time or paper to record more than a brief note of her awe. For this material I thank Lyman Van Slyke and his record in "Yangtze—Nature, History and The River." From my father's journals I cribbed descriptions of the old and new hospitals; here and there I added a fact from my own memory or made connective links. Historical notes were gleaned from various standard texts; some were supplied by Fred Drake, Professor of Chinese History at the University of Massachusetts in Amherst.

These resources were compiled into a document of more than a thousand pages for Hyla Doc's family and for various archives. It has been a joy to track down and put together Hyla Doc's remarkable story, adapted from these resources and told in her own vivid language as far as possible. Hyla Doc spelled Chinese names as they sounded to her, so with the help of Fred Drake these have been conformed to the Wade-Giles Romanization or to Atlas spellings. Of her time, Hyla Doc used words no longer approved, such as "coolie" and "amah," and spellings that today we would consider second, or English, usage. These I have left intact.

To complete these memoirs in Hyla Doc's absence I turned to many others for their help. Most generous with suggestions and corrections, and with his time, was Fred Drake. My indebtedness to him for helping to focus and clarify at many points is beyond adequate acknowledgment. Others who read the manuscript at various stages, and made valuable contributions out of their special expertise, include Douglas P. Fusonie, my surgeon; Corrinne Hardesty, former U.P.I. reporter and long-time friend; Kemp Tolley, Rear-Admiral, U.S. Navy Retired, who served on the Yangtze Patrol; Peter Wan, former Professor of American Literature at East China Normal University in Shanghai, now at Phillips Exeter Academy; and Indiana Governor, Edgar Whitcomb, whose life Hyla Doc saved during the war with Japan and with whom she shared internment in Shanghai.

Elise Bernier-Feeley and Elise Dennis, reference librarians at Forbes Library in Northampton, spent hours checking facts; Deborah Friedman typed the manuscript into a word processor; Martha Gordon drew the maps and Jennifer Curry took the cover photograph of Hyla Doc in 1987. Others who helped in various ways include Nancy Neill, Margaret Berry, members of Hyla Doc's family, my children, Peter and Ruth, and my sister, Lois Anderson.

To each of these generous people, and to patient and skillful members of Q.E.D. Press, especially my editor, John Fremont, I give thanks. Where errors are to be found, I alone am responsible.

My husband, Norman, gave unflagging, generous and wise support and counsel throughout. Before learning that the book would be published, he died suddenly while I was in China representing Hyla Doc at the Centennial celebration of Wuhu I-chi-shan Hospital.

Elsie Hayes Landstrom
Conway, Massachusetts

Hyla Doc's parents, Philip M. Watters and Ada S. Watters, at Tupper Lake.

Getting to China

1893-1924

The ship started to roll on the increasing swells that precede a storm, and scud blew across the deck below as I went top speed up to the crow's nest of the S.S. *President Van Buren* before anyone could change his mind about giving me permission to do so. Getting to China in my day was a marvelous adventure, and I had a most wonderful time mid-Pacific, high above the well deck where I could look down on the bridge and stay there through a heavy squall. Later the captain invited several of us up on the bridge, where I longed to take a try at the wheel, but had sense enough not to ask.

I spent a lot of that first Pacific crossing in 1924 up in the fo'c'sle, and did lookout there all afternoon as the storm came on. Its wind was Force 8, a moderate gale, but by supper it was too lively for even the official lookout.

He was sent to the flying bridge and I to a lower deck as the rolling of the ship set loose several big barrels of oil in the after well deck. They became animated, to the real danger of crew before they could capture and lash fast the runaways. Then the waves stove in one of our lifeboats and wrecked the radio aerial.

That night I watched the crew working in the brilliant light and black shadow of an electric torch to fix the aerial, with the boat rolling hard over, and the tops blown from the waves thrashing across above us. We were all soaking wet, and our Malay bos'n looked like an animated bronze dashing in and out of the light, barefooted, in a streaming red-brown rubber coat that matched his

1

face, hat gone, his wet, curly hair shining as it blew in the wind. The heavy water was inspiring, as big water always is.

I was lucky to be born with a zest for adventure. My earliest memory is of a tall ladder set up against two young maples, the summer before I was three. I managed to climb to the top rung, where I hung onto the two trees and called, "Mama, what shall I do next?" Mother, who had a horror of heights, climbed up the ladder, calmly told me to put my arms around her neck, and then, to my great disappointment, instead of going on up, she took me back down.

At six I undertook my first marine expedition. With a three-year-old cousin as passenger, on a very small raft with a piece of board for paddle, we pushed off from New York with our eyes on the blue hills of Vermont across Lake Champlain. Our parents had taken the two rowboats and gone fishing; our aunts couldn't swim. But they discovered what we had done and knew that once we got out of our sheltered bay the big waves would wash us off the raft.

They called and called, but we did not recognize the aunts as constituted authority, and kept on paddling. By the goodness of God, the oldest of our generation of cousins was in camp. He could muster a big bass voice when needed, and besides, we knew Carl could swim. So when he ran down to the shore bawling at us to come back, with the greatest regret we turned around and headed back.

Ours was a happy family, and took it for granted that with rare exceptions that was the nature of families. My mother, Ada Stowell Watters, was of old New England stock, her family strict Puritans down to her time. They lived in Peru, a small town in western Massachusetts, where Mother's family farmed. Her grandfather honored the sabbath, and insisted all the maple sap buckets must be turned upside down on Saturday nights. Mother's brothers felt that since God was giving the sap it was sinful to waste it. Nobody argued with Grandfather Franklin, but after the old gentleman was asleep the boys turned the buckets right side up again. Monday mornings the buckets were all as grandfather ordained, and were righted in his presence. Mother used to tell us this story to teach us that other people's beliefs must be respected though not necessarily accepted.

Peru was a country community, but classically-minded. Relatives and friends were named Cyrus, Darius, Socrates, Augustus Caesar, Solon, and among the women, Monica, Statira, Semiramas, Vespasia, and my own grandmother was Hyla Cleopatra. Her father had preferred Greek to Latin, so chose Hyla in preference to Sylvia. I'm glad I missed the Cleopatra.

The Stowells were strict, law-abiding people, but in one thing they broke the law of the land. Their farm was one of the stations on the Underground Railway, and all but the youngest children took part in helping runaway slaves escape to Canada.

Among many other visitors to the isolated farm was a young Japanese stowaway in a Yankee sailing ship whose captain let the boy work his way around the Horn, taught him English and put him in school in Massachusetts. Somehow Grandfather Stowell heard of him, so Joseph Neesima* came to spend vacations at the farm, where he was greatly liked. He told the Stowells that his great dream was, if the Emperor would pardon him for running away, to go back to Japan and set up schools like those in America. Long afterwards, in Japan, Mother was honored as a friend of the founder of the Dōshisha University.

My father was Philip Melancthon Watters. At least two lines of Father's were Staten Island Hollanders. Two others were Huguenots who escaped from religious persecution in France. Another ancestor was Peter Müller, a German musician who brought to America before the Revolution the tower bells for Old Trinity Church in New York. He played the Trinity organ, and after New York and the church were burned during the Revolution, both Müller and the bells, which were unharmed, were installed in the new building where the bells still sound from its tower. A young

---

* Niishima Jō (1843-1890), celebrated Japanese educator. A samurai from central Honshū, he reached America in 1864, received his B.S. from Amherst College in 1870 and was ordained a Congregational minister. He founded a school in Kyōto in 1875 that grew into Dōshisha University.

woman descendant of his was taken from Virginia to London for the "season," where she met and married a young Irishman named William Watters. They lived for a time in his home in Tellamaginna in County Carlow, Ireland, then moved to New York City where their son, Philip, grew up to meet and marry my Simonson grandmother.

Father was born in Brooklyn in 1860 and studied in the high church Episcopal prep school of Old Trinity, under Peter Müller's bells. In 1882 he graduated from Congregational Amherst College. We children were more impressed by his pitching baseball at Amherst than by his fine scholastic record. He took his theological training at Columbia's Presbyterian Union Theological Seminary, then became a Methodist minister, and was so nondenominational in his preaching that whoever heard him was apt to claim him.

Just before graduation from Amherst he and two classmates went fishing in Peru, in a fine trout brook on the farm of Austin Stowell, where he met Mother. They were married in 1885 when he graduated from seminary, and together they tackled the complicated problems of parish work. Florence, always known as Sally, was born at the first parish, Philip and I at their third, in Dobbs Ferry, New York. By the time I was two and a half we had lived in Poughkeepsie and had moved to West 104th Street in New York City. We accepted the fact that a minister's family could not have all the things our neighbors had. Once when there had been a burglary in our neighborhood I asked Mother fearfully what we should do if a burglar came to our house. She just laughed.

"Don't worry, Hyla," she said, "burglars know we don't have a lot of money or valuable things."

I thought that was fine. We had a piano and music lessons, and bicycles, and we went to Tupper every summer. We had each other and our dog, and what more did anybody need?

There were certain family rules. We knew we should eat what we were given, or we wouldn't get what came next. Squabbling was not acceptable, nor misbehaving at the table. A camping family, we knew that "a good camper always leaves the trail better than he finds it," and we knew that applied to all of life. We were expected to be dependable, and two other rules, which Father, who had done a lot of sailing, usually combined to remind us were, "Tell the truth and tie square knots."

Our parents never gave conflicting decisions, and I remember only once when they differed in reaction. That was when I beat up the bad boy of our neighborhood for calling my grandfather an uncomplimentary name. Mother was chagrined that I had behaved so badly, "right on the front lawn of the parsonage." But Father wanted to know who won, and grinned when I said, "I did."

Summer always meant camping. Father first took us to Lake Champlain in 1894, when I was ten months old, and we camped by the lake every summer until I was eight.

Westport was five miles to the north, Fort Henry five miles to the south, and Stevenson's Crossing merely a level crossing; but that was where Father and our cousins' families, the Snedeckers and Tildsleys, wanted to get off the train. So Father would write ahead to the railway company for permission for the train to stop at Stevenson's Crossing, and the engineer would invite him into the cab to show him where to stop. Then Watterses, Snedeckers and Tildsleys would descend from the train complete with tents, cots, deck chairs, blankets, cooking utensils, clothing, while other passengers peered curiously out the windows. A farm wagon would take everything to Presbry Point. After a while gear was stored at Stevenson's over the winter, and tent platforms and an eating shelter were built over a permanent table and fixed benches, one bench built extra high for smalls.

One of our last summers at Champlain, Father hired a horse and rig and we five went on a gypsy trip through the Adirondacks, eating picnics by the roadside and putting up at farmhouses at night. One day Father took us all up McIntyre, now known as Algonquin, the second highest peak. I was five, and can still remember the taste of blueberries and wintergreen leaves, and the beauty of the view from the top. On every side it was beautiful, except to the west where it was full of smoke. Father and Mother told us that the village of Tupper Lake was burning, and everybody's house was burning down. We had never heard anything so dreadful.

The campground at Lake Champlain got too populous. A good friend of Father's heard that there was good fishing at Tupper Lake. So in the summer of 1901 our two families rented a house together at Tupper and lived most of the time out of doors. We loved it.

Up to that time we had never lived long enough at any one place to put down roots and feel that that was where we belonged. Our parents talked over the whole unsettling business of moving around and decided to find a piece of land at Tupper. Together they bought a couple of acres with a fine view near the Raquette River. With the help of relatives and friends, two simple cottages were built. Sally and Philip were big enough to measure and cut boards, and I nailed on shingles along a blue chalkline.

Since that time, camp at Tupper has been home, and many branches of the family converge here in summer. Here there are mountains for climbing and a river and lakes for fishing and boating and swimming. Here we deal with what is real, and feel, as the Indians before us, that in the water and winds and stars and mountains and the wild creatures is the close presence of God.

We moved to Kingston when I was eight, where I had a dog named Rube. I believed Rube could read the clock, because when I was due home from school he would jump up on a chair where he could watch out the window with his chin on the back of it. Then I would take him for a run. Rube was a pacifist and never fought, so when other dogs attacked him I would jump in and fight them for him, keeping my guardian angel busy. I always liked birds and animals, big dogs especially, and took care of any that were injured. I splinted legs, bandaged wounds and sorrowfully buried those that did not survive.

In Kingston Father tried to get some grass to grow, without much success as a neighbor boy named Jackson walked all over it. So Father put up a polite sign asking him to stay off. Soon a second sign appeared: "IF THEM WATERS WILL KEEP THAR MOUT SHUT

THEY ALL BEE BETTER OF. Goodbye." Father spoke to Jackson's father who said, "Jackson is a good boy; only thing is, he's full of the devil!" But Jackson was right about one thing: All "them Watters" *do* talk too much and sometimes should "keep thar mout shut!"

My interest in China began in Kingston, where I read a story called, "Who Will Open The Door For Little Ting Li?" It was about a Chinese girl who wanted to go to a mission school in her village but it cost too much. On the back of the booklet it said that a dollar could keep a little Chinese girl in a mission school for a year. I was much impressed, and loaned the story to a number of my friends. We formed a Girls' Missionary Society and thought up lots of ways to earn money; as a result we supported a whole day school in China for some years.

In 1906 Father was appointed District Superintendent of the New York area, and we lived in Yonkers, five years most noteworthy to me for the night the whole family sat on the roof to watch Halley's Comet. I went to high school in Yonkers and, when Father was appointed to Washington Square Methodist Church in New York City in 1911, commuted back to Yonkers to graduate with my class and entered Smith College that fall.

I loved all the outdoor fun at college, the games, hiking, punging, walking the range, and I yearned for snowshoes but couldn't afford them. Finally I bought them anyway, and rented them out for twenty cents an hour, my only experience in investing for profit.

College days were, of course, questioning days, and Father had prepared us for many of the problems that were difficult for other students. Evolution he called "progressive creation," and natural selection was God's wonderful way of determining which species should survive and how they could gradually improve. He had taught us not to be afraid to doubt or question.

My major was philosophy, and comparative religion was an especially important course. All through my years in China I was thankful for its training in appreciation of the truth in other religions. Zoology was a great help to me in medical school, although

I didn't yet know I was going there. But the course that did the most to open my eyes to what was around me was geology. Up to that time I had supposed that mountains and lakes were "just that way," and always would be. The fact that they were constantly changing was a great illustration of "progressive creation." Even the courses changed as understanding changed. The big three-toed tracks Father studied while at Amherst as those of a huge prehistoric bird, were known to us as dinosaur tracks. So knowledge, too, was incomplete, and minds had to be kept open.

For one of our term papers I wrote, at the request of a friend in China, a simple explanation of the basic relationships between the earth and its neighbors in the solar system and other heavenly bodies. I felt foolish writing that paper, to be translated into Chinese for use in schools in a country where knowledge of astronomy began long before ours. But the friend who requested it said the students there rushed out at times of an eclipse to make as much noise as possible with tin pans and firecrackers to frighten off the heavenly dog that would otherwise swallow up the moon.

While I was at Smith there was talk of establishing a sister relationship with some girls' college in another country: India, Africa or China. I wanted it to be China, and wrote to the bishop about it, and he suggested Ginling College in Nanking. I out-argued the others, and Ginling it was. In 1983 I was present at Ginling's fiftieth reunion, held at Smith College.

All through my college years, 1911-1915, I became more and more conscious that because much had been given me, much would naturally be required of me, that my responsibility for "leaving the trail better than I found it" meant to use my whole life in service. And that, I began to see more clearly, would be as a medical missionary. One of Mother's Frissell relatives had been, we were told, the first woman doctor in New England. If she could do it, so could I.

In the autumn of my senior year Father was appointed President of Gammon Theological Seminary, the school of our church in Atlanta, Georgia, for training Negro ministers. The family was in

Atlanta when I graduated from Smith, and Father urged me to join them there and teach at Atlanta University, also a school for Negroes. I wanted to go straight on to medical school, but Father knew it would be a long—and expensive—grind, and that I'd had an irregular heartbeat since childhood.

I finally agreed to try teaching and arrived at Atlanta University very late, and taught whatever the rest of the teachers had not already chosen: psychology, first aid, and general history beginning with Babylon and ending with 1916. I was also asked to teach botany. I said yes, I could teach botany, but when I got the textbook, it was about crop rotation, animal husbandry, field enrichment; in other words, agriculture.

One time I went out into a field and got a sheaf of stalks of some kind of grain and gave one to each student, who wanted to know what it was. I didn't know either so I told them to find out. Then, like a poor fool, I forgot to find out myself. The students guessed everything from corn to oats. Finally one big boy at the back of the room got disgusted. "Oh, Miss Watters," he said, "that is rye. It couldn't be anything else." When I asked him how he knew he said, "I helped plant that field. Is it rye?" When I ventured, "Yes, it is," he triumphantly said, "I told you!"

When it came to plowing, we went down to where the plow was hitched to a team of mules. One of the boys said, "I can plow." Relieved, I told him to go ahead and show us, and he plowed a fine straight furrow. Then he said, "Miss Watters, now you do it." I'd never plowed in my life, but thought I could drive a team of mules since I had driven plenty of horses, but when I laid my hands on the reins the mules knew better. Fortunately, I had the sense to laugh.

It was a great shock to our family to be plunged into a way of life where who you are was determined by the color of your skin. We hadn't had any experience of the color line, and Father wasn't about to let it alter his own attitudes. When he first reached Atlanta, the bishop down there said, "Now Mr. Watters, you have come down from the North and don't know our way of doing things. Your students are all Negroes. A number of your faculty are

Negroes. You must never let any of these people come to your front door. You must never invite any of them to a meal in your house. You must never accept an invitation to take a meal with them in their homes. You must never sit down with the students in the refectory. If they have a reception at which they stand around each holding a plate and a piece of cake, that you may do. But put your knees under the same table—never."

That went on, with a lot of other details. When he had finished, Father said, "Well, Bishop, there are two things I can do. Either I can live and work here and be a brother to my students and friends, or go back North. But live and work here under the conditions you have outlined, I cannot and will not do." As it turned out, Father was there under appointment of the New York Conference, so that bishop had no authority over him. He stayed, and was very much a brother to all.

The library in Atlanta was a Carnegie Library, but supported by taxes. Negro landowners paid part of its upkeep, but were not allowed inside the building, much less to take out a book. I had a card. Mother had a card. Father had a card. Aunt Carrie, Father's sister who lived with us, had a card. Each card was good for several books. So I would go to the library and take out the books requested by various Negro faculty members. The people running that library never learned what I was doing, and I took a wicked joy in doing it.

There was a weekly prayer meeting at Gammon that I usually could not attend because of my own schedule, but one autumn day I did. As we started up the hill I picked up a most beautiful leaf from a red oak, carried it along in my hand and held it during the meeting. Afterwards one of the students asked, "Miss Hyla, why did you bring that oak leaf with you?" And I said, "Because it is beautiful." He said, "Beautiful?" I held it up, "Yes, look at those beautiful curves and that color, that rich dark brown. It's wonderful." He took it and held it up and looked at it and asked, "Would you give me that oak leaf?" I laughed and said, "Of course." Then he added, "Nobody ever told me before that color could be beautiful." I looked up at it as he was holding it, and it was exactly the color of his face.

After I had taught for a year and knew that I still wanted to go to medical school, Father was satisfied. The question of cost was settled by Dr. Edward C. Perkins. I believe he paid my way to Smith. All I know is that he said to Father, "Let's handle it the same way we did Smith," and there was no question of cost after that.

Edward Perkins was the son of a Hartford banker, a graduate of Yale, where he made a name as a high hurdler and captain of the track team, and of Columbia Law School. He hadn't any particular goal, but was uneasy with the well-to-do life he was living. Around 1903 or '04 he went to Kingston to help a young friend of his get settled in medical practice. While in Kingston he went out one stormy night to look for a church service and a passerby suggested St. James. Father, Mother and the sexton were the only persons present, and they held the meeting as though the church were full. By the end, everybody was shivering, and Mother took Edward Perkins home to warm him up.

When he first met Father and Mother he was in great distress of spirit. Then at a camp meeting he happened to see one of those illuminated texts that read, "Whosoever will, let him take the water of life freely." And he thought, "Whosoever WILL, why that means ME!" The burden on his heart rolled off and never came back.

He wanted to give his life in service to others, and thought he would go to China to be an orderly in a mission hospital. But Mother was incensed. She said, "You'll be no orderly! You will go to the best medical school you can find and graduate at the top of your class and then you will go to China and have a hospital of your own." Edward Perkins was aghast that anyone would have such confidence in him, but that is exactly what he did.

He graduated from the New York College of Physicians and Surgeons in 1910, spent two years as House Surgeon at St. Luke's in New York City, then went to the London School of Hygiene and Tropical Medicine. In 1913 he went to China and worked with Dr.

11

Mary Stone* in Kiukiang before building his own Water of Life Hospital. He served forty years in China without salary and often helped at our Wuhu hospital.

It was because of Dr. Edward C. Perkins that I chose medicine and the London School, and China. He and Georgie, his wife, who was business manager for their hospital, were my family in China.

To get into medical school, I thought all you had to do was walk up its steps and present your college diploma. It didn't occur to me that there were some courses I hadn't taken that I would need, so I spent an extra year at Cornell taking biology and organic chemistry.

There were not many women in the profession in those days. But Ezra Cornell was a far-thinking man, and when he gave his money to start the university he specified that there must be both men and women in all its departments. There were six women in my 1921 class of thirty-six, and we didn't have any problems being women.

That first year of pre-med the college was thinking about only one thing: would it be war? The men each had two years of military drill, and would probably be among the first to go. Some were in the New York State militia, which had already been called out to guard harbors, forts and arsenals; some were on sentry duty at the two campus armories. In February, as diplomatic relations with Germany were broken, I saw two boys marching and wheeling and saluting in a corridor and was suddenly struck with how ghastly it was that soon a large percentage of Cornell boys might really be in it. And they were.

I got through those first years and went on down to the New York City Cornell Medical School campus for the rest of it. I

* Dr. Mary Stone (1872-1954), first Chinese woman to obtain a medical doctorate in the United States (University of Michigan, 1896). She founded the Kiukiang Women's Hospital, under Methodist Foreign Missions, and for twenty-five years headed it and personally trained more than 500 nurses. In 1920, with the help of American friends, she founded the Bethel Mission of Shanghai, which included a high school, orphanages, theological seminaries, and nurses' training schools where more than 2,500 nurses had trained by the time of her death.

enjoyed interning at Bellevue, and especially riding the ambulance.

There were lots of pneumonia cases at Bellevue then. A young German sailor named Bierman died of it, while an American sailor, Jones, was deathly sick and didn't want to live as "there's nobody cares." But the whole crew at Bellevue worked to bring back his will to live, and he did.

When Jones got well, and the war was over, I gave him Bierman's mother's address in Berlin and asked him to tell her what kind of place Bellevue was and how we had worked to save her son. Bierman's mother welcomed him into her home on the other side of the Atlantic, and Bellevue was his home on this side. Every time he came back to New York he came to visit us. That's the kind of place Bellevue was.

Tony was a little Italian boy with sarcoma of the bones of one leg. He was an unhappy little boy, but we all liked him and wanted to help him. One student got a pair of white mice from the lab for him to play with. Tony loved those mice, and his whole attitude toward life changed. Then a new nurse came on the ward who was afraid of mice and said they must go. Everyone helped to hide them, sometimes tossing them like a package from one to another to get them out of sight. One time I took them into the lab off the ward so the nurse wouldn't see them, and Dr. John Augustus Hartwell* came in and found them. "What are those mice doing here?" he asked. He listened to Tony's story and said, "Don't let anything happen to those mice!" so I had to tell him about the new nurse. He went to the nurse and asked plaintively why he couldn't have his mice. She was flustered. "But Dr. Hartwell," she said, "I didn't know they were *your* mice!" That saved them.

Years later when I visited the same ward, I found it full of canaries and learned that Dr. Hartwell had put them there. When I

---

* John Augustus Hartwell (1869-1940), renowned New York surgeon. He was Director of the New York Academy of Medicine and its President for two terms; Clinical Professor at Cornell Medical College where he was on its staff 1898-1908; and at Bellevue, as Director of Surgery 1916-1928 and Consulting Surgeon 1928-1940.

saw him, he remarked, "Dr. Watters, there aren't enough white mice and canaries in this world." That's the kind of place Bellevue was.

The Methodist Board of Foreign Missions wanted me to go right out to China after Bellevue, but I didn't feel ready. There were so many big-name surgeons at Bellevue that I didn't get half the practice I thought I needed, and I decided to take a second year in surgery at Morristown Memorial in New Jersey. There I got lots of practice, especially at night when attending physicians weren't eager to be called out.

One time at Morristown the head of the Mayo Nose and Throat Department demonstrated tonsillectomies, which he did under local anaesthesia, with the patient sitting in front of him. Many of the townspeople volunteered as patients. When the doctor had finished he asked, "Anyone else?" So I ran up and sat down in front of him, thinking it would be better to have mine out before setting forth for China. When I was finished I grabbed another second year student and he had his out. Then as the two of us walked down the hall, we met the hospital superintendent. "I hear you had your tonsils out," he glowered at us, "Now just who do you think is going to do the work around here?"

"Why, we are," I said. "There was nothing to it."

For me that was true, but the other student went to bed for days, and I had all of his work to do as well as my own.

With Morristown behind me and Dr. Perkins' example to lure me on, I applied to the London School of Hygiene and Tropical Medicine for their three-month program. So in the fall of 1923 I had thirteen glorious days at sea which confirmed my belief that a sea voyage at frequent intervals ought to be a regulation part of everybody's existence.

After three months' saturation in tropical diseases it was back to New York to appear before the Candidate Committee at the Board of Foreign Missions. The ordeal I had been dreading was suddenly upon me, then over before I knew it. Nothing was decided then, as funds were woefully short, but the following

September I was summoned to New York for my physical and booked to sail for China.

In Los Angeles I learned that there was a war going on in China. When I went on board ship, a steward with whom I had traveled before said, "Oh, Dr. Watters, I've got a telegram for you." I was so afraid it might be from the mission board telling me that because of the war I couldn't go to China, that I took leave of my senses. I told him to keep it until later, and I went to the boat deck and hid behind a lifeboat until after the pilot had left us and there was no chance of sending me home.

That telegram might have been important but luckily it was a bon voyage from a friend. I was still worried however, that the Board might recall me, and when I got to Nanking I asked one of the older missionaries about that war. He said, "Don't worry. I've been in China forty years and there's always been a war. A little more war in China won't keep anyone home."

There was always a war on, all those years I was in China. Finally a war came that did send me home.

Dr. Robert E. Brown (courtesy, General Commission on Archives and History, The United Methodist Church)

Hyla Doc at Tupper Lake camp before going to China.

China Was Where I Belonged

1924-1925

The landing of the *Van Buren* at Shanghai in 1924 had us steaming past the most remarkable lot of shipping I had ever seen: liners and freighters from all over the world, schooners and other regulation sailing craft, great junks standing like half-moons on the water, with their split bows and hollowed-out sterns and painted after-structure way above water and their gun'ls almost awash midships, bamboo slatted sails set rakishly on their masts, each at a different slant; all manner of peculiar small boats propelled by great sweeping sculls aft, or by viciously-handled boat-hooks when near enough to grab anything bigger and take advantage of its greater inertia for a pull or shove; and among them all the gunboats of the foreign nations, silent, with steam up and ready for action.

Our ship landed way above the city and we went back to the customs jetty on a tender, where we were through in no time and en route to the interdenominational Missionary Home in a rickshaw. On the way up from the jetty I had a jolt when a woman passed by hobbling with a distressing, wooden-legged gait. Instinctively I looked to see what was wrong with her feet, and recognized the pitiful stumps of "golden lilies" I'd heard about all my life, not over three inches long, the ankles humpy and distorted. I suddenly realized how impossible it is to make people at a distance understand such things, for the reality hit me as the idea of bound feet never had. There were a lot of those feet, even in Shanghai, many of them on young women.

With the compass Mother gave me and a pith helmet to ward off the sun, I prowled around Shanghai to my heart's content; around the waterfront, the small Chinese city, through all sorts of food shops, a joss-house,* and the bird market where hundreds of birds were for sale. Dogs and cats were a half-wild lot and caged birds got the attention. Cages were everywhere, over doorways and shops, sometimes hung from low tree branches. On pleasant afternoons, the gentlemen of my neighborhood took their birds out for an airing. One of my language school teachers later told me that before a bird could sing well its tongue was rubbed gently every day until finally the skin rubbed off. Then the owner put some blood from his own hand on the bird's tongue, and when it healed the bird sang far more beautifully.

Next to the bird market I heard a piercing but musical chatter, and found crickets and locusts and grasshoppers and other insects in miniature cages cleverly constructed of wicker for the big ones and cardboard for the tiny ones. Each was fed rice or beans, and lived sometimes for a month in captivity.

Bubbling Well Road was such a beautiful name that I went out to the end of it by trolley to see what was there. It was a well with a marble coping and carved lions, doubtless of great antiquity, and it did bubble, but it was a scummy green hole.

A Buddhist monastery across the way was more interesting. A big bell was rung and monks came filing in, each with a piece of sackcloth draped gracefully over his black garb. They had taken an oath of poverty, and looked it, but the Buddhas were gold-leafed, the josses down in the lesser shrines had ornate and costly decorations, and there was no lack of incense. Very solemnly the monks came in, with bowed heads, and took their places on each side of the chapel, facing the center. The leader struck a rich-toned bell and they knelt facing the great central Buddha until their heads were on the little grass mats before them. Again and again they stood up, only to kneel at the sound of the bell.

---

* The word "joss," from the Portuguese *dues*, god, was pidgin English for a Chinese idol.

Then another bell sounded and, with hands together like the angels of Fra Angelico, they recited in chorus while one monk kept up a rapid drumming on what looked like a great gourd painted red. With that to hold the rhythm, they droned on and on and on. Occasionally at the sound of the bell they folded their hands or changed them back to the original position, drew a deep breath, and started over. The musical tone, rising and falling, the droning voices, the drumming, softer and louder, the scent of incense, each man in dead earnest, was very impressive.

There *was* a war on when I got to China, but most of the local fighting between warlords was in the area back of Shanghai. We new missionaries rolled bandages and folded gauze for use in the hospitals, and heard ghastly accounts of suffering, of wounded men left untended for days. I saw occasional wounded soldiers about the streets, others doing police duty, and we Westerners weren't allowed on the streets after nine at night. Some river boats were delayed, and the rail line between Shanghai and Nanking was cut so that I got a glorious boat trip to Nanking instead of a stuffy train ride.

I had heard accounts of travel up-country on junks with pigs and geese, and had some misgivings as to what this S.S. *Kung Wo* would be like. I was set to make a lark of whatever came along, so imagine my surprise to find it the new showboat of a British line, varnished and polished like a yacht.

The Yangtze was café au lait, with low-lying banks, sprinkled with small sailing craft sporting brown, patched sails. It was so wide that as we looked upstream or down, brown water formed the horizon. Occasionally a pagoda on shore let us know we were in China, but it might have been the Mississippi. As we went upstream the river narrowed and the country visible to each side grew hilly. After we passed Tung-chou the engine stopped, but the boat went on. An exchange of passengers was effected with a flat boat, both boats in motion but held together by boat-hooks, then the engine started again and we left the flat boat behind.

After a few days in Shanghai and Nanking I was convinced that

China was where I belonged. The people seemed solid and dependable, and were easy to get to know. What impressed me most was that they were always working, exchanging laughs meantime, and apparently enjoyed hard work, even the men who did the heavy work that would be done by horses at home.

The first day of language classes at Nanking was a circus instead of a hill of difficulty, but I wasn't fooled into thinking there wasn't a lot of steady work to be done. The direct method, whereby we students sat in class and had the language shouted at us and shouted it back louder, was great fun. We weren't allowed to take notes, and that made us pay one hundred percent attention. Our teacher began by holding up a book and saying "*shu*," then other objects, with a Chinese and foreign sample of each. Then he gave us "this" and "that," and personal pronouns and a couple of verbs and so worked up to sentences, with no English. He frequently played tricks on us, giving us wrong words, and after we'd been caught napping a couple of times we kept alert. There was a lot of satisfaction getting to the point where we could say a whole sentence in Chinese, and finally really converse.

I expected the people to keep us at a distance until they made sure we were friendly. But not at all. Everybody smiled and many bowed and greeted us as they passed, and the children shouted their two words of English, "hello," often metamorphosed into "kello," and "goodbye." Everybody was patience personified with our attempts to use their language, usually very clever at guessing what we wanted to say, and took a part in teaching us. My favorite rickshaw puller named every new and interesting object we passed without my asking.

Our teachers were marvelous people. One was a Manchu,* and carried himself with an air of lordly superiority that reminded us his civilization was ancient and noble while ours was new and rough-cut. He was the personification of courtesy and savoir faire, able to handle any situation without being the least ruffled, and to put us at ease in spite of our barbarian blunders. He

---

* The ruling ethnic class of the Ch'ing dynasty, 1644-1912.

played volleyball and played it well without losing his dignity. We arrived in China convinced of the superiority of everything American, but accepted his attitude as natural and right, and enjoyed it.

That first year of the interdenominational Nanking Language School was important for us to get acquainted with a whole new culture without the distractions of a job, and I found China far more attractive in every way than I had any idea it would be. I was all set to find a country bleak and brown, with all its vegetation grubbed out by the roots. Doubtless some parts of it were, but where we were the fields in October were as green as the fields at home, the trees much greener, and the garden beds, thriftily though unsanitarily enriched from household chamber pots, flourished like hothouse beds. It was truly a Flowery Kingdom.

The chief vegetable when we arrived was *pai t'sai*, white vegetable (Chinese cabbage), which stood up on a clump of white stems like celery, except that the leaves at the top were more like spinach. When washed and piled in big flat baskets for market, it was very beautiful, if you didn't remember what sort of pond it had been washed in. The dishes and children and laundry and rice, vegetables and everything else got washed off the end of the same plank on the shore of the same little pond; and the ponds had to be seen to be believed. But the marvel was that everybody went on washing and that they made such a success of cleanliness. And the food got cooked, so it didn't matter. As for the children and the men who waded into the ponds to fill the wooden buckets hung from two ends of a long bamboo yoke, schistosomiasis* wasn't in the popular vocabulary, so it didn't worry anybody.

I'd had the idea that whereas the Japanese were artistic and loved the beautiful, the Chinese were not. Perish the thought. The very buckets in which the water of the duckweed-covered ponds was dipped up were beautiful. The pottery was beautiful; the kind I

---

* Schistosomiasis is a severe endemic disease caused by parasites which multiply in snails as intermediate hosts and are picked up from fresh waters. These bore into the body, migrate through causing much damage, to start a new cycle of infestation in snail hosts.

liked best a light tan dull ware with landscapes and poetry done in dark lines graven into the clay.

I bought a most ingenious paper lantern for getting about at night. Its candle was stuck on a spoke on a bottom directly suspended from the handle, so that its thin, white paper sides could slide up for the candle to be lit. The light that shone through was lovely, and the whole lantern cost only three coppers, or less than a cent of American money, candle and all.

Chinese money was one thing about which I was not enthusiastic. The system was a wonder, the various relationships between coins constantly changing. One day a silver dollar "Mexican"* would be worth thirteen dimes and four or five coppers, another day exchanged for 216 coppers. The dime of "big money" existed only in theory, yet was the basis of a lot of the quoted prices. It was one-tenth of a dollar, therefore equal to twenty-one coppers. But the dimes actually used were "small money," and sometimes worth about sixteen coppers, except for those coined in certain years, worth a copper or two less. The Chinese shopkeepers worked it out by a complicated calculation on an abacus, but my brain lay down on the job.

Chinese love of beauty cropped up everywhere. Police stations kept great bunches of chrysanthemums always in evidence, and flower boxes on their porches. We often saw cops stand and gaze with rapt admiration at the blossoms, and on cold nights they took the flowers in with great care. Men walking the streets, often very poor men, frequently carried flutes and played as they walked. For fifteen coppers I bought myself a Chinese bamboo flute wound with black silk thread like a trout rod, finished with bone at the end, and strung through it a knot of blue cord I'd have paid the price of the flute for alone. One of the teachers showed me how to play it and in the process I acquired great respect for the people who played beautiful melodies with apparent ease.

Everyone seemed to like Mandy, my mandolin, and I was

* Mexican peso, often called "Mex," circulated in many countries, and was known as a "dollar," by English speaking peoples.

often asked to play. One day I was invited to help with a school entertainment. The place was jammed, and it was hard to reach the platform, but once there the master of ceremonies gave a flowery introduction and, counting on my unfamiliarity with the language, went on to say that whether or not they understood the music, I'd come a long way from home to help the Chinese people and play foreign music for them and they must clap to show their appreciation. And they did. But there was no doubt they liked some of it, particularly "Dixie."

One night I heard a man singing something that stopped me short. The words were Chinese, but the tune, "Auld Lang Syne." Someone explained to me that the Chinese were fond of Scottish and Negro songs and learned them easily, since both were pentatonic like the Chinese.

One of the things I marveled at was the way in which Chinese combined their love of music and of birds by fastening whistles to carrier pigeons so as to make music while they flew. Another whistling sound I heard in crowds was made by something like the "buzzers" we used to make of buttons on a long string. These were of wood and carved plum pits that whistled as they spun, a beautiful sound that one peddler said was like the voice of a goose.

The two copper pieces to which the handle of my tea kettle was fastened broke, and I took the kettle to a little shop to be mended. The man used copper coins to replace them, and put them both with the dragon side out, and turned so that the dragons were both right side up glaring fiercely at all beholders. The kettle was distinctly improved, and I was glad it got broken.

There were eighteen of us women in my Nanking Language School class, all American except for one English and one Australian. The mission boards were beginning to be hit by the economic depression and were sending out mostly medical people, so the greater number of our group were nurses, with one lab technician, and one dietician. Meigs Hall, where we lived, was two-storey grey brick, foreign in most respects but finished with a tiled roof, ornamented ridgepole and turned-up corners so characteristic of the Chinese. Floors and finish were wood, covered with Ningpo varnish. When freshly applied and not quite dry, Ningpo varnish gave people a rash like poison ivy, but when dry was harmless and so resistant that if hot water or tea were spilled on it, no harm was done.

We had hot and cold water in the faucets, a great luxury, and electric lights, unless something went wrong with the current or the company thought there might be looting, in which case the lights went out all over the city. We all had candles, mine in my cow-vertebrae candlestick, which caused comment by the servants.

The servants were most kind and patient and willing to work. They took great delight in teaching us new words, which we loved to spring on our teachers, but since the servants, like the varnish, all came from Ningpo, we soon learned our pronunciation was often wrong.

The food was almost all foreign and served foreign style. Most of us would have liked to have Chinese food, but some couldn't eat it, or thought they couldn't, so we had to depend on meals elsewhere for Chinese food and chopstick practice. In New York I had thought I was pretty handy with chopsticks, but watching the Chinese use them changed my mind. They thought nothing of holding a chicken bone in theirs, and picking it as thoroughly as we would holding it in our fingers. They served food from a main dish with chopsticks as efficiently as we would with a tablespoon.

I bought delicious dainties along the roadside, an oblong cake made of dough with a liberal sprinkling of little sweet seeds on the top. The baker had a big earthenware jar, about three feet deep, with a glowing charcoal fire filling about a third of it. He would reach down and plaster rectangles of dough inside the jar above the fire and close the neck of the jar by setting a kettle on top. After the cakes had baked he hauled them out with long iron tongs and delivered them piping hot, before germs had a chance to settle with the road dust.

It surprised me to find some people in my class who would have been saved a lot of trouble and worry and would have had

24

smoother lives in China if they had had the kind of background I was lucky to have had: not to be afraid of thinking and of truth, even new truth. And it would have been easier for Chinese to know that some things are essential to real Christianity and other things are not. It astonished me how the very people who battled so valiantly against "idolatry" of an unfamiliar Oriental kind failed to see the incongruity when they set up other gods, in the shape of traditional dogmas, and actually let them interfere with personal relationships and brotherly love.

In afternoon sessions at language school we learned much of interest besides the language. One was the cause of rabies. Before he went into hibernation, a snake took in his mouth a fragrant thing that grew in the ground. In the spring he spit it out and the first dog to come along would eat it and get sick from the snake's poison. The people he bit got the same sickness. There were two cures for leprosy. One was to eat a certain kind of snake deadly to anyone without leprosy; the other simply to give the disease to someone else. Everybody seemed to have malaria pretty straight, and perhaps it was politeness, but they seemed convinced that foreign doctors knew more than those Chinese-trained, especially in surgery. My teacher told me one day that he had heard foreign doctors had a device by which they could look inside people to see a sickness, and wanted to know if that were true. So I took him an x-ray print.

Another teacher told me an interesting way to keep mosquitoes from biting at night. He explained that he was a Christian and this was Taoist magic, but he had tried it and it worked. One drew a circle on the wall, then spoke magic words into that circle. The mosquitoes would all go and sit in the circle and leave one to sleep unmolested. In the morning one had to say other magic words to free them, for if you swatted mosquitoes in the circle the magic wouldn't work again. Another trick was to keep rats from making a noise at night. You took a picture of a cat, any color cat, but his eyes had to be blue, and said magic words to the picture. Then you set it on the floor opposite the rat hole and the rats didn't dare come out. I asked whether he had tried that one, but he said unfortunately his humble home had no rats, so he hadn't.

We also shared with our teachers stories about the way things were in America. Once I told about a hike and the pancakes we made for breakfast. They asked a lot of questions. Pancakes weren't hard to describe, as the Chinese had a sort of pancake, but maple syrup was new territory. So I knocked up my precious cake of maple sugar and took chunks over to the school where I had to expound the process of its production in minute detail, with questions that went over my depth as to the percentage of sap used and the number of spigots that can be put into one tree and the length of time it takes a tree to heal over after they are taken out, and the age of a tree when it can begin to be used. But they did like that sugar. Cautious at first, the teachers readily came back for seconds. One teacher looked doubtfully at his piece, and then asked, "If I eat this, when it's time to play ball will I have a lot of . . ." then launching into English, "pep?"

My family sent me nature magazines, which were very popular with the teachers and they took them home to show their families. One, on returning a copy, sighed, "This book has lots of flavor! If only I could read English!" Pictures of big woods were of special interest, as in central China there were only small groves, planted and protected with care.

Once I showed my teacher some pictures of aigrettes, and he told me that just as in America the Chinese used aigrette feathers. They had been the distinguishing badge of one grade of high official, and a picture of the bird was embroidered on the front and back of the official gown. When I said that we didn't use aigrette feathers any more, he smiled and said, "Just like China." When we came to an article on opossums, he was greatly interested and asked, "Those are rats, aren't they?" I explained that opossums were different and much bigger, and very good to eat. "Good to eat!" he exclaimed, "I've heard that in South China there are also people who eat rats. Surely the people of all countries are alike!"

That last remark was the conclusion to most of our conversations. Customs, proverbs, ideas—the parallel was most uncanny. But sometimes my teacher would remark sadly, "Your honorable country, although new, is ahead of my humble country, although my humble country is so old. We must learn more of the good customs of your honorable country, particularly American technical training, to make China independent of Japan in manufacturing." Western foreign goods were so expensive that far too much Chinese money went to Japan, which seemed to be doing all she could to keep China from developing her own manufacture of glass lamp-chimneys, for instance, and good quality cotton cloth.

No matter how far afield into economics or religion or politics or legends our conversations traveled, we always arrived at the same conclusion, somewhat like this: "Surely the differences are not great. The clothing in different countries differs somewhat and alas, men do not all speak the same language, but with regard to really important things, surely the people of all countries are alike." It was a tremendous courtesy for them to be willing to class our country in its newness on a level with their own land, where anything that happened a thousand years ago is comparatively recent.

It was astonishing what we students could get used to. Before going to China I thought I would be continually miserable with the smells. For the first few days they were a bother, but we developed a selection by which disagreeable odors no longer reached our consciousness. One morning I walked along enjoying the crisp autumn air thinking, "How fine this air is!" then suddenly realized I was going along beside a very green pond, stopped to analyze the air and reversed my opinion. But people who put on a long face and told doleful stories about the smells of Chinese streets told only one side of the truth, and not the side that impressed me most strongly. Along our nearest shopping street about six in the evening the fragrance of cooking food, of tea and incense and raw hemp and freshly-cut wood had a variety and richness one couldn't imagine except from the joy of experiencing it.

In Nanking we set our watches by the noon gun, which varied considerably from day to day, and Nanking time followed the gun in its deviations. If we failed to hear the gun we could be on the right time in the morning and way off by afternoon. Many things fixed at home were variable and approximate in China: the time of day, length of a mile, number of dimes in a dollar, having a subject or predicate in any complete sentence. Perhaps the "more or less" attitude was part of the explanation of the endurance of these marvelous people, which made it possible for them to come through hardships and worries that would drive Americans, with our need for precision, into brainstorm.

It was the custom of the country to put a bride on exhibition because the more people who came to see her, the greater honor for the family. So five of us students went one evening to a well-to-do home, well built, lighted with electricity, with a balcony overlooking one of the courtyards, and many servants. From the street we went through an archway and a courtyard and another archway and a room and another courtyard, and so on, deeper and deeper into the intricate geography of that complicated building. Finally we reached an inner room with big red banners and gilt inscriptions, incense and ancestral tablets. Along the way crowds of merrymakers were eating or gambling or sitting around chatting.

From the banner room we went through a small door into a bedroom where guests were crowded into a very small space thick with incense. In the center was an ornate four-poster bed with heavy gorgeous silk hangings, and by the edge of the bed stood the bride. Her headgear looked like a tower, with all sorts of dangling beadwork and tassels, paper flowers in among the chains, and from the top long pink veiling hung down on both sides. The whole thing was top-heavy, and she looked exhausted from holding up the weight of it. Servants on each side helped to hold her up while guests made remarks about her. One of our crowd suggested she sit down and rest, and a young man laughed, "She doesn't need to sit down, her feet are plenty big enough."

But they brought seats for us, and for our benefit a servant sang a long song of many verses in piercing falsetto while we admired the high pile of silk quilts, a set of foreign dishes on a table and a whatnot with shelves and drawers and a looking glass. There among all these foreign things and under an electric light stood that little bride, eyes and head down, living bravely up to an ancient tradition.

After the song someone suggested we shake hands with the bride. That wasn't Chinese custom, but they seemed to think it was a fine thing for us to do, so we did, each of us racking our store of words for some comforting thing to say. A Christian wedding always struck me as an ordeal, but this custom, in which the bride was on exhibition three days, supposedly without food or water, must have been torture. After that came the attempt to be happy with someone picked out by a third party, and with a mother-in-law who considered the bride her rightful slave.

When we went to Purple Mountain near Nanking, we went in great style in carriages built somewhat like the old victorias, but the front seat for passengers, facing aft, was short and narrow, so that whoever sat on it hung on for dear life. The driver sat up front, on high, and sometimes there were footmen up behind as well, but nearly always only one little horse to do the pulling.

Purple Mountain, a few miles outside the city to the east, appeared to be of stratified rock, partially metamorphosed and steeply tilted, the tip of it overhung to the north so that it looked like a wave with a curling crest. The lower slopes were well sprinkled with fine young pines and cedars planted by the university students; they hadn't taken kindly to the idea of using a shovel, which involved work they'd been trained to look down on, but were persuaded that it was a patriotic privilege. On the slopes were also goldenrod and harebells and many kinds of asters, small wild chrysanthemums and a rock pink in various shades of cerise and magenta, fragrant honeysuckle-looking pink flowers on a bush in the rocks, and a spire of fuzzy pink blossoms with practically no leaves that grew in rocks, and all over the tile roofs in the city.

As we toiled up the path without any shade, the sun looked down on the tops of our heads and fried them, even though it was late fall. I had to be careful about old friend, actinic ray, and decked out in helmet and dark glasses looked something like a locomotive or a strange species of beetle on the march. With a white sweater draped over the top of the helmet, it was still a lot stiffer sunshine than I like to take. Hot isn't exactly the word; the temperature didn't matter most, just the straight rays of the old sun.

We rested thankfully in the shade of a rock for some time, and traced across the slope the trenches that were dug and used in the 1911 Revolution. Then we went on to the top where below us to the south we could see the Ming Tomb.* To the north and west was the big brown Yangtze. I looked in the direction of Wuhu and wondered what lay before me.

Another day another student and I got a couple of horses to ride to the Ming Tomb. They were short-legged and solidly built, and we half-expected them to be anti-foreign. But not at all. Mine was intelligent and lively, and responded well to suggestions. We had a beautiful ride across the city and through the old Manchu city within it, most of its wall down but the old gates with their round arches still in place. We passed a number of threshing floors, like those in the Old Testament and probably as old, and watched the good grain being beaten out and separated from the chaff. We passed a mill being turned by a blindfolded donkey that walked around and around a circle. Then we clattered through the great gate of the city wall and turned out through a smaller opening further on.

The big stone animals that guard the approach to the Ming Tomb were an interesting lot, the horses and dromedaries apparently Chinese, but the long-maned lions and elephants not. There they stood, and stand today, those old stone guardians, two by two, facing each other solemnly across the road. I don't know what they thought of our levity, but that road was soft dirt and too good to miss, and we went past their noses at a gallop. The broad backs of the elephants were piled high with stones pitched up there by women who believed they could determine the sex of a coming child in this manner. Beyond the animals were three pairs of human figures, soldiers and civil officials.

---

* Burial place of Chu Yüan-chang, founder of the Ming dynasty, whose capital was at Nanking.

Beyond another turn was a very old stone bridge, and a slanting approach to the outer gate. Some boys waited for a chance to earn coppers by holding the horses, so we walked into the enclosure overgrown with small yellow wild chrysanthemums and trailing vines, where we found a stone tortoise with a big tablet standing upright on his back to tell the emperor's glories.

From him the way led straight down twin flights of steps with a slanting, carved spirit wall* between, through a garden to the mound where rests the emperor and those followers buried with him. The earth for the mound is said to have been brought from every province in the empire. It is wooded, without tablet or monument, and behind it rises Purple Mountain.

We stayed longer than we should have and once back inside the city gate went at a good trot to get back before dark. Suddenly my companion's horse stumbled and she with him. He scrambled up and bolted, and I stopped long enough to be sure she wasn't badly hurt, then took off at a gallop, tearing around corners and yelling at pedestrians before I caught him.

Both horses were winded, and we started back slowly when I suddenly realized I hadn't any idea where I had left my friend. I tried to ask some soldiers who had seen me tear by which direction I had come from, but they just stared at me. Fortunately my friend came along in a rickshaw and insisted on getting back on her horse. It was dark by then, and we were lost. We went slowly, using Mother's compass, and finally found our way back to the school.

I was seething over the fact that at no time did anyone offer sympathy or help. Later I learned that in China it is very discourteous for a person riding either a horse or a rickshaw to address a person on foot without alighting, and that if one is riding and passes a friend on foot without stopping, one always begs his pardon by way of greeting. The teacher who told me this also told me that the soldiers who infuriated me by their lack of response may well have been from some area with a different dialect, or had

---

* Spirit walls were to deflect evil spirits, thought to travel only in straight lines.

difficulty understanding my limited Chinese spoken in great excitement, and would have helped if they had understood.

Later a friend and I hiked to the Nanking city wall built by the Ming emperor and said to be more impressive than the Peking wall. The story went that whenever a workman was found who had left so much as a knife-blade crack between the massive squared stones, his services were ended by chopping off his head and building him into the wall. It was as high as a three or four-storey building and about fifty feet wide at the top, widening toward the base. Along the outer edge was a high battlement with loopholes. The top was grassy, good grazing grounds for the donkeys and goats. Over the big arched gates were very old two-storey buildings, formerly used as lookout stations, ammunition storehouses, perhaps as barracks.

We had a great view from the wall, down into the streets and courtyards of the city, and out into the huddled region that the Romans called the "suburbs." From the top of one gate we watched a long train of donkeys below, each with a great sack of grain carefully balanced across his back; and the little donkeys went their way so placidly that the loads stayed on. Perched on the last donkey was a man with a stick to discourage stragglers.

Outside much of the wall was a stream that served both as moat and as "water road." Along it sailed sampans with patchwork sails and tiny matting-covered cabin homes; skiffs with squares of matting rigged as sails to supplement the scull; tubs poled by men herding big flocks of ducks; barges loaded with long, plumed grass that served as fuel for cooking-fires. Along the shore large square nets were slung from what looked like well-sweeps. Whatever fish happened to be in the net when it was lifted got gathered up in long-handled landing nets and dumped into a pack-basket standing in water, where they gasped and flopped to prove they were fresh.

Above the South Gate we were stopped by a soldier who asked where we were going, then courteously escorted us down a long flight of stone steps into a courtyard, in through a barracks and out to the street, a way we would never have found. He was kind as could be, and much interested in my compass. Chinese compasses had the important end of the needle red, pointing south, so mine looked strange to him. On his account I put down a good mark toward Chinese soldiers, which offset my earlier impression.

Everything about this great and astonishing country fascinated me, from methods of cutting children's hair to military ethics. On the latter, soon after our arrival in Nanking two of the most estimable generals in the area cleared out and left their troops in the lurch. Everybody understood that thereby they relieved the soldiers of the necessity of fighting an unnecessary battle.

The opinion was prevalent at home, and we'd all been told many times in missionary talks, that whereas the people of some western lands were dreamers and poets, the Chinese were rank materialists. I soon learned differently. My teacher, the son of an artist, told me a story on which Chinese children were brought up.

Before the Han dynasty,* Pa Wang, the most powerful general fighting for control of the nation, led an army against Han Hsin. Pa Wang's soldiers were big and strong and well trained, and there was no army capable of defeating them in combat.

One moonlit night Han Hsin ordered his soldiers to sing songs of Pa Wang's homeland. The wind carried the songs down to the stalwart soldiers of Pa Wang as they sat around their campfires, homesick soldiers who had been on the march for years. The music wavering through the moonlight stirred memories of wives and children, and as Han Hsin's soldiers sang, Pa Wang's soldiers grew more and more melancholy until finally they began to desert and slip away into the surrounding darkness, which was what Han Hsin had intended.

Pa Wang thought his homeland had been captured by Han Hsin and men from his homeland had joined Han Hsin's army in large numbers. He rejected an opportunity to escape alone, gathered a small band of loyal soldiers and attempted a breakthrough. When he failed, rather than suffer the humiliation of

---

* Former Han dynasty, 206 B.C.–8 A.D.

being taken prisoner, he committed suicide.

Doesn't that sound like the sort of thing Homer would tell of his heroes? Entirely unexpected to me was how frequently the Chinese men reminded me of the Homeric Greeks: their love for extemporaneous debate and keen sense of the dramatic; their appreciation of the beauty of nature about them; the impromptu courts that the policemen held on the streets with hoi polloi for jury and themselves for judge, similar to the Athenian assemblies; the frequent expression of affection between men. We often saw men walking along the street hand in hand or even with their arms around each other, that was reminiscent of Achilles and Menelaos or the later Athenian friendships.

The more I saw of the country and its people, the more I liked them. I kept feeling that the foundation stuff of which they were made was good stuff.

Old Friend Unexpected

1925

The day before Christmas 1924, I found myself before dawn in a horse-carriage headed for the Nanking boat landing at Hsia-kuan, the old moon and a gorgeous planet low in the sky. It was the first of several surprise trips I made to Wuhu during language school to cover for Dr. Robert Brown, who had to represent Wuhu Hospital at meetings to consider rebuilding the hospital that had burned down in 1923.

At Wuhu, the hospital and other mission work were outside the wall and some distance from it, on hills that rose from so flat a river-valley that one got a fine wind, and view, from any of them. The hospital itself, or what was left of it from the fire, was on a promontory jutting out into the Yangtze river where it is about a mile wide. It runs north at Wuhu, with the city on the east bank. From the hospital we could hear waves on the shore below, the splash of oars and voices from many small boats always passing. There were big boats too. Standard Oil and other companies had landings along the bund, the embankment along the waterfront, and ocean-going freighters unloaded midstream. The hospital had contracts with several companies to keep a foreign doctor in port at all times, which brought in money to help keep it running.

The hospital was remarkable chiefly for its possibilities, in the form of an ugly excavation on top of the hill. One wing of the old hospital was saved, and was being used for a women's ward upstairs, administration, carpenter-shop and kitchen downstairs. Other small buildings housed the nurses, other helpers and the

Chinese doctors. At the bottom of the hill was a very small new stucco building for men's wards and operating room and laboratory. Another small new building was being erected beside it for offices, x-ray, examining and admitting rooms. Across the road from the gatehouse was a long, narrow mud hut with thatch roof for convalescents. Most equipment had been rescued from the old building.

Much of my time was spent planning what furniture we would need for the new building. Office furniture had already been made by the clever and able local carpenter, and it was more fun to work out what we needed in local material with local talent than to order from catalogues. But I used the catalogues to help with drawings and specifications, and was mighty glad to be going to a place where problems were tackled head on.

Chinese was the language of the hospital, and it spoke well for the language school that I was able to get on with what it was necessary for me to say and catch the drift of most that went on around me. My speech was the most rudimentary, but the words we had been taught had been so cleverly chosen that they covered simpler conversations. In operating we used Chinese except for a few words such as "sponge" and "cut" and anatomical names. I had been terrified, as I didn't know scissors from sutures, but the hospital staff had discovered by experience what words green foreigners were likely to know, and spoke accordingly. Two of the operations were for things that would have been grabbed for demonstration if they had turned up at home, but seemed to be ordinary in Wuhu. One was an odontoma, a jaw tumor, that would have figured in our textbooks.

The surgeon who was operating as the old hospital burned down, was packing to leave Wuhu on my first visit. He was highly able, well-liked by his patients and the genius behind plans for the new hospital. But he had not been able to run a tight ship with a crew that worked together, and was being replaced by Robert Brown. So there was a beastly hard situation when I first arrived, one that those still on the job met with heroic spirit. Foreign families on I-chi-shan had me to meals, and a Chinese feast was held in my honor by the business manager, who had been in the restaurant business in Indianapolis. The feast was of dishes unnumbered, from lotus root and sea slugs, which I found delicious, to sesame-seed cookies, peanuts and some things I couldn't diagnose.

I left Wuhu for Nanking at three one morning in the hospital rickshaw with the Brown's kitchen servant, Wang, running behind. When we reached the waterfront the boat was not in sight, so we sat down on a doorstep under a blinking electric light and Wang expounded to me the names and uses of everything in sight as well as the unsatisfactory nature of steamboats. Finally he began to haggle with the ferryman who was to take us out to the hulk (literally an old hulk used as a wharf) where the boat would tie up. After maintaining an air of indifference as to whether we ever got on any boat at all, a rate was at last fixed. Wang helped me into the sampan with a gallant flourish, and we rowed out into the beautiful dark river where the broken reflections of stars and ships' lights wavered across the water.

On the hulk were numerous other travelers, some eating food bought from a traveling restaurant hung from two poles across a man's shoulder. It looked and smelled good, but Wang said, "Not clean." There were men with enormous open-work reed baskets with live ducks inside, and others with big loads of dead ducks, drawn and plucked, all with their drumsticks pointed stiffly at the same angle. There was a "frozen-stiff" look about the marketed birds and fish that was quite gruesome. About five o'clock the Japanese ship ambled along and a mad scramble took place, everyone swarming over the rails at once. I spent the next few hours wrapped up in my big green blanket, sitting on something that looked like a ventilator, watching the morning come along the Yangtze.

In January the Nanking city gate was still closed the morning I set off on my second trip to Wuhu. I hopped out of my rickshaw and asked the soldiers in charge what time the gate would open, and three or four of them got hold of the big gate and pulled with all their strength and very slowly it swung back. I felt like Cleopatra as I sailed on down to the hulk at Hsia-kuan. The servant with me laughed and said, "You are very lucky; most times they don't do that."

Others were ahead of me, waiting for the boat, and had probably been there all night, for none of the boats had much of a system as to when they came along, the Japanese boats none whatever. Four men had laid their straw mats on the floor and unrolled their bedding on top and were sound asleep. Others were on top of some piles of sacks, more perched on boxes. A watchman paced back and forth with great show of importance.

There was nothing to sit on and nothing to do, so after I got over the first jolt I followed suit and curled up on some sacks with my duffle beside me and my head on my rolled-up green blanket. At six, when the lights went out, I fumbled around and got out my torch to avoid being stepped on in the dark, and only cat-napped. As it grew light I felt like walking around, as others were doing, and as I rose into view somebody exclaimed, "A foreigner!" It was fun to listen for awhile as they discussed where I had come from and where I might be going. I asked when they thought the boat might arrive, and from then on we had a lot of fun carrying on a conversation. It wasn't quite fair, though, because there were quite a lot of them to compare notes as to what I might be trying to say, whereas there was only one of me. We were lucky, for our boat came along about half past eight; some people often had to wait until eleven, or even afternoon. On board was an international assortment of passengers, including an awfully hard-boiled looking bunch of Europeans, and when Europeans in China were tough, they were beastly tough.

That first evening in Wuhu, just as I was thinking it would be well to turn in, along came a man with a note saying a doctor was needed on an Asiatic Petroleum Company (A.P.C.) boat. I hadn't thought before of combining joys and having an ambulance ride in a boat, but there followed a glorious launch ride down the moonlit river to the A.P.C. landing. There we went across the deck of a tanker and down into the fo'c'sle of a freighter, and aft through the crew's quarters to the cabin of the Chinese day pilot. The Scottish captain kept apologizing for the sort of place he was taking me into, but if he could have seen some of the places the Bellevue bus went to, he'd have saved his breath, for his boat was shipshape and clean and orderly, and the crew watched quietly.

All we could find out about the pilot suggested opium or malaria; if opium, very mild, and the man would be able to go on to Hankow; if malaria, the malignant kind and the man in immediate danger. So we took blood smears back to the hospital, found them negative and sent back word that the man could go on upriver.

Next morning, while making rounds with the Chinese doctors, a man arrived with two notes, one from the A.P.C. superintendent, an Englishman named Morton-Smith, and the other from Dr. Brown's wife. I read hers first: "Herewith 1 goat" (I looked at the man and noted that he looked fairly intelligent) "of a very fine flock belonging to Mr. Morton-Smith of the A.P.C." (Apparently this was some troublesome employee of the company; looked again and didn't think he looked the part). "Two have suddenly died and he fears poisoning. If you have a little time could you do an autopsy for him?" Then I read the other note and learned that this man was not the goat, but the goat's escort. The goat had arrived with him, riding in a rickshaw, and was that minute lying on the floor of the corridor as dead as could be waiting for a postmortem. It was a very big, fine goat, one of a valuable little herd Mr. Morton-Smith kept so his children could have raw milk. Pathological findings were few, rather pointing to poisoning but not definite enough to prove it.

Chinese New Year 1925 fell on 13 February, when I was back in Wuhu covering for Dr. Brown a third time. He was sick, and it fell on me to play the cruel and heartless person to tell all who wanted to go home for the holiday that it couldn't be done. It was amazing how many homes simultaneously developed crises; sick parents and dying grandparents were the order of the day, and the person to whom the story was brought was expected to go through all the formalities of being courteous enough to at least pretend to believe it. I hadn't been in China long enough to develop the art of using "polite words," but I realized the failing was mine. When one of the nurses said to me one day, "You Westerners aren't at all like the Chinese," and elucidated, when I asked, "You never learn to be courteous," I huffed that perhaps it was because in America courtesy as a virtue ranked definitely second to truth. He agreed there was a difference, and that he had been trained to feel courtesy was more important than accuracy.

I thought that very difference was to blame for a lot of misunderstandings and hurt feelings that result from superficial contacts between East and West; one side offends the other by its blunt rudeness, and is in turn offended by the evasions of the other.

The older missionaries told me that some things weren't expected to be taken literally at all but were polite ways of saying, as we say, "previous engagement, so sorry," and a few days later my raw thoughts as to veracity versus courtesy were altered further. A Chinese for whose opinion I had great respect said, "I have found that it is often unsafe to trust the words of foreigners. Too often they say one thing and then change their minds and do another. Nobody has any right to do that; word once given should always be kept!" I guess I came to the same old conclusion: that we can't make general statements as to racial differences, because the variations are individual rather than racial or national. The man who made this startling statement was scrupulous in living up to his stated ideal, and did *not* deal in "polite words."

In all the Chinese homes there were great preparations underway for the new year, when the Kitchen God, who kept the higher powers posted on the family's behavior, was sent back to heaven. As the time drew near for his annual report, it was wise to see that he went off in good humor, with firecrackers and celebration, so that he would deliver a good report and bring a lucky new year.

I didn't expect to watch the new year in, but did after all. There was a difficult maternity case pending; a midwife had already failed and the woman was worn out. I urged that the woman be brought into the hospital, as it was doubtful we could do anything in the home and it was dangerous to try. But the husband reported that the family had argued it all out and refused to follow our advice, so there was nothing for it but to go to the home and do our best. Dr. Chow, an intern on surgery, and an American nurse at Wuhu for a few months went with me.

Aside from the difficult nature of the job we were going to do, I was glad to be out on the eve of the new year. The streets were full of what the Chinese called "hot noise," the gaiety and celebration that we call a "hot time." All the doorways were decorated with red paper posters with auspicious quotations and hung over most of the doorways were variously decorated *Fu* characters meaning "happiness," or "good luck," according to the context. In front of many doors were incense-holders of wrought iron about four feet tall, holding a special incense made of many small sticks combined into one more than an inch in diameter. Such incense cost about a dollar a stick and was always burnt under the open sky in worship of Heaven, the household equivalent of the worship of Heaven by the emperor (before 1912) for the nation.

The home to which we came at last did not share in the general merriment. Everyone was worried, and they welcomed us into a courtyard, through that into a guestroom, and then into the bedroom where the family was assembled. A very frightened woman was the center of attention and the husband's face was full of trouble as he begged us to help and kept repeating that even if both mother and child should die they would not blame us.

The family was intelligent and cooperative. They prepared boiled water over little charcoal stoves, fastened back the carved-bedstead draperies of rich embroidery, and the old grandmother, so often the household person most likely to hinder efficient work, was a helpful colleague.

We got scrubbed and ready, appalled at the prospect of the job ahead, fearful of the results. As was our custom, we prayed, and my Buddhist intern added his amen to that prayer. Then our nurse started the ether, and the fight was on. Well, our prayer was answered; it was not so difficult as we had feared, and the child was delivered, dead, the father thought, but mouth-to-mouth insufflation started its breathing, a process that amazed the family. The

41

mother, too, was saved, and when she regained consciousness, was pleased with the baby, even though a girl.

The new year had been with us for a couple of hours when we got out again into the street sweet with its incense smoke and firecrackers. I had hated to take Dr. Chow out on a hard job on Chinese New Year, but he rejoiced all the way back to I-chi-shan and said he wouldn't mind a case like that every night. A success made up for any amount of work put into language, and for a whole lot of sorrow over cases that came in too late to be saved.

We had one of the other kind not long before this happy one. We were giving some treatment to a woman who had just been brought in and as she began to feel relieved her husband explained, "Yes, what the *p'u-sa* said was right!" The *p'u-sa* are Buddhist saints who have given up their own hard-earned chance of attaining oneness with Buddha for the privilege of helping suffering mankind in its upward struggle. But the term *p'u-sa* is also loosely applied to the images representing these beneficent spirits, so to any temple images. The one he meant was the *hu-li-ching*, or fox fairy, no saint at all but a mischievous spirit that goes about burning down houses and doing other nasty things. He said he and his wife came in from the country and put up at an inn, and the following morning he went to burn incense to the *hu-li-ching* and ask advice about his wife's health. He received a slip of paper with some characters on it and was told he should take her to our hospital, and that when she had recovered he was to take back an offering to the temple. Alas, the *hu-li-ching* was no diagnostician; the woman had an advanced carcinoma, and there was no hope for her. All we could do was to make her last days a bit less dreadful than they would have been without help.

In March 1925 I was again headed for Wuhu. I wished it didn't have to be the week before exams, but as the philosophical Chinese say when a thing can't be helped, *mei yu fa-tzu*, and cheerfully accept whatever they can't change; if they fretted as most Westerners do, they'd simply perish. It gave me a chance to get more into the swing of things at Wuhu.

While there I was called to the telephone to answer a call from one of the British steamboat landings. A man at the other end said, "Is this the doctor? We have two cases here that just came off the boat, and we'd like you to tell us what to do with them." When I asked, "Cases of what?" he replied, "sulphuric ether." I racked my brain to think whether I had ever heard of that kind of poisoning, and wondered whether there was a stomach pump that could be gotten quickly, as I'd left mine in Nanking. With a view to finding out how long before the poison had been taken I asked, "Where did they come from?" and was horrified to get the reply, "Rotterdam, Holland." Then he went on, "You see, we can't get the ether through customs until we know the amount of ether in each case and its value." So it was boxes, not people!

On my way back to Nanking I traveled on a small boat known as "The Launch," though it seemed to me a young steamboat. There wasn't a cabin to spare, but the chief engineer offered me the use of his and watched with great interest as I pounded out a family letter. He asked me to pound again as others clustered at the door to watch, then tried out the machine to the great admiration of the crowd. He was expected to be able to expound all about the process, and in fact asked very intelligent questions. Then by request I was off on another demonstration while the crowd inspected the first sheet of my letter and thought it a great circus to hear the bell and watch the carriage shoot back to start a new line.

By then the door and window of the stateroom were both jammed, and what light got in came around the corners. The crowd began to guess my age and ask where my husband was, so I explained that in America it was a matter of choice as to whether one has a husband. Then a policeman took up a position on a bench on the other side of the suitcase holding my typewriter and extended the conversation to religion and on through various topics to cigarettes, and offered me one. They were all friendly people, anything but boring.

I tried to use my Yangtze trips to write family letters, and those trips turned into more or less a continual reception, with such sociable companions as drifted by, people possessed of lots of imagination and always polite. On one trip there was an exceedingly impolite little dog who wasn't averse to sampling some of my lunch, but then stood at a safe distance and yapped what sounded like "*Wai-kuo! Wai kuo!*" which meant "foreign, foreign." But he was the only impolite creature I met, which is probably a lot better than a Chinese would be able to report for an average boatload of passengers in America.

When I got back to Nanking, old friend unexpected turned up in the shape of rain, most important as we had been having a serious drought. In January the ponds all over the city had been reduced to shallow, thick muck, many of them so dry we could walk across them without getting muddy. Vegetables were for the most part nonexistent, and everybody wondered what people would eat. Ponds and wells were dry, and water-carts worked early and late bringing in very expensive and very bad water from the old moat outside the city wall. Dust lay in drifts along the roads and filled the air so that we hated to breathe or to open our eyes while the wind blew. It was next to impossible to keep our hair clean, so I bobbed mine. Our teachers told me they knew all about the queer new feeling of it from their memory of the time at the change of empire to republic when they got their queues amputated.

I had been astonished to see the green fields at Wuhu. There the plains were almost level with the Yangtze so that when the river was high the plains flooded and the little mud huts melted down into the muddy river. But this low ground, although a danger, assured a constant water supply. Nanking is high and out of danger from floods, but suffers in dry weather.

When the rains came in March, the Chinese spoke of "full *p'iao* (the gourds used to dip water from large water jars) of water coming down," similar to our idiom, "coming down in buckets." So often their idioms were similar to ours. Of a stupid person they said, "his head is made of wood," and of an unimportant thing, "it doesn't count." Questionable ideas they labeled, "half raw, not cooked," much as we said, "half baked." And a common saying about someone not paying attention was, "in at the east ear, out at the west."

By March it was really spring, with rain enough to turn the fields of young vegetables and grain a vivid green. Fruit trees were in bloom and kites numerous. Wild flowers at our door, an exquisite wisteria-colored blossom that I took for sand-violets, I learned later were some member of the cruciferae. If they grew at home people would rave over them and make verses about them; perhaps they did that in China.

By April, although we hadn't had enough rain to more than cover the bottoms of the ponds, the face of the country around Nanking had changed completely. It was like a garden, the fear of famine was over, and our hearts rejoiced in the green and the violets that popped up everywhere through the grass and with them a lovely yellow potentilla. Along the edges of compound walls trailed sprays of coral and crimson corydalis, while the fields were glorious with an herb of the mustard tribe grown for greens that reminded me of the cloth-of-gold in Tennyson's *Idyls of The King*.

With the coming of spring we students went to the ceremony in honor of Confucius, that occurred each fall and spring. The word our teachers used for it was not the one used for worship, but meant veneration, or honor, much as we might in English mean by hero-worship.

We left the school about 1:30 in the morning and walked a mile to the Confucian temple where soldiers were on guard and many of the literati had assembled. The hundred best-educated men of the city were supposed to be on hand. We gathered in a big courtyard with stars shining down through ancient pine trees, big drums and musical gongs sounding. At the north end of the courtyard was a terrace and above that the temple with its long sweep of roof curved against the stars. Wandering about in the courtyard were groups of bright-looking students from the Confucian school who were to take part in the service.

While we waited we were permitted to enter the temple where a big portrait of Confucius was on the wall opposite the door. He appeared wise and benevolent, and his portrait was flanked with tablets listing his honors. To either side were tablets with the names of his chief followers, and still further to the sides the names of well-educated men, eligible to be listed if their lives and characters qualified them for the honor. Nobody who believed in demons could be chosen. If a man's name was posted about whom it was afterward discovered that he feared demons, his tablet was promptly removed.

A big gong sounded the start of the service. Up across the courtyard and up the side steps of the terrace came the officials, the orchestra, and two big groups of boys to perform the ceremonial dances. The orchestra had flutes, fifes and a kind of miniature pipe organ played with the mouth called *sheng*. There were also gongs arranged in a musical series, and a set of surprisingly musical stone chimes. A set of strange things somewhat like the necks of enormous violins, strung with a lot of gut strings across a big bridge and apparently intended to be played like a harp, were laid out in place as in the old days, but no one knew how to play them. It was explained that they were *ku shih-hou lai te*, "come from the ancient time."

At the sound of the biggest drum the service started with an intoned announcement from the master of ceremonies, then the orchestra began to play, in marvelously rich harmony, chanting singers combining their tones in a way that was exquisitely beautiful and different from anything I had ever heard before.

Presently the first group of dancers of sixty-four students, perhaps eight to fourteen in age, who were deeply impressed with the importance of the occasion, began their dance. They were dressed in dark blue silk gowns with heavy embroidery, and each held a small axe-like implement in his right hand and a small wooden shield in his left. The shield was a sign of imperial rank, and this group of dancers signified that Confucius had been officially raised to imperial rank. In strict time with the music they turned and changed positions, never moving from their fixed places.

Next the civil governor appeared, escorted by various attendants, to present offerings in memory of Confucius. His costume, alas, was the one discordant note, for he had donned a foreign frock coat and high plug hat that in contrast with the Chinese garments looked atrocious. He went up to the temple and made an oration in honor of Confucius, then dedicated offerings of slaughtered young buffalo, three pigs, a couple of sheep, various baskets of vegetables and other foods and a bolt of fine cloth. Again and again he went up into the temple, kowtowed before the tablets and held up the offerings before them.

The second group of student dancers was dressed in plain dark blue cotton gowns and held in one hand a bamboo case two or three feet long with holes in it, perhaps some musical instrument, and in their right hands slender bamboo wands. Set into the top of each wand was the most beautiful golden-pheasant feather, long and shining, that bent like tall grain with their dance and with every breeze that blew. Those feathers were precious and saved for this particular ceremony; it was against the law to buy or sell them. Even more beautiful than the first, this dance seemed to illustrate the old archers, then the dancers stooped and seemed to plant their feathers, and as they slowly rose the feathers seemed to grow from the terrace like tall rice stalks.

We students had one more magnificent event before final exams, our trip to Peking. We traveled north by train, in boxcars, each person equipped with a bedding roll consisting of a thin mattress and some blankets roped up in heavy oiled canvas, of a beautiful orange-brown shade, called a *yu-pu*. At night we spread the *yu-pu* on the floor of the boxcar and our bedding on that. The weather was dry and we had a number of dust storms along the way, so were loaded down with Gobi dust and ate quantities of it. Also among our stuff were enormous baskets in which we carried our food. These big baskets had a net of string over the contents, and riding proudly on top of each pile was an inverted enamel washbasin which served as dishpan and safe site for our Sterno cooking outfit in addition to their specified purpose.

I could go on and on about the beauty and mysterious charm of Peking, the still-magnificent city of ancient history, wavering present and undoubtedly great future. Several times we got to ride real horses, not the short-legged, tough little animals of Nanking, and if ever there were an interesting place to ride, it was under the shade of the old city wall, out through the great gates and along the willow-fringed moat. Sometimes we passed strings of camels, and my horse, who objected on principle to anything so outlandish, registered disapproval by jumping sideways in full gallop while the camels scorned even to notice our existence.

We went first to Pei Hai, one of a chain of lakes made for the pleasure of the Mongol rulers, a beautiful lake with pines leaning over it and paths winding about, trailing parrot's-feather in masses in its shallow water, great flocks of ducks sailing proudly on its surface and one old heron poised on a rock.

On the north side of the lake were palaces and temples and the famous dragon screen of many-colored tiles, and Coal Hill, where the last emperor of the Ming dynasty chose to hang himself rather than fall into the hands of a rebel peasantry that overran the capital.* We found it occupied by a squad of soldiers doing a goosestep so that they looked like poorly made mechanical toys, then wall-scaling at a rush in a way that proved they weren't.

As we climbed Coal Hill, the astonishing expanse of yellow roofs of the Forbidden City came into view and made us gasp with its marvel of rich shining color between yellow and burnished bronze, but with a warmth that metal could never have. Those lovely roofs must have been copied from tents, their corners flung up in a gesture that reminded me of the abandon of strong waves flinging themselves one after another against a rocky coast, or of great clouds piling themselves up in a glorious sunset. Sunset it was, and afterglow, for the glory of the Manchus and their Ch'ing dynasty was departed.

There were still many Chinese in those days who wondered whether the taxes that supported this luxury were not a fair price for the peace and security of empire, and in the huge audience room in the Forbidden City where the Empress Dowager Tz'u-hsi once held court, we saw a touching reminder that for some the

---

* The Manchus defeated the rebels and founded the Ch'ing dynasty.

empire had not yet passed. A lot of Mongolians were in the city who had journeyed from the northwest to pay homage to the Panchen Lama, then in Peking. The Mongolian men were gorgeous in long robes of yellow and purple and plum and orange, and wore huge ornate boots turned up at the toes. The women wore head-dresses with chains and fringes of coral and silver and jade. In the throne room we came on a large group kowtowing before the empty thrones.

We had a strangely unreal feeling in the Forbidden City, where so many generations of men had longed to be allowed to see the glories but had been denied. We were amazed and awed by the glory of those golden roofs, the brilliant white of marble-paved courts and carved marble balustrades, the unbelievable blending of rich colors in painted pillars and cornices. The halls and courts were empty except for sightseers and a few caretakers and guards, and I wondered what it must have been like in the days when the courts were thronged with officials in their gorgeous embroidered silk robes.

In the small palace overlooking Pei Hai, we visited the rooms where the old empress and her court favorites spent so much of the nation's money on their own pleasures, and were surprised to see how small was the theater where she watched plays.

Down at the boat landing we boarded an old flat barge and were ferried across to the north side, remembering the story of how the empress was disturbed one day during a boating party by the noise of guns besieging the foreign legations, and ordered the guns to stop until the party was over.

The Winter Palace was an apparently interminable aggrega-tion of buildings all in the same style, with painted pillars and beams, and up-turned golden roofs. Everywhere was ornate detail, a wealth of symbolism in dragons representing the emperor, phoenixes the empress, flowers and landscapes everywhere. But nowhere, except in the guard-towers over the walls and the occa-sional pagoda, was there more than one storey, and all decoration was secondary to structure and never allowed to run riot. The simplicity of plan and structure, I believe, explained the restfulness and impressiveness of the whole.

At the National Museum's marvelous collection of ancient treasures, the thing that impressed us most was not the ancient vases nor the court costumes nor the musical instruments nor the curious carvings in wood and stone, nor the screens done in jewels and kingfisher feathers, nor yet the jewel trees, of semi-precious stones, made in exquisite imitation of real flowering plants; it was the scrolls with characters written by emperors and scholars of hundreds of years ago that made us stand in rapt admiration. I don't wonder the Chinese have the feeling they do that paper with characters written on it is sacred. Those ancient characters, with the strokes done before the time of Christ, would be fine models for present-day writing. We stood and looked long and silently, hoping that somehow those beautiful sweeping strokes might sink deep into our consciousness and help our poor efforts at characters to improve. We felt new and raw by contrast.

We had autos for a day trip out to the Western Hills, taking the flat road that the Empress Dowager Tz'u-hsi used to go back and forth to her Summer Palace. It was bordered much of the way by willows, with strings of camels coming in from the west. Built at the foot of the Western Hills, on a hillside overlooking a beautiful lake, both said to be artificial, the Summer Palace was a great many scattered buildings with covered passageways between. The millions that went into it were from taxes levied to build up the navy and the famous marble boat moored by the shore. The old Empress Dowager certainly had an exaggerated idea of the part her own pleasure played in the affairs of the empire.

When we climbed up on the Great Wall, we could see great snow-capped mountain ranges, and the lure of that which is beyond laid hold of us. With some difficulty we climbed down the Mongolian side of the wall and walked out into the great silent land beyond, vast and barren and still. In our imaginations we peopled it with the hordes of fierce barbarians that had swept up those slopes against the wall.

One afternoon we went to a Lamaist service conducted by lamas with high yellow headdresses like Roman helmets, attended by a great many monks and a group of Mongolians. The service was most impressive with chants and prayers and something like our communion with little cups from which they drank. In the temple courtyard a fair was in progress. On cloths spread on the ground were little brass cups made to hold oil and a wick, to burn before the Buddha, beads and jewelry, porcelain, lacquer, carved jade, many sorts of craftwork and little idols to carry home to far-off villages, and horrors—American buttons and garters!

It was a relief to come into the simplicity of the high, empty hall of the Confucian temple, with only some beautifully carved characters to tell of the virtue and wisdom of the great sage, and side boards listing his disciples. In the same enclosure was the Hall of the Classics, a long pavilion built three sides of a square, surrounded by ancient pine trees, and under the pavilion roof stone tablets carved with the classics that have been the basis of Chinese civilization and education for so many centuries. Once, China's first emperor, too strong-willed to be bothered with the limitations the classics imposed, tried to destroy them all, and the men who had committed them to memory. He very nearly succeeded in eradicating all traces of Confucian literature, but in one temple the classics were saved by building them into a wall. Later they were brought out and copied, then the stone tablets were carved to make them safe forever.

The boxcar that we had on the trip back to Nanking was a fine big new one, with baggage racks around the walls which provided sleeping space for a lot of us. At T'ai Shan, the sacred mountain in Shantung where T'ien, or Heaven, was worshipped, we were side-tracked for a day to climb the great mountain.

It was of jagged rock, with clumps of ancient pines and cedars and occasional flares of flowering fruit trees clinging in crevasses. Steep stone stairs with frequent carved gateways and shrines led upward. Halfway up the trail was hidden in thick fog. The chair coolies told us it was about to rain and dashed into a little hut and couldn't be pried loose. Then the rain did come down and kept up for hours. We finally gave up the attempt to reach the shrine to Lao-tzu and went back down those slippery stone steps at an appalling rate. Back at the boxcar we pulled out what dry articles of apparel we had and were a weird outfit, in bathrobes and blankets and all manner of mismatched rigging, and the populace came from afar to look and wonder. The missionaries in the town sent down for our wettest things, built furnace fires in three homes to dry them out, while we strung our *pu-kai*, bedding rolls, on ropes between our car and another freight car and hung out a lot more things until the place looked like Solomon's backyard on wash day.

Throughout our language school year, rumblings between warlords continued their prelude to Chiang Kai-shek's Northern Expedition. The Nanking military governor was replaced and had to get out of the city, and one night we heard drums beating a long time, supposedly indicating his departure. But his soldiers, who were legion and had not been paid, surrounded his home demanding payment. Eventually he did get away, and the indignant soldiers who were left behind burned and looted about a hundred shops. The new military governor promptly executed some who might have been responsible, and left their bodies lying around the streets as a warning.

For a time it looked as though there might be some action around Nanking, but long-time missionaries laughed at the *yao yen*, the rumors, and our consul, an able and canny man, the son of missionaries and well-versed in things Chinese, thought it unlikely.

For us martial law was on and that was about all except for the entertainment we had reading home newspapers, which reported that General Wu P'ei-fu had marched into Nanking in November 1924 with 4,000 troops. That was news to us. We had heard he was in the city for a day or so to confer with the military governor.

Then on 30 May 1925 Shanghai International Settlement police, officered by the British, killed thirteen demonstrators against a Japanese cotton mill. This act fueled the nationalism and anti-foreignism that had been stirring into what was to become known as the May Thirtieth Movement, in which students and

52

workers across the country joined in demonstrations, boycotts and strikes that stopped shipping and rail lines, disrupted commerce and industry. In Nanking, where Christian schools' students were numerous and swayed students in the direction of moderation and non-violence, we had less disturbance than in many other places. Yet it was a tense time.

Students at Nanking University issued an open letter to the foreign community explaining their point of view of the whole affair. They assured us their protests were against only the Japanese because the mills were theirs and it was their jitters that set off the police, and the British because the police who fired were under British control and exempt from Chinese laws because of extraterritoriality.

One afternoon word came from Nanking police that there was some looting in the south end of town. Streets cleared and shop-shutters went up like magic. The language school campus had a high wall around it and was obviously foreign, but everybody considered it a refuge and a lot of our teachers and their families slept in the school that night. Some of us stood out where we could see our iron gate silhouetted against the streetlight and watched silent figures arrive by ones and twos, each with a bundle of bedding.

Mr. Chia, our chief teacher, his wife and three little daughters camped in the gatehouse and I took them my extra cot and blankets and got to meet Mrs. Chia, a lady of the old school. Most charming and gracious, she was a marvel to us unpolished occidentals. The children were subdued and a bit apprehensive, but quiet and polite and watched with interest the setting up of the cot but weren't enthusiastic to sleep on it. A rickshaw puller wanted to leave his rickshaw within our gate for safekeeping, so our matron let him stow it away. Then she told him she wanted to see his face so that she would know him when he came to get it. He stepped into the light from the gatehouse door, took off his hat and made a graceful bow and went silently out into the city.

After all that, nothing happened. The teachers were all dead for sleep the next day, but took great care to let us know they distinguished between personal and patriotic feeling, and were especially nice to our English student. Although under pressure to leave the school, they came loyally day after day, and the whole situation brought us a lot closer to them than we would have been without it.

We Americans found people on the streets as friendly as before. Sometimes they asked which was our honorable country, but always took our word for the fact. When I remarked about that to a Chinese friend, he replied, "They know that Christians speak the truth." What a reputation to live up to.

We were fast approaching the end of language school, and I marveled when I remembered the glib way I once spoke of taking the first year "to get the language." In the first month or so I altered that formula to "get a working knowledge of the language." By spring 1925 I realized that all we could possibly do was break through the edge of it. The further we went the more we realized the marvelous complexity of it and the more we wondered at the brain power of the people who could really handle it.

Language school closed toward the end of June. Everyone survived the examinations, but farewells were harder. We tried to tell the teachers how much their efforts and their spirit did for us throughout the year, but our attempts foundered in our vocabulary and we could only hope that as keen mind-readers they gathered more than we could express.

We were headed for the mountains known as Lushan, but steamers and trains were stopped, workers on strike. We had to get off campus as our old building was to be torn down and rebuilt, so we packed up all our worldly goods wondering where we could unpack them, and were variously distributed in Nanking homes.

Later in July, when travel was once more possible, we got ourselves and all our luggage down to Hsia-kuan, where I sat on an upended trunk with my typewriter perched on another to write my family letter. What a crowd gathered to watch, many of them pedlars. One was a very pretty woman selling fragrant blossoms, another selling bananas of a deadly green color, another some very good-looking peaches that made me regret I didn't eat unscalded fruit. One hawked little crocheted bags for coppers, still another crullers a foot long. A boy by my elbow had a big bunch of chopsticks for the use of people who bought their food on the hulk while waiting for the steamer, another had a rack of what looked like small featherdusters, and that they were, for the ears. These seemed to be used as much as toothbristles, and the populace considered us remiss not to use them. The pedlar who interested me the most had a basket of beautiful hard-boiled blue-green duck eggs. Then along came a man with little lacquer bowls, to watch the strange machine pounding on top of the trunk, and those who had been watching longer expounded for the benefit of new arrivals. All sorts of questions were ventured. One who asked my friend's age and was asked to guess, raised a laugh by guessing forty-four. That was a compliment, putting her age ahead by about twenty years.

The audience inquired about carbons, and it appealed to their practical mind to be able to knock out four letters at once. Then they wanted to know about the red half of the ribbon, so I did part of the letter in red for them. I asked if any of them would like to hit a few letters, but they all laughed and declined.

A man with a great handful of fans stood up on some luggage to watch over the shoulders of the rest. Everybody used fans except a few foreigners who hadn't yet acquired the habit. The question of pockets big enough for long fans was easily solved by sticking the fan down the back of one's collar. I hadn't realized how we have always wasted the backs of our collars by not using them as a place to carry things.

Every one of the crowd around me was the soul of courtesy. It seemed to be inborn, and there was real kindness a-plenty at the bottom of it, in spite of reports to the contrary. One day not long before that I saw what I had been told I'd never see in China. A woman by the side of the road was very sick and I wanted to get her into a rickshaw and to the hospital. Immediately there were many people in the by-standing crowd ready and anxious to help lift her into the rickshaw.

The crowd at Hsia-kuan told me that they could always distinguish Americans from the British because our noses are longer. But when I asked them about my short one, they replied that it was like the difference between the Chinese and their neighbors to the east: sometimes one can't tell!

Along about midday the boat hove in sight. After we'd gotten ourselves and all our stuff aboard, the captain said we'd have to get off again as there wasn't room for us. But when we told him we had camp cots and would be more than delighted to sleep on the deck, he let us stay. We had a glorious trip, two nights on the boat, and more breeze than Nanking had boasted for some time.

When we reached Kiukiang, Dr. Edward Perkins, who had made my education financially possible, was there with some of his hospital crew to welcome us. It was well they did, for we were a big crowd with loads of baggage to be seen to and bargained about, and in the scrimmage that followed we'd all have "perished miserable" if it hadn't been for Dr. Perkins.

We were supposed to have gotten in the night before, but since it was morning we went right up the hill. And some hill it is. Lushan is a very grown-up mountain, and the coolies who cheerfully carried us in carrying chairs from the bottom certainly deserved credit. They were a wiry lot, with very little arm development but thick cushions of flesh on their shoulders and tremendous muscles in the calves of their legs. There weren't any middle-aged men among them, as packing loads like that every day couldn't be kept up for more than a few years. One man carried up a steamer trunk by himself.

Kuling, the foreign settlement on Lushan, after the valley heat was simply heaven. In Nanking we had no relief from heat at night, and had all been sick from it. Once we got to the mountain I didn't mind admitting that it had not been a cheering prospect to look forward to a summer in the valley. Some of the Nanking missionary families who arrived after we did had been having a bad time, parents standing watches during the nights to fan their small children. Some couldn't afford the increased expense of the trip since the cheap Japanese ships had been taken off the run, but the bishop decided that if they stayed in the heat all summer there would be a lot of breakdowns. In the Chinese idiom, he "thought out a way" to make up the difference in steamer costs, and sent them on to the mountains.

Once, after the British and Japanese boats stopped, the Hong Kong-British Jardine-Matheson line manned a boat with a Russian crew and started it up the river from Shanghai. It was a risky thing to do, and they knew it. The boat ran aground near Anking, just above Wuhu, and there it stayed. When the next China Merchant boat came upriver, its captain tried to go to the assistance of the other boat. But he had a lot of students on board who had more intensity of patriotism than they had perception of nautical ethics. They raised a row and made the captain go on and leave the other boat behind. Eventually the steamer got off the bar, but the British didn't try that again.

The plains below the mountains were dry, so dry that rice yellowed in the parched fields, the time when a last-minute rain could save it nearly past. That meant famine in central China in the fall. Transportation difficulties made things a lot worse, for whatever rice could be brought in from other districts was sure to be too expensive for the poor to buy. It was already too expensive, and some merchants made it more so by hoarding it for famine prices.

Down in the valley, processions went through village streets, lines of men with carrying poles with green leaves on them topped with bottles of water to suggest to the rain gods that water was needed. A high Kiukiang official made a pilgrimage to the city temples to make offerings to all the gods for rain. He wore the rain costume of the country folk, straw sandals and straw-thatch coat and hat, and carried in front of his chair a big jar to catch the rain. He visited all the Kiukiang temples without success. Even a few drops would save face for him, and he came up to make the rounds of Kuling temples.

One of the temples he undoubtedly visited was a little Taoist temple in a cave in the side of a great cliff that went down very nearly straight to the Yangtze plain. When we visited it we sat on an ancient stone bench overlooking the many-terraced valley that stretched across to the western hills, and watched the wide Yangtze with sailboats working slowly upstream, the city of Kiu-kiang close to the river. Tiny blue supper-smokes rose through small clumps of trees here and there from little mud huts with thatched roofs. It was such a peaceful view and so cool was the breeze that it was hard to realize that down there it was blistering hot, that in those villages below us were fear of famine and fear of the unrest that was spreading throughout China.

We followed a narrow path along the face of the cliff to the little temple in the cave, a poor little affair with no roof but the overhanging rock and no front wall at all. An image stood looking out across the wide valley, before him a table with an incense jar, a small wooden drum, a bamboo holder with bamboo slips inscribed with fortunes and admonitions, and two blocks of wood, almost semi-spheres, for divination. In the back of the cave, where the ceiling rocks came down low, was a famous spring. A long-handled dipper rested in the spring, and the saying was that whoever drank of the water was sure of long life. My teacher was surprised to learn I did not drink of it, for it is always done, just as one kisses the Blarney stone or throws one's lei into Honolulu harbor.

We took several other short hikes back over the ranges behind us toward Poyang Lake. One day we climbed in rain and fog following little well-worn trails used chiefly by the men who gathered brushwood to sell in Kiukiang this side of the mountain, or Nankang the other. The hills were covered with orange tiger-lilies and blue lilies something like harebells.

We looked out over layers of mountains southward. Banks of mist rose between them, and there was a silvery light on the hills and mist and a strange indefiniteness of hill and cloud that made it impossible to guess where the horizon might be. It gave me a strange, detached feeling, of having gotten back into something awesome, primitive and tremendous, like the creation of the world. Sometimes when the mists parted we could see a great gap in one of the hills, and a high promontory called Lion's Leap that looked down on Poyang Lake. Then the silver mists would close in again and we would trace mountain ranges where there were none, for the clouds were as real as the hills and the hills as unreal as the clouds.

Our hike to Nankang Pass, about five miles to the south of us, was all on stone roads or good paths, hundreds of years old, trod through the centuries by the many pilgrims who have come from all over China to this sacred mountain. Nankang Pass is the place where the path goes through the range of mountains between us and Poyang Lake, an enormous lake over a hundred miles long. The shoreline must be many hundreds of miles long, for it has lots of irregular bays and twists that go shooting off into the country both sides for long distances. It stretched to the horizon, and far beyond the farthest point that we could see lay Nanchang at its far end.

On the nearest shore was the old city of Nankang, with its two pagodas standing straight and tall out of the plain. Three small sailboats made their ways slowly down the lake, and a small steamboat towing some barges came out from behind a point. The lake is very shallow, so that nobody who sailed it felt really initiated who had not been hung up overnight on sandbars at least once.

To our right the range of mountains climbed westward in a series of peaks, a real sawtooth with jagged rocks all along the peaked crests like the back of some prehistoric monster. Parallel to that range we could see another, rather better-wooded, with a row of wind-twisted pines along the crest, like the ridgepoles of some Chinese temples. So close was the likeness, with rows of small ridgepole animals to guard the temple from evil spirits that go flying about in the air, that we wondered whether the idea for Chinese temple ridgepole animals didn't come from such mountains as these.

We ate our supper sitting in a cranny in the rocky side of the mountain by the pass, where we could look down and watch men go by on the road below, carrying brushwood to Nankang to be fuel for the blue supper-smokes. Nankang was not too friendly to foreigners in those days, but as we looked down from our rocky perch it was hard to imagine anything but peace and contentment there. We returned by moonlight, following the road around the shoulders of the mountains, over old stone bridges, across rocky ravines, back to where we could see the lights of Kuling again.

"We" included Dr. Perkins and Georgie, his wife, and our chubby, smiling servant, Lo, who went along to carry the supper-basket and lantern. Lo's smile was not always evident at the start of a trip, for he thought it very serious business, this trudging off to some place miles away to eat supper. But when we would arrive at some gorgeous view, his smile appeared and broadened.

Another good hike was over to Lion's Leap, where the rocks go down a straight four thousand feet to the plain. From there we could see, not far from the foot of the cliff, a school known as the White Deer Grotto, that claimed to be the oldest university in the world, and still had a library and a number of students. I had no desire to stand close to the edge of the precipice, but by lying down flat and sticking my head over the edge I got a marvelous view of the rocky wall and the plains far below. There was a pinnacle of rock standing straight up from the plain for a couple of thousand feet, like the tower of some great cathedral. In the crevices of the cliff below me were wind-stunted pines with their branches reaching out over space. It was on top of Lion's Leap, with the great cliff and wide plains below, that our smiling Lo grew enthusiastic and asked with proud assurance of a negative answer, "Do you have anything like this in America?"

There were a number of good-sized caves nearby, and we explored one so large and dark and with such deep recesses in two directions that I worried lest one of the mountain lions or tigers should appear and object.

On another hike we went westward along the main valley to the famous Three Trees, which are big enough and ancient enough to rate their fame. All three tower up like California redwoods, and indeed two are of some similar species of conifer. The third is a gingko.

Almost under their shade stands the Yellow Dragon Temple, so named from a resoundingly hollow rock in the paving that resembles a dragon's head. The temple was in better condition than many, the images freshly gilded and free of dust. One day we found the doors of the temple closed and a service going on inside. A monk told us that at regular intervals the priests and monks from all the little temples on the mountains assembled there, as they had that day, for general meetings, a manifestation of the revival of Buddhism, of which we heard much but saw little.

Some of our teachers went along to Kuling with us so that we could continue to study mornings. Mr. Li, my teacher, was a keen observer and full of fun. One day he made an interesting remark in reply to something I said about Chinese being opposed to foreigners, "But the Chinese also oppose themselves," and went on to say that one of the greatest difficulties China faced was the lack of cooperation within China, the wars between provinces and selfish manipulation of officials.

I had some flute lessons during the summer from one of our teachers who could write our kind of musical notation, a mystery to most Chinese. He wrote down and taught me two Chinese tunes, and one day when he and I were playing together on two flutes pitched alike, we suddenly realized there was a third playing with us. We stopped, and the third went on for awhile, and we discovered smiling Lo sitting on the steps with his *hsiao*, a sort of bamboo fife, using the opportunity to learn a tune from a good teacher.

We took our teachers for a picnic, and as good sports they all came and ate heartily of both fried chicken and ice cream, and manfully tackled everything else that came along. One thought boiled beets belonged on top of the ice cream but was rescued in time. The unquestioning way they ate everything implied a confidence and sporting spirit that were truly remarkable, considering the horror most Chinese felt for our kind of food. It made us suspect they had all agreed beforehand to do or die to demonstrate that their friendliness had not been affected by politics.

After that I did a lot of medical work in an attempt to ease up some on the amount Dr. Perkins had to do. People started to leave the mountain, and the dryness of the early summer was relieved by wet weather. The brooks rose from trickles to raging streams that dug out their banks and pulled down bridges. Fog and clouds we had always with us.

By September first the China Students' Union was urging all students to return to their classrooms when schools opened, so the prospects for peace and progress looked good. I was eager to get into my real job in Wuhu and enthusiastic about China.

Perhaps I hadn't been in China long enough, but I couldn't agree with some of the missionaries that China was depressing. I had found it anything but. Pitiful in its poverty and suffering, yes. Perplexing and often astonishing in its reactions, yes. Difficult in interpretation of some of its moods, yes. Tragic in its domination of the many by the few, yes. But always, beneath the difficulties and sometimes in the midst of things that would discourage, you could feel the great potential power of the people to overcome, to work out a way to escape approaching calamity, or, if calamity fell, to gather up the fragments and carry on.

I liked China and the Chinese, and the more I saw of them the better I liked them and the firmer faith I had in them. It wasn't that they were going to make good. They had already made good. There was no end to the things China could do for the world.

Getting Into the Game

1925-1926

E arly in October 1925 I went down from Lushan to the plains, alone except for the chair-coolies, and was glad of a chance to revel in the beauty of the winding way along the ledges, the rivers and homes by the wayside. There was no sound but the soft pad-pad of the coolies' grass sandals, their good-natured jollying back and forth, and the creak of the chair. At the foot of the mountain came the bus trip across the few miles to Kiukiang, and after months of nothing faster than a chair or rickshaw, it seemed as though we were tearing through space.

Georgie Perkins was waiting for me, and as soon as I had gotten rid of the road dust we started out for the Water of Life Hospital down a lane banked both sides with high-plumed pampas grass, past the future building site for the new Water of Life Hospital. At the end of the lane we came out into an open street with a big drillfield on the far side. To the left and down the road a ways, past an army barracks, we walked along watching the soldiers drilling till we came to the door of what had been a *yamen*, a local seat of government. Through the doorway we could see a court with palm trees and blooming flowers and a lawn beneath the palms. Beyond that was a trellis with masses of wisteria, then a doorway and a glimpse of a second court and a class of student nurses listening intently to a teacher. And the teacher was Dr. Perkins. So this place of green courtyards and many flowers, of rambling buildings totally Chinese in structure and design, was honestly and truly the Water of Life Hospital that Dr. Perkins had established and financed on his own.

When his class was over, he joined Georgie and me to tour the hospital. Inside the front gateway along the wall of the first court, hung a number of "merit boards" that had been presented to the hospital in recognition of its services. These were plain black or a dark rich brown, each with four big gilt characters, some quotation from the Confucian classics expressing a thought appropriate to the feeling of the donor. At the ends of each board were small characters with Dr. Perkins' Chinese name, the name of the hospital, the date, and the donor's name. One was presented by the Chinese government at the time of the pneumonic plague, and bore the seal of the president of China.

The rooms, built between courts, had fine ventilation, and a lot of work was actually done out-of-doors on the covered walks. Some of the walks had been walled in and made into wards, but they took kindly to their new form and did not shriek that their structure had been changed. As I enthused about the building, Dr. Perkins called attention to how small the rooms were and the scattered nature of the plan, to the way white ants had eaten away much of it and the difficulty of supervising work effectively in that sort of building. All true, and I could see why a new building was to be constructed, but in spite of the difficulties the hospital was accomplishing wonders.

I was allowed to get into the game and saw cases the like of which I had never seen before, and in incredible swarms. There were operations, too. It gave me a queer feeling to assist at an anthrax case, but all went smoothly and the man recovered. The ire that always rises in me at needless suffering certainly rose for a child that came in with a big abscess of the abdominal wall. He had had some pain, and an old-style practitioner had stuck in a needle and some germs in his efforts to let out the demon.

One evening Georgie and I set out on a walk under a full moon. It was a time to honor the spirits of departed relatives, and there were numerous little fires along the roadside where people were burning paper replicas of all sorts of things that the souls might need in the spirit-world: money, houses, servants, clothing, horses; and always by the fires the sweet smoke of incense.

In an old temple court being used as a barracks, soldiers crowded around a bit suspiciously until they learned that we were Americans, then pointed out what appeared to be an old stone horse-trough but was, they said, a boat of stone that had flown in ancient times through the heavens and lighted down at that place to be a wonder for succeeding generations.

From there we walked over to the foot of the Kiukiang pagoda which stood like a shaft of silver in the moonlight, with its crowning tuft of shrubbery dark against the sky. In the bottom of it was a tiny temple. Its priest came out and brought benches, inviting us to sit down. Then he stood talking with us, going in at intervals to strike a deep-toned bell. We wandered on down one of the streets to look at an octagonal shrine that stood at a crossroads, and quite a crowd gathered to ask questions and listen to our efforts to use their language. It wasn't many weeks earlier that the Kiukiang concessions had been looted and some of the buildings destroyed, but the crowd was as genial as could be, especially when they heard the name Pei, Chinese for Perkins. It was a name well known throughout the city, and a magic password.

Soon after I got down to Wuhu Dr. Robert Brown returned from a Finance Committee meeting in Nanking to tell us the great news that construction of our new building had been approved by the Methodist Board of Foreign Missions and could start immediately. Foundations had been dug two years before.

Dr. Robert Brown, superintendent of the hospital, and his family were one year along on their second term in China. Mae Brown, whom we all called Brownie, supervised meals for foreign patients and had a hand in the school for staff children, nursing and greenhouse programs. When I went back in 1925 to start my first term, I lived with Paul and Helen Hayes, who were just completing their first term. Mr. Hayes was District Superintendent of Southern Anhwei and was gone much of the time, traveling the countryside, where there were fifteen outpost churches. Later he became our pillar of strength as Secretary/Treasurer of the Central China Conference. Helen Hayes taught English to the nurses, who didn't have any textbooks in Chinese.

There were two resident Chinese doctors when I arrived, both men of experience. Dr. Wang, the surgeon, was unusually fine. As Dr. Brown put his major time into supervising construction, Dr. Wang was my strong standby and source of information and advice. The medical resident, Dr. Huang, was a much younger man, but very good. He and I divided the work at first, for Dr. Wang was off on four-months' postgraduate work at Peking Union Medical College (P.U.M.C.), and I was in charge of surgery.

The two interns, Dr. Chou and Dr. Chang, had both done their medical work in the government naval medical school at Tientsin, and were both fine doctors. Dr. Chang was from Borneo, spoke English more easily than the Anhwei dialect, and was quite foreign in his outlook.

We had no foreign nurse. Our head nurse was Mr. Jen, a P.U.M.C. graduate, and head of our nurses' training school of six men students. There were three graduate men nurses besides Mr. Jen, and three graduate women nurses. The service was rushed, with cases the like of which we wouldn't see in America in a long time, and on surgery the most astonishing things were the tumors; their name was legion and they were of all kinds and sizes. One man came in with an enormous one on the side of his face that he'd had some twenty years. He wouldn't have come in then but that he fell on it and injured it. The facial nerve was in the tumor and of course he got facial paralysis when we took it out, but he had been warned and didn't hold that against us.

I began to miss autumn coloring, but enjoyed the mild days, and Helen Hayes told me that the violets bloomed all winter, that snow was unusual and they could play tennis on Christmas Day. Someone gave Helen two geese for Thanksgiving, and each night they had to be brought in from the pond, which they had no intention of leaving. Helen and I finally devised a system of swinging a rope across the pond, which gave the geese the choice of swimming peacefully to the steps and coming out or else jumping rope. For outdoor hilarity, I recommend the jump-rope. The geese raised a rumpus, but seemed to enjoy the game; they finally gave up each night and came ashore.

The arrival of foreign mail was always an event, and when our *sung-hsin-te*, mailman, finally delivered it we all settled down to a real feast of home news and papers and magazines. Other news we got spasmodically by way of the one Wuhu radio, which was in the Bank of China. Mr. Hayes took on the job as correspondent for *The Shanghai Evening Post*, which we then got free, although some days late.

One day a goat wandered in through the I-chi-shan gate, and nobody knew whose it was. It made itself at home, and explored the little garden patches each family had at the back of the hill. Each garden had one cauliflower growing in it, and if that miserable goat didn't go and take one large bite out of each cauliflower.

But that goat gave me an idea. Goat's milk would be good for some of our patients, so when an English business family left Wuhu and couldn't take their beautiful milk goat, Capella, along to Peking and asked if I'd like to have her, I said yes. I had helped my cousin, Carl Snedecker, get in hay one summer when I was young, and he had taught me to milk his cow. So at half past six every morning, Capella was brought to our front door and I milked her. Later we got a whole herd of goats for the hospital, and by then other people had learned how to milk them.

The only auto in Wuhu was an old Red Cross ambulance somebody gave the hospital. It couldn't go into the city, for the roads weren't wide enough for it, but there were several miles of roads out our way where we could use it, and it was a help to reach the dispensary.

The dispensary was known as T'ieh fang-tzu, Iron House, because it was made of corrugated iron roofing sheets, awfully hot in summer and cold in winter. It was located down near the city wall on an island in a little lake, with trees and grassy space about it and a little bridge leading to the island from the big road.

Over that little bridge came all sorts and conditions of suffering humanity. Our medical and surgical crews alternated going down three afternoons each week, where we treated what we could and referred others to the hospital.

Dispensary work was excellent language practice for me, as the only other staff person present was Dr. Chou, and he was down at the men's end of the building. It was much harder to talk with the women than with the men, for they had little contact with strangers, almost none with foreigners, and were unwilling to take a venture so rash as to try to understand a foreigner's talk. Usually women who had been in the dispensary before interpreted for new patients. It was great fun trying to get an idea across to a new patient, and then listen to how one of the old patients would change the wording just a little and get the idea across. The trick for me was to get the new phraseology and say it that way next time; but then next time I would again be looked at in bewilderment, and someone would say the same thing still differently. Usually the new patients were so sure they wouldn't understand me that they didn't.

One day down at T'ieh fang-tzu a woman who had been a patient for some time came in with a broad beaming smile and a basket. In the basket were three sweet potatoes, which with much ceremony she presented to me. She politely apologized for the meagerness of her gift; but for her it was not a little thing, it meant real sacrifice and she would go hungry for a day as a result. Another infirmary patient asked the nurse, after I had done something for an injured hand, "Would it be alright for me to kowtow to the foreign doctor?" We often had patients or their families go down on their knees to us, not in worship but a most intense form of respect. The dividing line was too vague for me to get over an uncomfortable feeling when people did it, and I got them up off their knees and explained that they must not kneel to us.

Another day at T'ieh fang-tzu I noticed a man floating about in a wooden tub on the little lake. He was sitting in the tub and leaning far over the water, propelling himself slowly along with his hands. I was puzzled, but the nurse and patients told me that he was feeling for fish, that people could catch good-sized fish that way and lift them into the tub.

It was noised abroad early that winter of 1925 that a general was coming to capture Anhwei Province and make himself its military governor. This was still during the time of warlord battles. It was proverbial that Wuhu usually escaped trouble when a war was on, probably because it had no treasure worth looting, but it hadn't escaped during the Boxer troubles in 1900 and gossip circulated that this also was to be an exception.

A few nights later I heard a heavy booming, and since Dr. Brown was in Nanking and I was responsible, I made the rounds of the hill to see what was happening. From the top of the hill I looked out over the city and upriver and downriver. It was gorgeous moonlight, with boats riding on the moonlit river and all the ships' lights reflected in it, but I didn't see any war. The noise seemed to be some distance away, so I gave up and went back to sleep. Next day all was quiet. Some said there had been a battle many miles away, others that a new ship in port had announced its arrival by firing salutes, still others that there had been a big celebration in town with firecrackers. We learned later that the military gentleman did arrive in town and capture us, but an escort of Wuhu soldiers met the gentleman and welcomed him to the city.

A day or so later, there was great excitement about a battle going on across the river, and sure enough, we could see a crowd of people over there and puffs of smoke, each followed by a report. So we got out the field glasses, and behold, it was a temple-celebration with banners and firecrackers.

In December it looked as though the impossible and unthinkable were about to happen after all. Word came that Kiangsi troops would take over Wuhu. I wondered why this city which, since it was destroyed by the T'ai-p'ing rebels in the mid-nineteenth century, had been considered beneath military notice, should suddenly rise into view. At any rate, our defending troops dug trenches back of the boat landings, the soldiers in town were put under strict discipline and a big bunch of soldiers was sent out to I-chi-shan to guard our point and keep troops from landing.

The Chinese Red Cross Society sent us a big Red Cross flag and asked us to be ready to metamorphose into a Red Cross hospital, and a big red cross was put up over our gatehouse. All hands were in a state of expectancy. The night the trouble was expected, our six young male student nurses decided their quarters at the top of the hill were too dangerous, picked up their beddingrolls and came down the hill to more sheltered regions. These young men had seen warfare at close range before, and had no illusions about it.

Next morning there were plenty of troopships headed upstream, but none of them tried to land. Day after day went by, and no blasting for new construction was allowed lest passing troops might think they were being fired upon and return the compliment. Our only excitement came about when a guard at the gatehouse dropped a cigarette stub into straw bedding in the gateman's room. Fortunately the floor was of hard clay, and aside from a lot of smoke and smudged uniforms, there was no damage. We concluded that once more Wuhu had succumbed to delusions of grandeur.

One of my patients about that time had been a farmer from north of the river until crops had failed the past summer. His fields went dry and he wandered about searching for odd jobs until he fell and broke a kneecap, and there was nothing left for him but to beg. His family scattered, and he gradually made his way down to Wuhu and drifted into our outpatient department. Repairing a broken kneecap four or five months after the break, when there's a gap of several inches between the fragments and the broken surfaces were smoothed over with scar tissue, wasn't a simple undertaking. We had to cut part of the tendon above the patella to get the upper fragments down, and finally got the two parts together after a fashion. I first used kangaroo tendon for suture, but it broke and had to be replaced with wire. I wasn't optimistic about the results, but several weeks later he had a working knee joint and walked with a crutch. He would soon leave to hunt up the remnants of his family, and I asked him what he planned to do. With some surprise that there should be any question, he answered, "Farm."

Soon after I got down to Wuhu we had a new baby brought in whose parents had put her out to die as they hadn't the food to keep her alive. By late December she had grown fat and was a charmer, and she needed a home. One offer for her was made, by a woman who lived in a mud hut down back of one of the wharves. She had lost heavily in gambling one night (mah jong was a curse in Wuhu) and tried to kill herself by slashing the top of her head with a big knife. She didn't die, but was brought in by the police to have her head sewn up. She took a liking to the baby, but as she would probably have sold it to pay gambling debts, we didn't take her offer and for some time had our hospital baby to ourselves.

One man came in with a knee that had been badly infected for some months. He wasn't at all willing to have his leg taken off, which is what was needed, and he waited and waited and grew thinner and paler and grayer until we wondered whether he would live if we did amputate. Finally he decided to let us do it, with the stipulation that he must be allowed to see the leg afterwards and be sure the bone had really gone bad and we weren't doing it for our own amusement. We promised, and took off the leg. He was very weak afterward and I sincerely hoped he'd forget to ask to see the leg for it was very rank. But the following morning he asked. I wanted to send him a small piece of bone to look at, but the nurses said, "That won't do; he'll think it isn't his. He must see the whole leg." So they took it in and showed it to him. He promptly went into shock and we had a bad time pulling him through.

But he survived, and in the following weeks gradually improved. Then he staggered us. He stopped me one day and said, "Doctor, about that leg of mine: I'll be going home soon and I want to take it with me." I told him it had been buried, that it was of no use to him and must be in even worse state than when he saw it. But he sat up with tears running down his face and said, "It isn't for my own sake; I know the leg is of no use, but my old father wants it and I must take it to him." When I looked puzzled, the other patients took a hand in explaining to me: "You are a foreigner and of course you don't understand. He is going back to his own village, and he can't leave the leg here in Wuhu. One can't have

71

parts of his body scattered about like that. Besides, it is very disrespectful to his old parents if he goes back to them without one of the two legs they gave him." I promised that I would inquire about the leg and try to find out where his treasure was buried. He didn't mention it for a long time, but undoubtedly did before he went home.

A student in the town who had studied in Boston invited me one night to his home for dinner. His family was strictly old style, and I was startled to see an American plough in their courtyard, alongside a gnarled old dwarf pine growing in a beautiful jar. This young man was a teacher in a government technical college and wanted to introduce this plough. It was smaller than the ones at home, and rigged with only one handle so that a man could use it driving a buffalo.

Such a meal as we had, every bit delicious. The dish that delighted me most was sharks' fins. When hanging in the shops they looked leathery and unattractive, but when cooked were delectable. Another dish consisted of paper-thin slices of liver and kidney and fish all boiled in a thin soup along with several kinds of vegetables and noodles. It was cooked in a dish made of copper and supported on a copper cylindrical base perforated with many holes in an openwork pattern through which the fumes of alcohol burned a gorgeous green. It stood in the middle of the table, and various people leaned across to stir and encourage it with long chopsticks.

After dinner my host took me to visit the big Hell Temple of Wuhu. I had been to the one in Nanking, where I found to one side of the door a large coffin on stilts waiting for an auspicious burial day. Two large paper figures stood at the head of it to ward off any evil spirits that might try to capture the soul of the departed. On the lid of the coffin were jars of food and a pair of chopsticks so the soul would not go hungry while waiting.

Images along two sides of the Nanking temple, representing the souls of departed sinners, were being put through all sorts of horrible tortures by a most human lot of demons. At one point as I walked along, a hand reached down to clutch me, and there was a life-size demon, more horrible than the others, apparently about to gather in whoever walked by. Some of the figures had animal heads, one flew through the air on a white goose. Doubtless there was significance in each, but all were in deep dust and the priests gave no evidence of reverence or energy on the idols' behalf.

The Wuhu Hell Temple was planned like that in Nanking, with various successive judgment-courts and torments of souls depicted in realistic and gruesome images, the souls and little demons about three feet high and chief demons life-size. A large sign overhead admonished us to "see clearly and understand," and another to, "remember there is still the present."

Two things impressed me that I hadn't seen, or hadn't noticed, in Nanking. The Wuhu temple was much larger and better kept up, so may have had in it features the Nanking temple hadn't. Fastened overhead in the rafters were two great *suan-p'an*, abacuses, perhaps ten feet long, their great beads on wires. One, slightly smaller, was red, for reckoning up all the good deeds men do. The larger black one was for reckoning up bad deeds.

The other feature that especially interested me was a group of gods and *p'u sa*. They were seated up in some fantastic clouds over each judgment-hall, and in several cases I noticed wires from their hands reaching down to some soul in distress. The wire represented the beneficent influence of the good spirit exerted on behalf of that particular soul. For instance, a wire led from the hand of Kuan-yin, the Goddess of Mercy, to a couple of lotus blossoms floating in a lake of blood. Each lotus blossom had a soul clinging to it, and was so being drawn in to shore. When you realize that the lotus blossom is a symbol of the spirit, the meaning is plain that the merciful goddess saves such souls as spiritually desire to be saved and cling to the means she provides. The images expressed a deep spiritual truth, one with which I could identify, and I understood the growing tendency among missionaries to explain great truths of Christianity in terms of some of the teachings of Buddhism.

Christmas in Wuhu started a couple of nights before with a community sing outdoors in front of the hospital where an evergreen grew that had been trimmed as a Christmas tree, topped with a lighted star and hung with colored lights. And Christmas Day started long before daylight when the men nurses came around to every house singing carols, several playing flutes. At least half of these young men were not Christians, all were intensely patriotic and had heard all the arguments about Christianity being a foreign importation, yet they climbed out into that cold night to sing at the doors of foreign homes, "Glory to the newborn King."

I took them out snacks in the shape of candy and cookies, exchanged greetings and wished my Chinese were equal to telling them what was in my heart. But perhaps I couldn't have told them, even in English.

After breakfast our household sat around a very pretty arbor vitae in a tub, which we replanted later, and exchanged gifts. Then we went over to the hospital where in each of the three wards our I-chi-shan school children sang and the meaning of Christmas was explained and red-wrapped gifts were given to each patient. In each service the nurses played, "There's a song in the air," on their *hsiao*, a long bamboo instrument played like a fife. The tone is so beautiful that the Chinese have a proverb, "If a *hsiao* is well played in the moonlight, the hearer, if he have true perception of beauty, will weep." This being not moonlight but Christmas morning, we rejoiced.

On Christmas night there was a big celebration out by the tree, with crowds from the town as our guests. In a pantomime of the nativity scene, there had been a blockade in rehearsals because everybody wanted to be angels and no one wanted to be a goat-coolie. Being a foreigner and therefore lacking in perception, I thought it would be fun to be a goat-coolie, and after I said as much some of the other girls agreed to join me. For realism we introduced Capella, and at rehearsals she kept things lively by jumping about and once broke it up by bucking an angel. I was detailed to manage her during the performance, and by keeping a firm grip on her horns and another on her larynx so that each time I felt a bleat coming I could stop it, trouble was averted. For the actual performance the shepherds appeared in goatskin coats with the furry side out, and straw coolie sandals. The angels were beautiful with their long black hair and white paper wings.

The play that followed was gotten up entirely by the men nurses, their acting ability truly remarkable. The last third was almost straight preaching, and while I realize that the introduction of propaganda into a play is hardly artistic, the significance of it was that it was put on outdoors where all the world could see, and on a Christian holiday at a time when anti-Christian feeling ran high. There had been an anti-Christian parade that very afternoon by a howling mob of young people with gongs and banners and two hundred soldiers following them to take action if there were violence. The Christian Chinese were called "foreign slaves" and "traitors," but the boys went ahead anyway, the assembled town citizens listened quietly, and when the pastor in the play appealed for money for poor people, the crowd contributed rather well.

So the day ended. Bits of carols, hummed or whistled or played on flutes, still sounded for some time, and on a nail high on a rafter over one of the wards hung two links of paper chain.

Climbing Lushan, 1926 *(Lewis L. Gilbert)*

The Impossible and Unthinkable

1926-1927

It did great things for our vision of the world and all that is in it to live in China when Chiang Kai-shek's Kuomintang (Nationalist) Southern Army marched on the Northern Expedition. Exactly what was happening was seldom clear to us until long after, when we could look back and see how many factions had been in the land and how the struggle went to unify China under one leadership and to free her from foreign domination.

In mid-January 1926, Dr. Perkins came down to Wuhu to get himself out of the rush of his hospital for a few days and to escort me back to Kiukiang for a rest. The Water of Life Hospital had been in the midst of a battle won by the Southerners, and he left when all seemed peaceful once more. By the time we returned to Kiukiang things had changed again.

Our boat, instead of docking as usual, anchored mid-river and we went ashore in a sampan. There we learned that foreigners living in the British concession had left. Americans living in the Chinese city, which included all our missionaries, were still there. On the bund, a crowd collected to witness the sight of foreigners arriving instead of leaving, and would have been hostile but for the shouts that went up from those who recognized Dr. Perkins: "There's no trouble, it's Dr. Perkins. He's not a bad man, he's a good man. He's not English, he's American." When some rickshaws appeared we set off with a former nurse of the Water of Life Hospital walking along beside us announcing loudly to everyone that we were harmless.

At the Perkins' house we found that the servants' union was holding meetings every night and threatening to put through all sorts of extreme demands. The Perkins' cook and some of the other missionary servants, influential members and officers of the union, persuaded the rest that some of the demands were foolish and impossible. In the course of a few days they simmered down to a three dollar increase per month per servant, not at all unreasonable.

That kind of problem followed in the wake of the Southern Army, for there was a Communist faction within the army that stirred up propaganda, and caused troubles for which the whole Southern Army was then blamed. But the Southern soldiers, the Nationalists, I saw in Kiukiang were different from the Northern, the warlord, soldiers in Wuhu. Most of the Southern soldiers could read, and the difference showed in their faces. They were intelligent and reasonable and less inclined to demand what they wanted regardless of custom or the rights of others, and with a few exceptions didn't loot. They did quarter their troops in any mission property they could get into, but that was all in the fortunes of war. They were remarkably considerate of the people in whose compounds they lived.

Georgie Perkins told how the Southern soldiers had invited the populace to help themselves to supplies deserted by the retreating Northern troops. Thousands gathered and swarmed past the hospital carrying bags of flour, sacks of rice, chairs, boards, tables, firewood, charcoal, dishes, uniforms—everything imaginable and unimaginable. Therefore the Southerners were in high esteem. At I-chi-shan we had to take precautions to prevent wounded Northern soldiers from rising up and going out to loot the townspeople.

Foreign concessions were a sore point and we were thankful at Wuhu that there were none there, and that America had none in China at all. In Kiukiang the row had started over some workmen carrying baggage for foreigners in defiance of the workmen's strike. The fighting was between workmen, but it was because of the foreigners, and of course the foreigners were blamed. Anti-

British feeling grew hotter until the British people were warned by their consul to get out. Then the soldiers took over the concession and a mob looted the vacant homes. American homes generally were not touched, but one of the more amusing incidents took place when soldiers walked into the Plummer home and carried off some of the children's clothing. Mr. and Mrs. Plummer were both in bed. When they heard the noise, he stopped to get some clothes, but Mrs. Plummer gave chase in nightgown and bathrobe, and after doing a marathon across their compound, recovered her goods.

The Hankow concession was also taken, and we began to wonder how long the British would stand for it when the rumor started that the warlord army of the North was going to follow the successful example of the Nationalist forces and take over concessions there. That news precipitated more unrest in Kiukiang, and the commander of the U.S.S. *Penguin* and the men of the missions gathered to consult with Vice Consul Paxton of Nanking who had come to round up foreigners from Kuling on the mountain. He and the commander urged that foreign women and children leave immediately. I, as a guest who might be underfoot in an emergency, was included. Georgie and a few of the single women elected to stay and take their chances with the men. The gunboats stated clearly that they would not send armed parties ashore to rescue anybody, since it was against U.S. policy to do so, especially in cases where warning had been given, but those remaining were able-bodied and among mostly friendly Chinese. They had a good chance of reaching a gunboat if need be.

The group that gathered to leave on the *Kung Wo* didn't in any way suggest flight. It meant the breaking up of families, leaving some to certain risk, but the children thought it was some kind of picnic and their parents gave no signs to the contrary. Dr. Perkins and their cook walked with me to join the group, and we fell in with a friendly detachment of Southern soldiers. Their intelligent-looking commander, who rode a long-furred pony at the rear, much resembled Chiang Kai-shek, who had sent a telegram to Kiukiang a few days earlier telling his own soldiers to "Stop opposing missionaries and Christianity and stop pestering churches and schools and Christians. Sun Yat-sen himself was a Christian, and so is our strong ally, Feng Yü-hsiang, and Christianity stands for many of our ideals."

We walked down to the bund, sending our baggage ahead to avoid being too conspicuous. The crowds were friendly, until we got to the concession where there was a demonstration against England and all imperialism and in favor of taking over the concessions. A man at the gate said to our escort, "Don't bring them in here; the crowd can't easily tell Americans from British, and something might happen."

We could hear the crowd shouting that foreigners had been killed in Canton and threatening that it could be done again. They were waving banners colored like Easter eggs, and I picked up a couple for souvenirs. The mission servants, even the cook who saw me aboard the *Kung Wo*, had marched in the parade earlier in the day for fear they would get into trouble if they did not. All the way down to the shore, in spite of stump speeches and yells and threats, no one made trouble and many people smiled at us. We knew that at the moment public opinion was strongly friendly toward Americans, but we had heard rumblings that Uncle Sam might pack a gun, and if that happened we knew the reverse would be true.

Back at Wuhu there was no war, but—did you ever hear of a pig that fell down from heaven? We had a pig, and that was the workmen's theory of its origin, for there it was, and they looked upon it and saw that it was good and proceeded to grab it. The Shanghai workmen who discovered the pig magnanimously said they would take only a third; the hospital workmen who might have claimed it all as hospital property agreed to a third; and the stonemasons who evidently had a weak claim strengthened it when the original owner of the pig came in the back gate and demanded his property. Up rose the stonemasons and made for that unhappy man with their stone hammers so vehemently that he beat a retreat. All difficulties thus being eliminated, the united group proceeded to slaughter the pig, in spite of its protests shrieked to high heaven, from which it had not come.

At about that time the rest of the hospital discovered what was going on, and the plot thickened with the return of the lawful owner, this time through the front gate and emboldened by reinforcements in the shape of six men with long sticks, and the law in the shape of a policeman. There might have been a battle royal but for the timely interference of Mr. Hung, our business manager, who politely intercepted the determined group and persuaded them to go to his office to discuss the matter. It was a fine pig, the owner said, worth all of twenty dollars. Mr. Hung bargained him down to sixteen, and paid with hospital funds. When the owner had gone off satisfied, Mr. Hung asked me to write a diplomatic note to the man in charge of building operations, explain the matter, state that the hospital had bought the pig and it was to be put into the hospital kitchen unless his men wanted to pay for it. The last was added rather as a joke, but we up-country people had forgotten that the Shanghai men were wealthy, and presently the letter came back with sixteen dollars enclosed, and the pig was theirs.

McGarvin, the man who built our new hospital, was an American ex-marine. We all called him Mac, and I never knew his full name. He had been building a hospital down in Hangchow on the coast, where his wife, who was Chinese and spoke very little English, was known to be wise and many people came to her with their troubles. One woman explained to Mrs. McGarvin that her husband had been a successful pirate up and down the coast, so successful that the local magistrate had put a price on his head. That meant that anybody who took his head to the magistrate would receive a bounty, whether or not his head was accompanied by the rest of him.

The pirate had a change of heart and wanted to be a good man, but how can you go downtown and look for a job when there is a price on your head? Mac talked with the pirate at some length and became convinced the man was in earnest. Then Mac talked the matter over with the magistrate, who asked if he were willing to take personal responsibility for the pirate. Mac thought that over very seriously, decided he was, and the magistrate said, "Then I give him to you. Wherever you go he must go, and you are responsible for whatever he does. Every three months I want you to write me a report about how he is getting on."

When Mac came up from Hangchow to build our hospital, he brought his pirate along. He called some of us together and said, "Here's something not for general knowledge, but I think you should know that I have brought a pirate with me, in process of being tamed . . . ," and after telling the story said if we didn't agree to have the pirate he would of course have to figure out something else. But Mac was so sure the man meant to be good that we let him stay, and he turned into one of our best people. One of his abilities we liked most was that we never found a lock he couldn't open. He carried on his watch chain three bent wires filed down at the ends until flat, and with them he could open anything. He learned to drive the hospital Ford some years later, and when a patient who was half out of his mind jumped over our wall and threw himself into the river, it was our pirate who drove down the narrow dyke that no car had ever navigated before nor ever did again, and rescued the man who by then had decided he didn't want to die.

For some time I tried to swing the administration of the hospital on my own, as Dr. Wang was at a medical conference in Peking, Dr. Huang took the first vacation he had had in years, and Dr. Brown was sick in Nanking. The house, instead of being half-empty around February as we had expected, was bulging. After a hard obstetrical case, when the patient's mother wished me, "May you live a thousand two hundred years!" I suddenly realized that to do that one must have sleep.

I wondered whether it usually happens that an administrative job brings one into contact with the less desirable side of things and people. It was certainly true that when a green hand ran the place, or tried to, the weather was less calm than usual. We had various minor squalls, and the sailing was accordingly interesting and perplexing.

One of our chief difficulties was with the nursing force. Mr. Jen, our head nurse, left us in the middle of February with the termination of his contract. He was a corkingly good nurse, with judgment and technique one could invariably depend on. He was so fine an operating assistant that I had come to feel that when he handed me an instrument it was the one I wanted, whether or not it was the one I had in mind.

But it's one thing to have the ability, and another to get it across into the heads and hands of a bunch of green recruits, and he had hard sailing instilling the same sort of ability and spirit into the students. At the same time he had to leave, two others of our graduate nurses went to Nanking to the annual conference of the China Nurses' Association. That left us, on the men's side, which was the active side of the hospital and the side where most of the happenings both auspicious and otherwise occurred, only one graduate nurse, Mr. Tsai, and the six student nurses. We thought that barring unforeseen events it could be managed. Then the unforeseen happened. The six horribly incompetent first-year students decided they weren't keen on taking orders from Mr. Tsai, who was a splendid chap, very thorough and conscientious, with high ideals. He was really up against it and came to me in distress.

Together we called a meeting of the students and outlined the sort of work and spirit necessary to be a nurse and exactly what was expected of them. It was put on the basis that a hospital is where people's lives are in the hands of the workers, and there wasn't time or place for anyone not willing to cooperate.

They divided into two camps; three decided to stay with Tsai, the other three that they would beat up Tsai if he tried to enforce his orders. So Tsai and I had an intensive session with the latter three, and when it was over they understood they were at liberty to leave, but that if they wanted to stay they had to get down to business. The non-cooperators were not bad fellows at all, their leader very clever and likeable, and when he awoke to his possibilities he became a joy, doing the sort of work one would look for in a second year nurse and in as fine a spirit as one could wish. The other two, without his abilities, took to plugging away in dead earnest. I held my breath, praying the metamorphosis would be permanent. It was greatly to their credit to have made an about-face.

Then one of the comedies, the foam over the swift current, took place. Years before Dr. Perkins had said to me, "Sooner or later you will find chickens in the hospital." One Sunday morning when I went into the women's ward, there was a hen tethered to a table-leg just outside the door of the delivery room. Purposely, I didn't ask whose it was until I had done considerable sputtering in a tone of voice that would reach the owner wherever she might be in that small building. She turned out to be one of our two women graduate nurses, and it took some persuasion to convince her that she must park the hen outside and get the floor cleaned up.

One day a girl came into the hospital for an operation, and with her came relatives and friends who talked with me at some length. One was a genial soul, always laughing and making jokes, and Mr. Hung, our business manager, told me he was Wuhu's famous joker, still known as "Little Dog," his childhood name, which most people gave up on going to school.

The girl's trouble was a bunch of tubercular glands high in one side of her neck. I explained to her relatives that there was some danger the facial nerve might be cut, which would make her face crooked. That threw them into a panic, and for a while it looked as though they wouldn't let her go through with the operation. But then the joker exclaimed, "We'll go ahead! At last we have found a doctor who tells us that it is dangerous. That means she knows the danger and will be careful. Of all the many doctors that we've seen before, there wasn't one that even knew there was any such nerve!"

We had a quiet Fourth of July, 1926, with tea and tennis at the Wuhu Recreation Club where the whole cosmopolitan community gathered. Our biggest event was to get an American flag flying over the hospital for the day.

We had only one flagstaff, and seldom flew a flag, as it seemed rather too bad to fly only a foreign flag, even though the American was the most liked. So on Chinese holidays we flew the Chinese flag, and on American holidays we flew the American flag. We planned to have two flagstaffs on the roof of the new building and to fly both flags together.

We were still in temporary housing as a hospital. The old flag was a wreck, and a new one had been so carefully put away that it couldn't be found. Then along came a sailor from one of the British gunboats who had been in earlier with measles, and whenever his ship was in port he came over to see us. We told him our flag predicament and off he went and presently came back with a good American flag. Since there was no American gunboat in port just then, his ship did not plan to dress ship for the Fourth and was glad to loan us their flag. So he hoisted it for us, properly tied and with due ceremony, and with some of the patients looking on and wondering what it was all about. We explained that the "seventh month fourth day" was our humble country's "pair of tens day,"* which seemed to make it quite clear. When the flag was up, I said that I thought it remarkable that we should have an American flag loaned from a British gunboat and raised by a British sailor in celebration of American Independence. Whereupon he grinned, "But it isn't every British sailor that would have put it up for you!"

By midsummer 1926 hospital personnel was in a great state of shuffle. Dr. Chang, our Cantonese intern from Borneo, finished his year and went on to work with Dr. Perkins in Kiukiang. Our Buddhist intern in surgery, Dr. Chou, returned for his second year, bringing with him a wife as small as he was and a two-year-old miniature of himself. The medical resident, Dr. Huang, a hard-working and sweet-spirited fellow with a scientific outlook, remained, for which we were thankful. But Dr. Wang, the resident surgeon, resigned. In spite of other reasons offered, we were certain he left because his nephew, who was one of the pupil nurses who led the insurrection against Mr. Tsai, had finally been fired. Good spirit and cooperative work had broken down after all, and the gang against Tsai had finally forced him out. Mr. Tsai got a

---

* "Double Ten," 10 October 1911, was the date of the Wu-ch'ang uprising that led to the fall of the Ch'ing dynasty in 1912.

good job with a language school classmate of mine upriver, but the troublemakers we still had with us. We fired one and suspended two others for a short time. After Mr. Tsai left, we tried women graduate nurses on the men's wards in charge of the men student nurses, but public opinion ran against this and the girls balked.

The operating room was run for some time by one of the men students who had been suspended for three weeks and was taken back after two, with new glasses and a new outlook on the world. Another of the men students, not one of the troublemakers, had also gotten glasses, and his work improved vastly. A graduate nurse finally arrived from Shanghai, another Mr. Kao, which made the third Mr. Kao on our force, and in a few days we added a fourth, increasing immeasurably our problems in keeping them all straight. Two more men and two women graduate nurses were expected. As I began to think I needed a card catalogue to keep everyone straight, two of our nurses who had been with us for some time, Miss Liu and Miss Lu, left to be married, their places taken by Miss Hu and Miss Ho.

One of our big problems was rabies, and we tried to get everyone to bring in their dogs for shots. With foreigners the idea got across, and among those to bring in their dogs was Baroness de Cartier, the wife of the Customs Commissionaire* and therefore the "first lady" of the port, who was really a likeable girl in spite of her title. But the street dogs, whose name was legion, were often without owners and what owners there were were a long way from caring about preventive inoculations. So that campaign fizzled out.

By September 1926 the new hospital was nearing completion. Its floor wasn't finished, nor the window-frames, nor the chapel, but it seemed fitting to have some use of the building. I-chi-shan prepared for the opening service for days, and everybody looked forward to a blessed experience, and so it was, except for some of us. Just as the bell was about to ring for the service, some soldiers brought in a poor fellow who was in awful shape. Ch'en was only fifteen, one of the many who, when the rice crop failed on account

---

* Chinese Customs was staffed at the upper level in large part by foreign nationals.

of the floods that year, had drifted down from the farms to the city looking for work. He came from upriver and had been adrift in Shanghai without a job or anything to live on. There were many like him, country boys out of their environment and helpless when grabbed by one of the many bands of soldiers that were capturing men to work for them, later to be turned into soldiers, the equivalent of the old press gangs and just as dreaded.

I had seen groups of soldiers with their catch, perhaps fifty men walking mournfully along, each with his right arm tied to a long rope that went the length of the lot, the bayonets and rifles of their guard ready to deal with anyone who resisted. They had no chance to send word home or take anything with them. Men disappeared and were killed or dropped by the way in distant places, and even if they did get away they had no money to get home and many had no idea how to find their homes. They were packed like cattle into boats to be transported upriver to the scene of war; and on the boats they were sometimes fed and sometimes not.

Ch'en and several others were not. When they saw some food being prepared, they grabbed for it, but the cook chased them off and in the excitement they stumbled into the machinery of the boat and two were killed. Ch'en was not, but broken and torn as he was, the astonishing thing was that he kept on living.

His gratitude at finding somebody who was kind to him spoke volumes for the awfulness of the treatment he must have been getting. He was mentally clear, and talked with us as we were getting ready to try to mend what could be mended. Somehow he gathered that this was a religious institution, and suddenly he turned to me and said, "If I get well I will believe in your faith." I asked if he knew what that faith was, and he said, "No, I don't know, but when I get well I will believe in it."

Almost the last thing before I started the ether, he repeated, "Yes, I will believe your faith." Poor chap, a faith that meant kindness was a faith to believe in. I found myself feeling almost glad that if he did get well the soldiers would never want him again. He lived through the debridement and waked up looking content despite pain and knowledge of his condition and of a poor prognosis.

One night I went into the ward to see Ch'en and found a cupful of meat soup standing alongside his bed. I fed it to him, and knowing it wasn't time for regular meals, asked him where he got it. He said, "One of the other sick men gave it to me." I asked which one, and one at the far end of the ward spoke up. He was happy at having shared his soup, and we rejoiced over that, for such unselfish deeds weren't common. The following morning I went to see Ch'en first of all the patients, and my heart sank when I laid my hand on him. I could feel bubbles crackling beneath his skin in the region of one of the worst wounds. That meant gas bacillus, and gas bacillus meant death in about twelve hours. We had had two cases of it earlier in the year. I called several of the crew to feel the bubbles, for gas bacillus, once felt, is never forgotten.

Three Chinese pastors all talked with Ch'en and were touched by his story and by his repeated statements that he wanted to believe in our faith, and decided that he could be baptized. He lay all day with his eyes shut, and all hands prayed for him, but I am afraid those of us who saw it from a medical point of view prayed only that he might be blessed in the few hours that remained. That evening I went to see how much worse the bubbles had gotten, and they were less; the following morning they had disappeared. His temperature was lower, his general condition better, and his poor flesh, which had looked about as much alive as a fur rug where his skin had been ripped off, was taking on color and beginning to look like real flesh. His appetite returned, and he drank a glass of goat's milk with relish. He was not content with rice gruel, but wanted vegetables like the others. We all felt to be in the presence of something past understanding and dared to hope for him. He lived a week but refused to have a splint on his broken leg and died suddenly one night, undoubtedly from an embolus from that many-times-broken femur. Mr. Hu, the head nurse, said, "I'm glad. He was suffering too much." We all agreed.

We were in the midst of a cholera epidemic, and the shining event of those weeks of turmoil was a visit from Dr. Perkins. He made rounds with us and joined our cholera vaccinating bee at Green Hill, the Woman's Foreign Missionary Society compound. We staged it at the gateway, where first the students crowded to see what was going on, then a crowd gathered to see what the students were doing and another crowd to see what the first was up to. Although we kept explaining, lots of the people didn't know what the shots were for, but amazingly and trustingly held out their arms to be jabbed. It would be hard to be sure that some of them didn't come several times, for there was such a mob we wouldn't have known if they had, and China was supposed to be full of hatred and fear and distrust of foreigners.

One blind woman came to get hers with such a happy smile that I asked her if she knew what it was for. I was staggered when she replied, "Yes, it is to make my eyes well again." A man I had given a cholera shot to returned in a few minutes for another, saying, "A pain I have had for months disappeared when you 'hit the needle;' please hit it again."

A couple of weeks earlier, at a vaccinating party over at our Second Street Church, our best advertising agents were a group of prostitutes. Their manager brought them all in to be done, and then they went out on the street and brought in bunches of passersby.

At Green Hill we culled out several who had abscesses, and after the vaccine gave out we had an abscess-opening party. It was queer how people trusted us to stick knives into them. One day I found a child by the roadside with a huge abscess over one eye and told his mother it ought to be opened. She said, "Please do a good deed and open it." So I did, right there, the child standing still as an image. And next day when I passed he ran out to ask me to change the dressing.

In spite of vaccinations, the cholera epidemic went on. People who brought in a relative one day returned next day as patients. Some starting to get well got up to go home to attend to funeral arrangements for relatives who had died meantime. The wonder was that, living in filth and flies and ignorance of simple hygiene, as the majority did, anyone failed to get the cholera.

It was great to have Bessie McCombs come to be our foreign nurse that fall. We had no face at all about the awful state she found prevailing in the hospital, and she was rather aghast. A lot of the procedures and refinements of technique that seemed to us essential didn't seem so to our Chinese nursing staff. I don't mean there weren't any good Chinese nurses; some were the best I've known. But even Mr. Jen never succeeded in getting the technique and sterile procedures over to the nurses working under him, and gave up the attempt. Mr. Tsai refused to give up the fight, and broke his heart and nearly his neck in the attempt. Team work under Chinese leadership was a goal which was yet to be attained, but Bess began to work wonders.

She had a hard introduction, for the first week was full of storms. The graduate girl nurse who had been longest in the hospital refused to come on duty in the evening to give anaesthetic in an emergency case, and on my insisting left the hospital. The other girl nurses went on a sympathy strike, but we got through that squall, and when they got back to work, things went more smoothly.

We had two star cases come in that September 1926. One was a man who ferried people in his sampan across the little river that comes in to the Yangtze at Wuhu. He had a complete intestinal obstruction of five days' duration and was in awful pain. We found an acute appendix which had plastered itself to everything in its neighborhood and thus compressed a part of the intestine. We got the appendix out and cut loose the adhesions and put in drains, fearing peritonitis as his abdominal wall was infected from much needling by native practitioners. But the peritonitis failed to develop, and after a few difficult days he made an uneventful recovery.

The other star was a woman who came in with a huge abdominal tumor and in very poor condition. She and her husband begged us to operate. We found the essential organs, while badly adhered in spots, were not actually involved, and we took heart. Eventually we got it out, a huge thing and beastly to look at, made up of numerous cavities full of thick brown fluid, but sterile. Her heart went bad, and we sent her back to the ward with the not very cheering word to her husband that she might get well. And she did. The resistance of the Chinese was simply marvelous.

The case that was not a star began with the arrival of a young student from the St. James Academy, the Episcopal school, with a note from B.W. Lanphear. B.W. had had some nurse's training at Bellevue, and I trusted his reactions to things medical, so looked at once at the small student and diagnosed him on sight as acute mastoid.

An older cousin was with him to whom I explained that if necessary I would tackle the surgery needed, but would much prefer to send him down to Nanking to an expert. A down-river freighter was in port, so the cousin returned to the school to fetch their things while I jumped into our rickshaw and took the boy down to the freighter. The captain was most obliging. It was against his orders to carry passengers, but under the circumstances he would.

At that point, along came B.W. and the cousin to report that the whole faculty had held a council, and had decided that, since the boy's father was a doctor of the old school and would make a lot of trouble if they had him operated on, it couldn't be done. So off they went, the cousin who knew what ought to be done but had no authority, and the small boy whose life could in all probability have been saved by a quick operation. I only hoped he would pull through.

October 1926 was perfectly gorgeous, with warm sunshine on the fields and river. There was no autumn coloring, but the empty rice-fields and stacks of rice-straw, the reappearing riverbanks, all spelled autumn and the end of the cholera epidemic. The building where we had had the emergency cholera hospital was cleaned up, its walls whitewashed, and it was readied for the school to move back in. The Red Cross officials held a feast and presented a silver shield to Dr. Brown in appreciation of the work done at I-chi-shan.

Then began the next chapter. The town fathers requested that I-chi-shan continue emergency work, as a lot of wounded soldiers were being dumped into Wuhu from the war area upriver. More beds than ever were gotten ready, straw bedding prepared and coarse quilts hastily made up in the town, one per bed, all the bedding each bed had, and then the soldiers arrived. The town fathers paid the bill for this work as they did for the cholera work, and students from the various schools in the town came out in regular shifts to make up dressings. Our nurses volunteered overtime.

Only the worst cases came to I-chi-shan; hundreds of others were being put into dormitories of the government schools, which were temporarily closed, and several Chinese foreign-trained doctors practicing in the city went up to see them but couldn't begin to fill the need.

We had an idea that since we were a day away from the fighting we wouldn't get many emergencies. But they were shot up *and* neglected, and even more urgently in need of care than fresh casualties. One of the first lot to come in had a gut completely gangrenous and died on the operating table. Another had an entire leg gangrenous, and for obvious reasons needed a room to himself, but even the small rooms with dirt floors down under the school rooms were all full. A great many of the men were wounded in the back—and why shouldn't they have run? No one understood why they were fighting, and everybody wished the whole lot would take themselves off and give the populace a chance to pick themselves up and hunt up the remnants of their scattered families and build up their poor little houses again.

We in Wuhu were in something of a backwater, but kept hearing from Georgie and Dr. Perkins at Kiukiang that their hospital was full to bursting; a battle raged right across the street from them, with shot going over and through their hospital. Non-medical missionaries were hard at work tending the wounded soldiers. Then a China Merchant Line steamer, loaded with troops and munitions lying at anchor off Kiukiang, took fire. Rescue boats didn't dare go near it under exploding ammunition, and about twelve hundred men died. All along the line the wounded soldiers turned to the mission hospitals confidently expecting help.

We got a new nurse, Mary Louise Pfaff, who came direct from

America, and was like a refreshing breeze. For instance, our ancient language teacher, popularly called Liu Hu-tzu, or Liu of the Whiskers, had a time-honored custom of coming to lessons with his watch twenty minutes fast. He would keep his watch in his pocket until the middle of the hour, then quietly set it down on the table and leave by his own time. Probably as a scholar he was bored having to teach elementary Chinese to foreigners, and we took the custom for granted.

Then enter Mary Louise. After her first lesson she reported that he had skinned her out of good time by having his watch set wrong. We laughed wearily and told her that it was as it had always been and doubtless always would be. She didn't look convinced, and set her own watch by the Customs flag. Next day, when Liu Hu-tzu pulled out his watch and laid it down on the table, she picked it up, compared it with hers, set it back twenty minutes, smiled sweetly and put it back on the table. That was typical of her, and the rest of us would gasp and ask each other, "Were we like that?" and watch to see what she would do next.

Mary Louise brought with her from Japan a little dog named "Naggie," short for Nagasaki, that was as little as my German Shepherd, Gyp, was big. Sometimes Gyp would open his big mouth and Naggie put in her head. We trembled to think what would happen if he shut it, but he never did. They ate from the same large bowl, and usually started together. Then Naggie would get into the middle of the bowl and growl, and Gyp would back out and let her have it alone.

Gyp was the soul of faithfulness during the two weeks I was down with the 'flu. He stayed with me night and day, and it was hard for anyone to get him to leave long enough to eat. Gyp thought I deserted him for keeps in November. The 'flu put my heart off stride, and while I was greatly improved, and had been up and about, and expected speedily to get back to work, the old heart kicked up a protest and put me back to bed again. That happened several times, until I was banished from I-chi-shan to learn wisdom and moderation, so I went over to stay with B.W. and Mrs. Lanphear of the American Church Mission. Whenever B.W. thought I sat up too long or got too tired, he would count my pulse and issue orders in a Bellevue tone that had to be obeyed. At I-chi-shan I rated as a doctor, but with B.W. my judgment didn't count and I had a chance to recover.

Christmas was approaching, and I had red Christmas cards made in Wuhu, the design at the top of the front page made up of ancient Chinese characters to mean Merry Christmas. Modern Chinese used this old type of character much as we used the ornate Old English letters, in places where decorative effect is the purpose rather than legibility. The copper "cash" below, with the square hole in the middle, symbolized wealth, and therefore wished the receiver prosperity. Red was used to wrap gifts, the color of festivity and happiness. A servant at Lanphear's, when he saw me doing up Christmas gifts in red paper, said approvingly, "Yes, that's just right. All presents ought to be wrapped in red." It must have seemed strange to Chinese friends to see gifts done up in white, because that was the Chinese funeral color.

On 27 January 1927, all over China, families were sending the Kitchen God up to heaven again, with gifts of good food to cheer him on his way, and fire-crackers to give him a good start. Alongside each Kitchen God was pasted a red paper that said, "Going up to Heaven, carry a good report; coming back to earth, bring us peace." And his mouth was smeared with sugar to ensure a good report. For days there would be no Kitchen God, and the families had to get along without him while he gave his report on them to the Court of Heaven. On New Year's Eve, February first by our count, he would return. How we hoped he would bring peace.

China needed peace so desperately, peace to carry out the many plans for constructive and reconstructive work all over the country, peace for educating a great people, most of whom had no chance for any school but for the hard school of experience, a much harder school in China than in Western lands. But there was no peace, and the semi-peaceful relations between China and other lands hung in the balance.

Anti-Christian sentiment was increasing and we knew, and our Chinese friends knew, that if we had to leave Chinese Christians would bear the brunt of hostility. So we were moved when one of the men nurses I had suspended in the spring for refusing to work with Tsai began to show an interest in the ward chapel services, and surprised everybody by one day suddenly leading in prayer. The wandering sheep whom we fired for a month during the summer was taken back on promise of good behavior because we were convinced he had more potential usefulness than any other man in his class. He kept his promise and did splendidly well. Then one day when Pastor Li in a special meeting asked those to rise who intended to live more in the spirit of Christ, he stood up. He began to help in the ward chapels, and even led one service and did it well.

We didn't experience any unfriendliness. When some of us went down on the business street while preparations were being made for the new year, people we knew showed us they were glad to see us, and people we didn't know were just as friendly. Two beggars got a bit overzealous in their attentions, and a policeman told them kindly that they mustn't bother us. We kept on meeting people who greeted us, ranging in rank from one of the Li family, who owned a good deal of Wuhu and were related to Li Hung-chang,* to a beggar who was so anxious for me to speak to him that he patted my shoulder and kept calling my name until I turned around.

Did you ever hear of a beggar refusing money? This one did. He had been a patient at I-chi-shan for months the winter before, with a crop of abscesses that won him the hospital nickname, "abscess-factory." We all thought he would surely die, and for weeks he and everybody else hoped he might. But he recovered, only to return in the summer with cholera. Again he nearly died but didn't. When he patted my shoulder, at first I didn't recognize him, he was so fat and round and cheery. After we had chatted a couple of minutes, I pulled out some coppers to put into his

---

* Li Hung-chang (1823-1901), Ch'ing dynasty scholar-administrator, general, statesman and diplomat, leader in China's early attempts at Westernization and modernization.

95

begging basket. But he put his hand across the top of his basket and said earnestly, "No, don't do that. That's not why I called to you. I just wanted to say hello and ask how you are." The crowd was flabbergasted when they heard that, and thought they must have misunderstood. I'd had rickshaw men turn down money, but never before a beggar. But I put the coppers into his basket anyway, and told him I wanted to give him some because we were old friends.

Whatever was true about anti-foreign spirit in other parts of China, it wasn't true in Wuhu. Agitators there were, of course, but the man in the street greeted us with a smile and exchanged jokes while doing business. We expected to go on working as usual. We knew we might have to get out later, but did not plan on it and couldn't have asked for a more congenial place to work.

Within a short three weeks things changed, and I found myself refugeeing down the Yangtze River. So much happened within that time that it seemed a great deal longer.

The Southern troops under Chiang Kai-shek had been hurrying in our direction and were due in town the evening of 6 March. A lot of Anhwei troops went out to meet them, and we all braced for a big battle. By a big battle, we didn't mean with gas warfare or bombing planes or liquid fire or barrage, the refined devilment that seemed to be used only by "Christian" nations, but we got horrible enough casualties. The Chinese Red Cross requested that we reopen the emergency hospital, Dr. Brown telegraphed Shanghai for more doctors and nurses, and because we couldn't look after all the wounded expected, the Red Cross and Red Swastika (the non-Christian equivalent of the Red Cross) prepared other places as well to receive them.

The long-expected day finally arrived and Wuhu was occupied by the Southern troops the first week in March without a battle. Our valiant defenders of the inter-provincial warfare of a year earlier went over to the South, and the Wuhu military leader, who had lived at I-chi-shan for a long time during the fall, accepted a commission in the Southern Army.

The beloved five-bar flags all suddenly disappeared, and the new Nationalist flag with its red field, a blue corner and in the blue the eighteen-rayed white sun, flew everywhere; a new flag that held promise of so much good mixed with so much hazard. The people said of the Southern troops, "They don't just shoot, they shoot *at* something; and they're afraid of nothing." Perhaps the basis of their spirit was that they had an aim, the building up of an independent, unified, sound nation.

The night they came in I waked to the sound of martial music. It was raining hard, and I knew the roads were deep in mud, yet there were the drums and something that sounded like cornets. I could see lights bobbing two by two, the soldiers marching along the little dykes between the rice fields to the east of I-chi-shan, coming into the main road south of us and going on down to the parade ground to set up their camp.

When they got down to the parade ground the march music stopped, and I heard the first three notes of "Mei Hua San Neng," my favorite of all Chinese instrumental music. I sat straight up in bed and listened, for it was beautiful. Men who could march in the mud and rain and play music like that were men with great possibilities.

After that troop ships brought in more and more soldiers. The local Southern general issued an order that foreign buildings were not to be used or disturbed, but our Second Street Church filled with soldiers, and the China Inland Mission (C.I.M.) church was damaged. The C.I.M. people were among the most sacrificial missionaries and were so utterly devoted to their work that we thought they would be exempt from harassment, but because they were British they had a hard time.

When the Southern troops came in, the Wuhu Customs building, under foreign control, refused to fly the new flag and a crowd gathered and smashed up the windows of both the Customs building and the Customs Club. A call went out for all foreign women and children to go down to the British Butterfield hulk for the night. We could see how those living on Customs Row might have been uneasy, associated with a system whose name was anathema to all patriotic Chinese, but we on I-chi-shan felt safe. Judging by the fact that our patients were loath to leave the hospital, we understood that I-chi-shan was a desirable place to stay. The one exception was a boy who wanted to leave the first day he had a normal temperature after pneumonia. I prevented his doing so by the imperialistic method of carrying off his shoes.

We had wounded soldiers as the army moved on. Then more and more of them. The chapel and school rooms filled up, and the rooms below them. All available space that could be begged, borrowed or stolen on the regular wards and private rooms filled to overflowing. The white building that we called Noah's Ark (the old women's ward left standing after the fire, which had been moved and rebuilt below the hill on the north side) was called into service, and straw laid on its floors for bedding. The Episcopalian Sisters opened a ward in their dining room and took cases that didn't need a resident doctor. Sister Constance was a splendid nurse, and B.W. piled into the job. At I-chi-shan we opened a second operating room, and when we could divide the crew ran two schedules at once.

Out in the town new organizations sprang up overnight. The Students' Union flourished like a green bay tree, and devoted itself to speeches and demonstrations beyond count. Farmers, tailors, servants were organizing. We ate meals at such times as the servants were not required at meetings, and the union of the foreigners' servants scheduled a lot of their meetings at meal hours by way of asserting their independence. Our household servants were distressed and frightened. They didn't like the imperialistic ways the union used to protest against the imperialism of the foreigners. Our amah wanted to return to her country home, then reflected that we would "eat great bitterness" and decided to stay. The union insisted on 100% attendance at all meetings, and subjected to ridicule any who failed to fall into line.

The hospital servants, much to our relief, were not included in the organization, nor were the hospital office staff in the clerks' union. People in the town had said, "No, I-chi-shan is special; the workers there are doing important work for the Chinese, not for the foreigners, and most patients are Chinese."

Then one night the Chinese hospital crew held a meeting and decided that in harmony with the prevailing tendency, it would be better to run the hospital under nine committees and do away with Dr. Brown's position as superintendent. This was by no means a unanimous decision, and some of the crew refused to be intimidated. At one meeting anyone who objected was challenged to stand up and say so, and up rose Mr. Kao of the operating room, pale as a sheet and with a look of determination gave his reasons for objecting. It was a brave thing to do, for it was with reason the average Chinese kept still rather than balk public opinion at such a time.

To our relief Bishop L.J. Birney arrived on the scene and talked the whole thing over with the staff at length, let them say all they had to say, then offered a compromise: to have them elect an advisory committee of four to work with Dr. Brown, Bessie McCombs and me, and elect three other committees to investigate and advise but not to interfere with the regular work of the crew. Bishop Birney talked everybody into good spirits, and it looked as though disaster had been averted.

The committee of four was elected, two of the four what we called "fire-eaters," but the other two were our resident doctors. One was an enthusiast over the committee form of government, the other a quiet soul eager to keep out of rows. But contrary to agreement, this committee was announced to be an executive committee. One by one staff members came to say that the hospital was headed for disaster; and one by one came loyal, frightened souls to say they were being terrorized and wanted to leave before anything happened to them. We urged them to stand by and try to save the hospital, and one day it came sickeningly over me that I was using the same arguments and almost the same words I had used in urging poor Tsai to keep on as head nurse the year before.

Meantime, the S.S. *Kutwo*, one of the Jardine steamers then under control of the British navy, bumped and sank a Chinese passenger launch in the fog off Wuhu bund. A good many Chinese were lost. We heard that the launch crossed the bows of the *Kutwo*

99

in the fog, but no one knew just what had happened. The *Kutwo* turned back to Wuhu and was tied up at the wharf at the demand of the military, which made landing and loading of other boats difficult as Jardine had only the one landing hulk. Then the military demanded the *Kutwo* be turned over to them by way of reparation, and the British gunboat in port got wireless orders to hold the *Kutwo* at all costs. The *Kutwo* stayed at the Jardine hulk and as far as we knew there was no attempt to seize her.

Soon after, Jardine seemed to have another fiasco. I had been x-raying the wrist of the Irish doctor from the British gunboat and went to the gate with him to arrange a rickshaw for him, to avoid a row, when we saw a group of people pointing out to the river. There we saw what looked to be a big passenger ship blazing. Jardine's *Loongwo*, a beautiful ship, had left Wuhu earlier in the day loaded with hundreds of passengers who had come down from Anking before the Southern troops had reached either port, and wanted to go home. We knew that one of the Standard Oil men was aboard, and that there were few lifeboats. It was a ghastly sight, and we prepared for casualties, but finally learned that it was not the *Loongwo* but a Customs station across the river.

Meantime, over at Green Hill, the Woman's Foreign Missionary Society compound, agitators came into the school and insisted on talking to the students without any teachers present, either foreign or Chinese. We later heard reports that the Russian-trained propagandists were spreading their pet doctrine of free love among the girl students, and demanded the patriotic duty of the girls to become concubines of the military officers. They also told the Green Hill students that it was an evidence of imperialism that the teachers insisted they obey school laws, that they should go out on the streets unchaperoned whenever they pleased and return when they liked. Finally Bishop Birney called a meeting of parents, who agreed that the school could not continue to be responsible for the students in their care, and it would be best to close down and send the students home.

We were well aware that there were two wings to the Kuomintang. At the time it seemed to us that the right wing was idealistic, patriotic and reasonable, and that it was the left wing, under Communist influence, that stirred up trouble. Foreigners were ordered to leave Wuhu and other river ports by their own agencies. The exodus had started some time back, and the business community had deserted us. But they were in a very different position from ourselves, and it looked unnecessary for us to run away from good friends.

At the hospital our crew learned from other cities that there was real danger for foreigners, and then they discovered that the rumpus over committees at the hospital had originated in the scheming of the same man who had been responsible for downing Tsai. He was disgruntled at having been fired and eager to put a monkeywrench into our machinery whenever he had a chance. Recent difficulties were forgotten and the whole crew pulled together most beautifully.

I was very proud of our crew. They worked their heads off, overtime and with complete disregard for meals and sleep, under real hardships. Our surgeon, Dr. Chou, was a hero in his devotion, and Dr. Huang stayed up till all hours every night preparing x-ray films to guide our operative work next day. Mr. Kao, the nurse in charge of the operating room, quietly worked days and nights without relief or complaint. He organized the work splendidly and worked without time off, refusing to be chased off the ward, even for meals. Jasper Liu, the man who had such a change of heart after he got his glasses, did the same in Noah's Ark, and when he was finally switched to night duty his place was taken by "the wandering sheep" who upheld the tradition equally well. It was wicked to let them work so hard, but short-handed and overcrowded as we were, there was no help for it.

In many other mission hospitals the troubles rose from the student nurses, and some people predicted our troubles would stem from that source too. But they were wrong. We had already gone through our troubles with the nurses, and the young men who were raw cubs a year earlier had reached a stage of real understanding and responsibility. I was so thankful to have been with them long enough to see them come through, for they were a marvelous demonstration of the potentialities of China's students.

So things were going when we learned of the 24 March Nanking Incident. Many foreigners had left Nanking before the turnover to the Southerners, to avoid trouble from the retreating Northerners. The incoming Southerners were understood to be opposed to banditry, and Chiang Kai-shek had promised protection to foreigners. But as the Southerners reached the city there were simultaneous attacks on foreigners in several places, eight people were killed while others were injured, badly molested, and homes wrecked, the Nanking Theological Seminary, Hillcrest American School and the Quakerage burned.

It was a servant at the British Consulate who brought the first warning of trouble. Cars were sent into the city to evacuate some people down to Hsia-kuan, the Nanking port, where they were taken aboard a gunboat. They were fired on, but no one was killed. Several people hid in the British Consulate overnight, fed and assisted by a servant and the policeman of that district, and escaped over the wall next day. The servant who helped them was shot. A group of about thirty business and diplomatic personnel and five missionaries at the Standard Oil residence could not get out, and were increasingly harassed by Chinese soldiers. John Wilson, an American sailor standing on the roof, dodged snipers' bullets to wigwag for help to the destroyer U.S.S. *Noa*. The *Noa*, the destroyer U.S.S. *Preston*, and the British cruiser H.M.S. *Emerald* laid down a barrage around the building that allowed the besieged to escape over a sixty-foot wall using bedsheets tied together and to reach safety aboard the warships.

The minute the barrage started, bugles were blown and, at this signal, attacks on foreigners ceased. By ones and twos from all over the city, missionary families, some of them shot and left where they lay, others beaten, all hidden by Chinese friends until the danger seemed over, were gathered and loaded onto the warships that then made the Shanghai run in record time, fired on by forts as they passed.

At first we got vague reports with indefinite numbers of foreigners killed and wounded and many unaccounted for. Bishop

Birney asked us all to get out and start down to Shanghai. What happened at Nanking, he knew, would have echoes elsewhere as soon as it was known that the British and American warships had fired. Dr. Brown and I felt that as doctors we should stand by, both because of our responsibility to the patients and hospital, and because as doctors we were somewhat safeguarded. I hadn't the slightest hankering for martyrdom; it merely seemed to me the obvious thing that a doctor can't pick up and go sometimes when other people can and decidedly should. For all that, it gave me a queer feeling when the foreign families left.

As far as I can reckon, there were only twenty-four hours between the time they left and I did, but it seemed ages longer. Nothing untoward happened. The hospital crew rallied more loyally than ever. More soldiers came in as patients, and we did a lot of operating. Our Chinese crew knew why we were staying, and that short interval brought us closer to them than weeks of ordinary work would have. It was heartbreaking to see how they went out of their ways to show us they cared. And back of it all was the realization we might have suddenly to go.

That last afternoon Dr. Chou was operating, with Dr. T'an and Dr. Ch'en assisting. Remembering how I had needed more surgery experience while interning at Bellevue, I had made it a policy to give them all possible operative work, assisting instead of having them assist me. I was giving anaesthetic and between times trying to do all I could to make up for the short-handedness of the crew by tying up gowns, getting supplies, mopping perspiring faces, and there was quite a bit of that last job as the operation was a high thigh amputation with plenty of difficulty controlling hemorrhage, and that always makes a surgeon hot.

In the midst of it all, I suddenly got a new light on Jesus' attitude of mind when he washed the disciples' feet. I had always thought of that event as an object lesson. Suddenly I didn't think so. I am quite certain Jesus loved those disciples and treasured every possible last chance he had to do some humble service for them.

When word came that foreign women had had a particularly

103

hard time at Nanking, Bishop Birney urged me to leave. It would be no kindness to the hospital, the patients or the crew to insist on staying and imperiling them all; and it might precipitate further difficulties between China and America. Trouble was expected all along the Yangtze. It was certain the Chinese would resent the firing by American and British warships, and just as certain the foreign warships off the ports would not stand for further injury of foreigners. It was even possible that a mob not even headed for us at all might be misinterpreted by a gunboat crew. Our Chinese friends thought I should go, and I didn't want the two countries I loved getting into trouble over my life, nor did I want the foreign gunboats to feel called upon to drop shells on the heads of my friends on my behalf.

To leave, to say goodbye with no way of knowing if I would be gone for days or weeks or years, was one of the hardest decisions I ever made. Dr. Chou would carry the weight of my work, and I was glad I had given him so much extra experience. He would have been pardoned if he had thought first of himself, but his first exclamation was, "I don't know what is going to happen to the patients!" It was certain the hospital organization would fall apart without Dr. Brown, and he stayed on.

I took along my clothing and bedding, some of my pictures and Mandy and Chatty, so I fared pretty well. But I hated the thought of a mob carrying off or, more likely, destroying my things, and gave my medical books and microscope to the hospital, several other books to Dr. Chou and Pastor Shen. Some books were boxed and left behind, as was the new Simmons bed I'd just gotten out from America and slept in for about a week.

It took several days to get down to Shanghai on the *Tatung*, traveling only by day and keeping behind the armor plates newly installed. We had a lot of evacuees on board and a number of us spent the nights in the Chinese section on the boat deck where we went to sleep to the soothing rattle of mah jong and money, and the sweet fragrance of opium smoke.

At Nanking we heard accounts of the trouble there from the marines who went ashore on rescue work, and later from Consul

J.K. Davis who was staying on a U.S. gunboat. The S.S. *Loongwo* joined us at Chinkiang, and the U.S.S. *John Paul Jones* escorted our convoy downriver, its guns trained on all the forts as we passed. We were fired on, but no damage done.

There was much confusion among all the stories about the Nanking Incident. Some believed it was caused only by the Hunanese, the Communist wing of the Southern Army, perhaps to embarrass Chiang Kai-shek who had guaranteed safety to foreigners, an effort to get him into trouble with foreign governments.

Hyla Doc with her mother, Ada S. Watters, and Dr. Edward C. Perkins, 1930.

Korean Interlude

1927

Shanghai bristled with barbed wire and seethed with rumors, momentarily expecting a blowup. Until we could arrange a crossing to Nagasaki, we stayed at the Navy Y, where our windows were across from the *Courier* office, a Communist paper busily spreading propaganda, and had front seats for a police raid that sent fugitives across the rooftops.

When we reached Japan in April 1927, we voted a unanimous thanks to the Kuomintang for kicking us out of China during Japan's cherry blossom time. And we were astonished by the orderliness, efficiency and cleanliness of Japan.

The day we traveled from Nagasaki to Shimonoseki, we took a detour to Omura and a beautiful park where there were many other excursions, including a group of school boys who had come to see the cherry trees. Imagine an American boys' school declaring a holiday so that students could go to where the cherry-bloom was particularly beautiful. The boys were not playing ball or racing around, but wandering about admiring the trees. A middle-aged gentleman, merry with saki, came along and started to make eloquent speeches to them. The boys saw the humor of it and applauded, whereupon he waxed more and more fervent and finally launched into an old Japanese sword dance. The saki, instead of disturbing his equilibrium, made him light-footed and graceful. In his stately dance his walking stick evoked a sword and his dark kimono the embroidered robe of a warrior.

We ferried across the Korean Strait to Pusan, and then it was a day's trip by rail to Seoul. All along the way we kept seeing things that made us feel as though we were back in China: poverty everywhere, mud huts with thatch roofs, and instead of Japan's gay kimonos, a monotone of white rather than the prevailing blue of China. Three things spoke eloquently of recent changes in Korea: the excellent railroad system that kept to its schedules, the truly beautiful roads, and reforestation of all the hills. I wondered how long it would be before China would plant trees wholesale and protect them from being instantly grubbed out by the roots for fuel, how long until China could control the terrible cycles of drought and flood that kept the country starving and drove farmers to leave their dead fields and join the wandering armies in hope of being fed.

At Seoul six of us were sent to East Gate Hospital, a Woman's Foreign Missionary Society hospital for women and children that had been in service for many years. Our sixth member arrived a bit late and was one of those who got out of Nanking in the grand scramble at the end, losing practically everything she owned. It was rather a point of honor with us not to bemoan things left behind, as we'd learned the truth of what Lao-tzu said, that in comparison with the spirit of a superior man, "the ten thousand things are as straw dogs." In spite of which one sometimes wished a few more of the straw dogs might have come along.

The hospital was well equipped with supplies and instruments and beds and nurses, and had three Korean doctors, but no surgeon, and it was put to me to build up a team for a surgeon expected in the fall. The Korean nurses had no idea of sterile technique, and I had only sign language to teach them, so at times I found myself longing for our good I-chi-shan operating team. Since there had been no surgeon for a long time, it was strange to have to drum up trade instead of breaking my neck to keep up with the work, but that was probably just as well with the unskilled team we had.

There was little to write home about: no plots, Red propaganda, violent demonstrations, looting or destruction, no battle, murder or sudden death; no wards full of wounded soldiers suffering and dying for lack of care our short-handed crew couldn't possibly give; no heart-warming demonstrations of brave loyalty in the face of danger.

We didn't write to our Chinese friends for fear of harming them, but news dribbled through to us. One delightful story leaked out from Nanking about soldiers who occupied Hitt, the Woman's Foreign Missionary Society Bible Training School. After their first night in the residence they went wild-eyed to the servant of the house and showed him a picture on one wall and asked, "Who is that?" He told them it was Miss Peters, the founder of Hitt, who had worked in China for thirty-five years. "Well," they said, "she was in every room of this house last night, and none of us could sleep. We had a terrible night!" They packed up and left the house empty and no one went back in. Miss Peters was in America, undoubtedly praying for Hitt, but you can interpret this as you like.

Korea is famous for its beautiful mountains, and we had plenty of time to become hardened hikers exploring the famous Diamond Mountains to the north of Seoul. But despite all that beauty we were sick at heart with longing to get back to China and all her troubles, and to our friends who bravely ate so much bitterness as "running dogs of the foreigners." Our hearts remained behind and sporadic news reached us of Chinese imprisoned for having befriended foreigners and others who fled for their lives. I-chi-shan was occupied by troops, artillery was mounted on the hill and horses were quartered in the basement of the new hospital.

When we evacuated, Dr. Brown was left alone with over a hundred wounded soldiers. Some kept their arms with them on the wards and threatened nurses and staff who wouldn't do as they commanded. But city friends got better soldiers to surround the hospital and disarm the unruly men.

At one time more than 50,000 troops crowded into Wuhu and were quartered in nearly every foreign home. There was some looting, but worse was the overcrowding, which made sanitary conditions very bad. Flies were a plague, and dysentery, typhoid and smallpox, always with us, got worse; cholera broke out in the most severe epidemic of recent years. I-chi-shan opened a cholera hospital in connection with the Chinese Red Cross, and the manager of the Bank of China assumed expenses. In a little over two weeks, of 400 patients admitted nearly all had been saved. Of course many died in their homes. The hospital overflowed so that patients had to be laid on floors, then out on the grass; day and night shifts worked continuously.

City authorities gave Dr. Brown what protection they could, and by staying on he saved the hospital from looting while other mission hospitals along the Yangtze lost thousands of dollars worth of supplies and equipment. Construction of the new hospital continued without one lost day of work.

Mrs. Brown, who returned to Wuhu from Shanghai after about three months, wrote that food was scarce, prices rising, but that people on the street were as friendly as before and often went out of their way to show goodwill. There were still a few who shouted, "Kill the foreigner!" but that was disappearing, and the spring avalanche of propaganda was also passing. When the army pushed on they left many chronic cases behind in the hospital, adding to the financial burden because the soldiers could not pay their bills and had to be fed when rice was scarce.

Dr. Brown wrote about the many fine men in the Seventh Army, but that there weren't enough of them to leaven the lot, and people who had been enthusiastic about the quality of the Southern soldiers in the spring were disappointed. As so often happens, a movement starts out with fine ideals and accomplishes much in its early days, then becomes corrupt and falls into dissension. So radical was the Communist wing that the party split* and seemed

* By the start of the Northern Campaign in July 1926, Chiang Kai-shek had emerged as the strongest proponent of China's military unification. In the political body of the Nationalist Revolution, the Kuomintang (K.M.T.), there was an uneasy alliance between the left-and right-wing K.M.T. leaders and the Chinese Communist Party (C.C.P.). The C.C.P. had lost the balance of power in the K.M.T. that it once held. By

to be on the decline. After so much success the first year, the Southern Army began to have reverses and Wuhu was once more in the fighting zone. But even with the daily possibility of a battle being fought at the city, life went on with farmers harvesting their crops and businesses open. Work continued on the new hospital to the accompaniment of rifle fire and the boom of larger guns. The hospital staff pulled together better than ever, and by fall the worst seemed to be over.

Father had died earlier in the year, my brother Philip was married and a pastor in Madison, New Jersey, while my sister Sally had married Bishop Stuntz's son, Clyde, and they were in India. Mother was sixty-six. I wrote to her that since she wasn't needed at home, why didn't she come out to be with me. What a crazy thing to suggest in wartime, but she came, joining me in Korea, and was with me for a year; then went to be with Sally in India and alternated back and forth, spending a total of seven years with me.

The first week of October we were allowed back to Shanghai. I left Mother with friends and caught a steamer for Nanking. There I was stranded when the boat was taken over for troops, and I began to look for other transport. Men had been allowed to return inland, but few foreign women, so I knew there might be problems. When I spotted the S.S.*Ngankin* anchored off Hsia-kuan, I determined to go upriver in her, but knew she had a British captain who might have other ideas. So I waited until she was about to sail, hailed a sampan and said to its owner, "Get me aboard that ship, and then clear out!"

From the cargo deck, where I scrambled aboard, I moved slowly and as inconspicuously as possible, but long before desirable ran into Captain Edwards. His language blistered the air as he raged about the trouble I would make for him, so when he finally

---

the time the great military campaign had reached the Yangtze, it had absorbed more than thirty warlord armies, only one regiment later proving to be under Communist control. The growing anti-Communism of the military led to a split in which right, and eventually left, wings of the K.M.T. turned against the C.C.P., and the Nationalists brutally purged their ranks of the divisive C.C.P. program for social revolution to focus on the goal of military unity.

shouted that he might have to go to jail because of me, I offered to do half-time.

He was so angry that he used up all his vocabulary, went away and thought up some more and came back and shouted again. Finally he said he would turn me over to the captain of whichever British gunboat was in port when we reached Wuhu. Knowing the American ship would welcome a surgeon on board, I asked, "Why not the American?" So he turned me over to the American gunboat whose captain was not the old friend I expected. He gave me a few well chosen words of wisdom but added that if I could arrange escort from I-chi-shan I could stay. That was easily done.

When the story of my escapade got around, Captain Edwards took a lot of ribbing and sent me a note, "Dear Hyla, I'll never again admit I know you!" But later, after an argument with his wife, told her, "Well, I've got a girl upriver willing to go to jail for me!" And we were friends.

Dr. Brown had done heroic work in our absence, and the new hospital was a wonder. There were electric lights and a heating plant, a pumping station and filter to bring water up from the river to holding tanks on the hospital roof, and inside finish work was well underway.

There were no signs of war except that there were always soldiers about, but they were respectful and didn't trouble us. A group of Red students in town amused themselves by putting up posters on foreign buildings, but they were out of favor with the town. The U.S.S. *John D. Ford*, the *Noa* or *Sicard* were anchored in turn off our hill, close enough so that we could set our watches by their bells, a British gunboat further upstream. As our ships patrolled, changing places frequently, they dipped their flags to us on leaving.

Mother reached Wuhu in November, and one day went shopping in the town with Brownie. They left the hospital car in a side street and darkness suddenly (as it does at that latitude) came down before they got back to it. Meantime there was a fire, their street was blocked and it was too narrow for the car to turn around.

112

Instantly the street filled end to end with a shouting mob, but it was a curious, not angry, mob that wanted to see how the foreigners and their gas wagon would get out of their predicament. There was not a single unfriendly word, and they most obligingly got out of the way as a policeman helped the car back down the long narrow alley.

Construction continued at the hospital, the grounds were graded, paths built, and by mid-December all the patients and equipment were moved from the temporary quarters they had been in for four years into the new hospital. It was with special joy we celebrated Christmas and brought the difficult year of 1927 to a close.

Wuhu General Hospital about 1930. Hyla Doc's home was the top house at left, the Brown's home next, Hayes' home at the foot of the hill. Taken from Yangtze River.

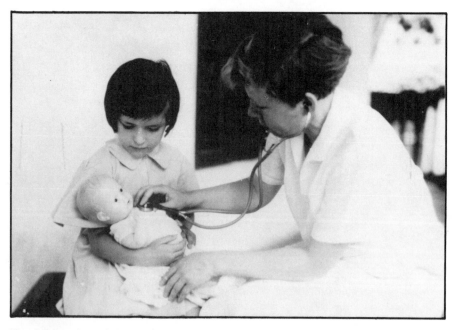

May Goldie, whose father was with the Socony Installation in Wuhu in the 1930s, brought dolly to the doctor because "she has been feeling seedy." *(Howard A. Smith)*

China Was Far From Standing Still

1928-1929

Working in the new hospital was a joy. Can you imagine what it had been like to work in the temporary buildings where all the water had to be brought in buckets carried by coolies, where the roof of the women's ward leaked so badly that on rainy days it was hardly safe to do dressings for fear of contamination, and where charcoal fires and a bellows worked by a perspiring coolie furnished the heat for sterilizing? To move from that into an up-to-date building with steam-sterilizers, an elevator, two wheelchairs and water to be had by turning on faucets, cold *and* hot, real bathtubs, a sure-enough operating room, two of them in fact, with big north windows and enough room to walk around without contaminating the sterile table? We even had a system by which patients in private rooms could call nurses, wonder of wonders. Every one of these things would be taken for granted in any hospital at home, but for a long time I wondered if I shouldn't wake up some day and find myself back in a thatch-roofed mud hut.

The new building was equipped to care for 100 patients and to provide for a school of nursing. On either side of the front steps sweeping up to the entrance were installed bronze plaques, one reading, "Who is my neighbor?" the other, "Not to be ministered unto but to minister." And over the front entrance was cut a round window I suggested, that got to be known as "Hyla's porthole."

There were terrazzo floors, modern plumbing, a water-filtering system, electric light and elevator, connecting phones, a steam plant and ice-making machine. There were administrative offices, medical and surgical wards, private rooms, classrooms for the nursing school, kitchen, dining room and pharmacy.

Below the main entrance was one for a hoped-for ambulance. A chapel with colored windows was in the center of the building, and the surgery on the top floor had two operating rooms, an anaesthetic room, nurses' and doctors' dressing and shower rooms, stretcher and appliance room. Large plate glass windows on the north and a sloping ceiling reflected light without glare to the middle of the surgeries. Between the two operating rooms shelved instrument cases and blanket warmers were accessible from either side. I walked on air, and people from well-to-do homes, who hadn't been willing to come into our old building, began to arrive as patients and thereby helped greatly with its running expenses.

From the British gunboats anchored off the bund and the U.S. gunboats that patrolled the Yangtze and changed ports frequently, we had many calls to treat illnesses and take x-rays; and since I did all the x-ray work I soon had sailor friends the length of the river. Boys from the U.S.S. *Sicard* brought in their Filipino cook so I could remove his appendix, and came in every day to see him. They seemed glad of a chance to visit Americans and hear English spoken, and one night brought over their movie apparatus and gave us a treat. All the hill coolies were at the show in their blue and white uniforms, and all the patients who could be moved, on crutches, with arms in slings or heads in bandages, in white hospital pajamas and jackets.

Among the most interested was Yung Kuei, who came on a wheeled bed. A good many weeks earlier this young lad had been brought in after having been shot through the pelvis and hips by a bandit. Complications were such that it didn't seem possible he could live long. However, his shattered leg was dressed and after weeks of suffering he began to brighten up and smile and the great resistance power of the Chinese pulled him through. A gentle and patient soul, he had won the heart of everyone who cared for him.

Another of our first patients in the new building was Mrs. Liu, whose fourteen-year-old son brought her in. She was most awfully sick, with amoebic hepatitis, a bad heart and cardiac asthma. We gave her anti-amoebic treatment, and she improved markedly. Then one day, when the nurses were all out of the ward for a moment, she jumped out of bed and ran away. We thought we had seen the last of her, but the next day she returned and explained that she had gone home to get money to pay the twenty-five cents a day (American money) she owed the hospital. She went home again, and returned in a couple of weeks having accumulated enough to keep her in the hospital for some time.

I had long wanted to start some handwork for convalescent patients, saleable goods that could help them earn money toward their expenses. I longed for a trained worker and a recuperative workshop such as we had at Bellevue, and decided to start something on a small scale for Mrs. Liu. Some years earlier a friend had sent me a Swiss bookmark with a doll made of yarn at one end. I showed it to her and asked if she would like to try to make one. She thought she could, so I took her yarn and other materials. The first ones were bungled and crude, but gradually they improved to where she made very attractive ones efficiently and quickly, and she was a lot happier for having something to do and feeling that she was helping to pay her own way. I sent the finished products to friends and relatives to sell in America, although all the first ones sold readily right in Wuhu. Soon other patients were at work; Mrs. Hsu, a woman shot by bandits, began to make needlebooks, and Yung Kuei began to make napkin rings of braided bamboo.

As for Mrs. Liu, she brightened considerably, so I was surprised one day to find her in tears. Someone had brought her the news that her dear son had disappeared aboard a passenger ship headed downriver, and hadn't been seen since. She was sure he had fallen into the Yangtze, and was eager to jump in after him, but we were able to persuade her that wouldn't help him at all.

Mrs. Liu needed consolation, so we said to her, "You have heard while you have been here about the God who loves us all and wants to help us. Pray to Him to bring back your son and take care of him, and we will all pray too." She said to me, "I do believe in the Heaven-God, and I know this thing has come to me because of my sins. I had two children. I sold my daughter for eight dollars, and now the other is taken from me."

Poor woman, it is hard for Americans to understand the economic pressure that would lead a woman to sell her daughter, but often that was done because the mother herself could not get enough food for her child and believed the person to whom she was sold would be better able to care for her.

Two weeks later Mrs. Liu's son walked into the ward. He had gone down to Shanghai and had a wonderful time playing around the great city and had then returned with the ship.

Every day Mother made rounds in the wards, and the patients looked forward to her visits and inquired with great anxiety if she didn't appear when expected. She was game about using the Chinese she learned, and listening in, I was amazed to hear the extent of the conversations she carried on.

Soon she developed a new indoor sport. She started to teach Chinese. She had a primer with six new characters on each page, and sentences using the characters. Each day she went to the hospital third floor private patients and got them to teach her a few new pages. Then, when she felt sure of the new words, she would go down to the men's surgical ward and teach what she had learned to Yung Kuei, who came from a poor farmer's family where no one had ever learned to read. This little boy so badly wounded by bandits was as keen on learning to read as she, and they had great fun together.

Then one day, before his leg was entirely well, Yung Kuei's father came several days' journey to see him, and Yung Kuei had only one thought, to see his mother. Away they went, Yung Kuei on his father's back carrying his crutches. It is possible that the joy of being home might have been enough to pull him into condition to help the leg heal, but we never knew.

One day a man at the dispensary named Ch'en asked me to look at his foot. I looked at his foot, but first at him, for although he was a beggar he looked less like one than any I'd ever seen, and

118

didn't sound at all like one. I told him his foot might have to be amputated, and that he ought to have it x-rayed. He asked what our price was for x-ray, and when I told him, instead of kowtowing and knocking his head on the ground and crying, as most beggars would have done, he merely said, "Then I'll have to do without it, for I can't pay," and started to leave. I was surprised, and told him to come on up to the hospital and I'd x-ray it anyway.

Ch'en appeared at the proper time, and a few days later returned for the report. When he heard that the bones were so far destroyed that the foot would have to come off, he considered it quietly and then said, "Well, then I'm willing to have it off. But how about the price of staying in the hospital?" I told him the ward price, the equivalent of twenty-five cents a day American money, and once more, instead of wailing and begging me to do "a good deed," he simply said, "But I can't pay, for I have no money." He was so earnest and so simple about it, and obviously in need, I couldn't turn him away and referred him in as a charity case. The foot was taken off, the wound healed beautifully by first intention, and while he was with us we learned his story.

He had been a farmer in Shantung, and like so many other able-bodied men had been picked up by troops in transit and carried off to serve as a baggage carrier. He came along as far as Wuhu when his foot went bad and the soldiers dropped him and there was nothing for it but to beg. He couldn't work and had no home or friends.

One day when Ch'en was about to leave the hospital, the man in the bed next to his said to me, "We've been talking here in the ward about this man Ch'en, and we have decided that he ought to be sent back to his home. We have taken up a collection and have gotten a dollar and some more toward sending him back. Do you think something might be done?"

I suggested that the Shantung Association in the city might do something, and we wrote to them. But the days went by and we got no reply. Finally our Pastor Shen said, "Why wait for the Shantung Association? Let's do this ourselves." A man who had come to visit another patient overheard our conversation and approved, "Yes, that's right, do a good deed." I said, "Alright, we're doing a good deed. Suppose you do a good deed too!" He was rather staggered at that, and protested, "But I am a poor man!"

"Yes," I told him, "and as for us there is not a single capitalist (a hated word) among us. Every one of us depends upon his wages to live." That raised a laugh, and when the man got his breath he smiled and said, "Alright, I'll do half a dollar's worth of good deed!" That was surprising, for he really was a poor rice-farmer. But that started the ball rolling, and in half an hour the hospital crew and private patients had contributed enough to send Ch'en home.

The hospital carpenter made him a pegleg, Brownie upholstered it, and we all helped him learn to use it. Then he made a request that proved beyond question that he was real: "I'm going home to my father and mother. I would be ashamed to go to them in my beggar's rags. Is there any way I could get some decent clothes?" A real beggar needs rags to advertise his trade, and wore an outfit that had to be seen to be believed. We took some gift money and had a new muslin jacket and trousers made for him. I was a bit dubious as to what sort of reception he would have, going home a cripple, where economic pressure was so great that another mouth to feed could break a family. I asked our business manager what he thought, and he said, "But don't you see, he has been away from home for many months and his parents don't know if he is alive or dead. Do you think the lack of a foot will make any difference? Of course they will welcome him!" I felt properly rebuked. Pastor Shen went down to the boat to see him on board, and the captain, on hearing his story, gave him free passage.

The Nationalist movement that had fought first against the warlords and then the Communists within its own ranks, had entered a period of constructive reform. As proof of that we received into the hospital two ex-officials who had been kicked out of their jobs because they smoked opium. Under the new regime there was a rule that nobody could do that and hold office, a rule based neither on sentiment or ethics. Opium-smokers can't get up in the morning, and the new government didn't want officials that slept all day.

We could see other projects taking shape under the new Nanking government: road-building on a large scale, which both increased communication and gave work to former soldiers to keep them from going bandit, school-development, licensing of doctors, illegalizing of drinking and smoking by minors, organizing active militia to protect the countryside from bandits. A system of national phonetic characters was developed that was thought to be about to revolutionize literature and the educational system. The phonetics were not popular with students, who feared that the beautiful old characters would be lost, but some sort of shortcut was needed to make it possible for the general populace to learn to read, which was out of the question with the old characters.

All the planned projects of the new government would take a long time, considering the difficulties to be overcome in a land of some 90% illiteracy, but wonders had already been accomplished. As the Chinese proverb had it, "Don't be afraid to go slowly; only be afraid to stand still." And China was far from standing still.

One of my favorite occupations on my days off was to go templing, to learn how the Chinese thought and worshipped. To celebrate my birthday in 1928 I hired a junk and took all the upper staff of the hospital and a few others for a picnic to two temples on the point across the river. One had been built in honor of a woman who had lived in legendary times. On her way up the river she fell into it opposite Wuhu, and her body floated upstream against the current and went ashore on the point. We were told that her body was still inside a great rock behind the main altar. There was an image of her, dressed in red silk and guarded by two ferocious servitors with weapons.

The images of the eighteen Lohan* in that temple were particularly lifelike and individual. Each has his own story, like the Christian saints, and in that temple it was particularly easy to pick out the ones we knew: the one with so luminous a face that he wore his eyebrows long to cover it; the one that was able to tame ferocious beasts; the one whose heart was so filled with the

---

* Lohan are Buddhist monks who have attained Nirvana.

spirit of the Buddha that the face of the Buddha was visible in his breast.

Nearby was an ancestral shrine of the Li family of Wuhu, whose most famous member was the nineteenth century statesman, Li Hung-chang. It was in marked contrast to the first: no images, no drums, no gongs, no priests, just the quiet dignity of ancestral tablets. Soldiers were living in the temple courtyards, and they gathered round to watch as we partook of our picnic.

Dr. Perkins' brother, Dr. Henry Perkins, came out to China for a visit. While he was with us we visited three of the Wuhu temples, one the small pagoda that shows up over the crest of a hill, to the southeast of I-chi-shan. On our way up the hill we suddenly heard a voice, "Bon jour, Monsieur!" Startled, we looked up to find a workman beaming down on us. He had learned his French during the First World War, when the Peking government sent Chinese laborers to aid the allies in France. Soon he and Henry Perkins were climbing the hill arm in arm, singing *La Marseillaise* at the top of their lungs.

The pagoda was full of soldiers who were very friendly and invited us to share their evening meal. It had lovely sweeping curves to the roofs, fish and little animals on its ridgepoles, its images better done and better kept up than most. The thing I thought about the most in that temple was in the uppermost of a series of buildings that climb the hillside. Back of the Buddha, in the very center of the back wall, was a high niche and above it characters reading, "True Light." I could see that the niche must be an opening into the lower part of the pagoda, and apparently there was supposed to be light coming down through the pagoda windows into it. But whether there was an image in the niche or it was empty, we could not tell. It was only a black hole with the words above it, "True Light." A woman was worshipping before the Buddha, and when she rose from her knees there was no light in her face. One thought of the words of Kim's Lama, how the truth of Buddhism is crusted over with ceremonies and superstitions until it is hard for the ordinary worshipper to find it, and of the wise answer of the keeper of the wonder house, "So may it be in any religion, my brother."

The abbot of the White Pagoda Temple on T'ieh Shan was a friend of ours. He came in as a patient and I made the terrible mistake of prescribing cod-liver oil for him even though he was a strict vegetarian. After he'd taken it a week, he asked me what was in that medicine. Then I realized what I had done, and apologized. He said, "I don't blame you, for you are not of our faith, but that has probably set me back about a thousand years in my transmigrations." I was horrified, but my mistake didn't affect his friendship and he would invite us to meals at the temple where his cook made up vegetables to look like roast chicken or baked fish or pork. I asked him why he did this and he said, "I know my friends are fond of eating those things, and while I can't give them what they really like, I can make my food look like their food." Sometimes he ate with us in our home. We would show him which dishes were only vegetables, and he always trusted us.

One day I said to him, "You know, the gods in your temple are the Goddess of Mercy, the God of Knowledge, the God of Literature, the God Who Fights Evil; all of them good gods." "Yes," he said, "all of them are good gods, not a bad one in the lot." Then I said, "Did you ever think of it this way: those gods are not really separate gods, but deifications of the qualities of one good God. God is mercy, is knowledge, is courage, is kindness, and He is the fight against evil. But He is all one God." He didn't answer for a bit, then said, "I've thought about that a great deal, and I am sure that is the way it really is. But we have to train up the young monks and can't explain it that way."

The White Pagoda abbot told me stories about some of the other gods. There was one about a god by the name of Ti Tsang, who was sympathetic with the poor suffering souls in hell. He began as a Siamese prince who came up the coast of China in a sailing ship, went ashore, probably in the vicinity of Shanghai, and came up the Yangtze in a junk. When he got to Anking, where there was a series of hills, he wanted to go ashore. The people of the town said, "Don't come ashore here; we have no room for you." But he said, "All the room I want is the size of my prayer mat." So they welcomed him.

He spread out his prayer mat on the ground, and his fame went abroad as the holy man who sat all day long on his mat with his bowl in front of him and his white dog beside him. People began to come to the holy man to ask his advice. He was a young man when he arrived and over ninety when one of the heavenly messengers came to him and said, "Ti Tsang, you have done all the necessary preliminary things for Buddhahood, which is about to be bestowed on you." Ti Tsang was very much pleased with the honor, but when he got to thinking about all the poor suffering souls down in hell he said, "Who am I to accept this great honor and become a Buddha when so many people have to suffer." And he sent back word that he much appreciated the honor but couldn't accept it.

Instead, he climbed a mountain until he came to a deep crevasse. He jumped into it and went straight down to hell, where he went to Yen-lo, the head of that region, and said he had come to offer his services to help the poor sufferers in hell to repent and change their whole viewpoint so that eventually they could be saved from hell. Yen-lo was a kind spirit, but he had to see to it that people got their just punishments down there for what evil they had done during their lifetimes. So Yen-lo gave Ti Tsang the job to help lost souls repent. Yen-lo was represented in some of the temples of the region around Wuhu, where most of the temples also had a figure of Ti Tsang. First in the people's affections, though, was Kuan Yin, the Goddess of Mercy, then came Ti Tsang, then O-Mi-To-Fu, the great god with arm extended in welcome to anyone wishing to come to him.

One day I met a figure standing among the other gods that was different, with a face that was not Chinese. I asked Pastor Liu Wei-i, who he was. "That is Ta Mo," said Pastor Liu, "Saint Thomas." What was St. Thomas doing in a Buddhist temple, I wondered. "Well," he said, "Ta Mo is greatly admired, and the Buddhists claim him as a great teacher from India who brought Buddhism to China. But the Christians say, 'No, he came from India teaching Christianity, not Buddhism.'"

Ta Mo, along with the other disciples, was told by Jesus to go to the ends of the earth and preach the love of God. He went first to Mesopotamia, then over to India where he stayed for many years. Many evidences of his teachings in India remain in the Church of St. Thomas, of which there are many branches, especially in southern India.

But St. Thomas realized that India was not the end of the earth. There were ships that went further. So he said farewell to his friends in India, boarded a ship and went down the coast of India, through the Straits of Malacca, past Singapore and Penang and headed north up the coast of China, where he stayed for many years.

They say he first knelt for about five years with a bowl in front of him, like Ti Tsang. People would bring him rice and other food. Personally I think this was the period in which he learned the Chinese language. Be that as it may, he traveled all over China and there are many stories of his travels and preaching.

One story tells how when he reached the Yangtze River and wanted to cross it (and the Wuhu people believed it must have been at Wuhu because of the reeds: the name Wuhu means Reed Lake), he looked for a boat but couldn't find one. So he went to the reeds that grew along the riverside and asked the reeds if he might have a branch. When he was satisfied that it was alright for him to take a branch, he took one and laid it down on the water and stepped out on it to cross the river. A student following him, who didn't stop as he had to ask permission to take a reed, just took one, started to follow Ta Mo but sank into the river and had to be rescued. The Christians said, "Ta Mo wasn't telling that story about himself crossing a river, but about Jesus on Galilee hauling Peter out when he fell in."

Another story was that Ta Mo died in South China, where the custom was to bury people sitting in a *kang*, a big round jardiniere. Ta Mo was put into one of these and the top sealed. Later his friends got to arguing as to whether his body was actually in there and broke it open to see. All they found was one shoe. So pictures and statues of Ta Mo show him carrying one shoe. But the Christians said, "No, that was the story Ta Mo told about Jesus and the empty tomb."

Among the many visitors to I-chi-shan was the central figure of China at that time, President Chiang Kai-shek. He arrived in a Chinese gunboat that anchored below I-chi-shan, and a salute of twenty-one guns set the echoes reverberating among the hills both sides of the river. He came up to the hospital next day with a bodyguard of several score of men, a quiet, unassuming sort of man with a smile that lit his face. He stopped to speak with wounded soldiers on the wards, then came with some of his officers to the house for tea. He asked how the hospital had come through the troubles when his army had passed through Wuhu, and we were glad to give him a reasonably good report. When he saw the unfinished wall that was being built around the compound, he made a contribution that made possible its completion and the building of a fine gate.

General Ch'en, who was head of all the troops that had been in Wuhu for some time and accompanied President Chiang to I-chi-shan, was our guest to tea and dinner at other times as well. One day he invited me to come down to the gate to see his horses. A couple of days later General Ch'en's secretary appeared with a military escort and the General's favorite horse, with the compliments of the General, who had been called away to Anking, and the request that I ride it. Now the General's horse was nimble of foot and light of step and heavenly of gait, and did anything from a prance and singlefoot to a gorgeous gallop, and was surefooted as a goat in following the little foot-wide paths between the ricefields. But he had a complex, and it had soured his disposition, as complexes sometimes do. He wanted all the world to remember that he was the General's horse, and insisted that the other horses recognize his position and proceed in the customary manner: one mounted guard in front, then himself, then an open space, then the hoi polloi following on behind. Not being familiar with this particular procedure, we did not follow it, and the horse decided it was his duty to instruct us, which he proceeded to do by means of his powerful hind heels. We had a lively time of it for a while, the only safe place being on his back. He did think he could accomplish more if I weren't there, but that was a passing fancy and it was a case of, "Where are you going, my pretty maid? 'Blamed if I know, ask the horse!' she said." We got back to the hospital without any real casualty, much the better for the exercise and determined to try again.

Next time the General was along, and insisted I ride his horse, since that was by far the best horse of the lot. We followed the customary order of march and had no trouble at all. We went for a considerably longer ride, and on the way back, while the horses were going at a good lope along the little roads between the rice fields, I began to be conscious of a pain in my appendix region. It wasn't severe and I didn't pay any special attention to it except to note that it grew increasingly uncomfortable when the horse galloped. That evening I walked a mile to the Advent Mission and back, to an entertainment given by the Customs people, and laughingly told the household that I was getting appendicitis. But it never occurred to me it could be the real thing.

Next morning the pain was gone and I started to make medical rounds with Dr. Liu. Then the pain came back, worse than before. Presently we met Dr. Chou, who was making surgical rounds. My old friend Frances Culley, who had accompanied me to China and was my fellow student in language school and was now Nursing Supervisor at Wuhu for her second term, told him what was up. He looked at me hard and said, "You had better go home to bed and stay there." I said I'd probably go after rounds, but he said, "No, right away." It still didn't hurt badly enough to feel like appendicitis, but I listened and asked him to come over and make a diagnosis. He did, and he diagnosed acute appendicitis, and to that he stuck, in spite of my disbelief.

On the strength of his diagnosis, Brownie wired to Shanghai for Dr. Brown to come back from a medical conference there and bring Dr. Perkins. Next afternoon they confirmed Dr. Chou's diagnosis. Meantime Mr. Kao, our operating room nurse, had kept the operating room set up, and Dr. Chou had been ready to operate if things became urgent. I would have been happy to have him operate, but he knew and I knew that I was a poor risk with a general anaesthetic.

It was decided that inasmuch as a doctor in Shanghai was doing appendices with local anaesthetic, it would be worth the risk to try to get down there. The trip downriver was a strange one with cargo delays, but we made it. The doctor and the ambulance were waiting on the bund, and in about an hour after we reached Shanghai the offending appendix was out and I was back in my room. It was queer to be wide awake and know just what was going on, drinking sips of cold water meantime.

Of the days and nights following the operation, I was convinced more strongly than ever that every nurse and doctor ought to have one major operation, as part of training. As the Chinese say, "If you want to know the road beyond the mountain, ask those who travel over it." I realized I had known very little about appendicitis before, and hoped I'd never again be "the butterfly upon the road preaching contentment to the toad." Yet I had no complications and made an uneventful recovery.

One nice thing about sickness is the discovery of how many and how fine one's friends are. They most certainly did everything for me that could be done, and as soon as I could leave the hospital took me to the Woman's Foreign Missionary Society residence and next day to a steamer for Kiukiang to recuperate at the Perkins' home. As it happened, I was the only topside passenger, and the captain was my old friend Captain Edwards, on whose ship I had stowed away, and he looked after me very well. The visit at Kiukiang was a great joy and complete rest, and I left feeling a hundred years younger than when I arrived.

When I got back to Wuhu there was only a week left in which to pack for my furlough, to catch a boat two weeks later than the one I had originally planned to go on. But when all the goodbyes had been said and by all that pertained to dramatic fitness I should have made my bow and exit, I did neither. There was no boat.

A couple of days before I was due to leave Wuhu, a passenger ship went aground on a mud bar above Kiukiang. Another tried to get past her, also went aground, and the channel was blocked with the very low water still falling. The ships going upriver couldn't discharge their cargo at Kiukiang and turn back, as the godowns were already full, and the army had made off with the loading coolies. Ships went up to the block and anchored; ships came down to the block and anchored; there was no detour.

It began to look as though I would miss my ship at Shanghai, so I decided to take the little launch that ran between Wuhu and Nanking, and to get a train from Nanking to Shanghai. We sent a coolie down to the launch to reserve one of the little two-by-four cabins. I got another boy to take my baggage down and supposed all was well. One of our head workers, Lao Ma, was to go down to Nanking to help me with baggage.

Next morning bright and early I was up and out, headed for the nine o'clock sailing with Lao Ma pulling the hospital rickshaw and our operating room worker walking alongside with a long string of firecrackers hanging from a bamboo pole. We arrived at the boat landing about seven, and saw the launch already out from shore and headed downriver. Enough passengers had arrived to more than fill her quota, and she was off. The hospital man on board holding my cabin waved wildly and jumped up and down in his agitation.

Dr. Brown, Culley and Miss Pon, who was our Chinese Super- intendent of Nurses, had walked down to see me off, and Lao Ma hustled us all into a sampan in the hope we might catch the launch when she stopped at Customs for clearance papers. Lao Ma got up on the bow and urged on the rowers, and so effective was his urging that one pulled too hard and broke his oar. He picked up a floorboard and paddled with that, and we caught up with the launch as she steamed around in circles in front of Customs, trying to keep clear of many sampans loaded with other hopefuls. She was already overloaded and listing.

Dr. Brown persuaded the captain of the launch that since I had my ticket I should get on board, and he agreed. So Lao Ma and I got on, and the man who had held my cabin got off in great relief.

As we boarded, I noticed that buckets of water were being

passed to the engine room, and some were being poured on deck, but I supposed the engine was thirsty and the deck dirty and paid no attention, and waved goodbye to all my friends.

We had gone a few miles and I was settled down for the nine-hour trip when I heard the sound of chopping. That seemed strange. There was also the smell of smoke that was neither engine nor tobacco. Lao Ma and I put our heads out our window, and to our horror found some of the crew chopping up a part of the deck. Smoke poured from below it, and I feared a panic, that the people would all rush to the other side of the launch and it would turn turtle. There wasn't a life preserver aboard, and almost no Chinese in our region knew how to swim. But the people who, over a little thing such as getting off and on at a landing could do a terrifying lot of shouting and hustling, were dead quiet in the face of real danger. A country woman near me said under her breath, "Scared to death!" and a Buddhist priest with his rosary in his hand kept repeating in a low voice, "Dangerous! Dangerous!" I don't doubt he was praying. So was I.

Gradually the smoke changed to steam, and finally up from the coal-bunkers, through the hole in the deck, came a sorry-looking figure black with coal dust, streaked with water and red of face, but grinning broadly. One last bucket of water was dipped up and poured over our hero amidst great cheers.

At Nanking Lao Ma and I went over to the railroad station and checked the baggage, then got on one of the new busses and rode into the city, the first time I had been back since the 1927 troubles. I dreaded to go lest it be too mournful, but was cheered all the way by evidences of progress. The bus had a definite limit to the number of passengers it could take, and a set fare for given distances, and a set custom as to where the bus did and did not stop. To those of us accustomed to the usual utter lack of system it was remarkable to watch the conductor-girl politely but firmly stick to all these points; even when army officers wanted to board and the passenger limit had been reached, she stuck to regulations. The much-discussed Middle Mountain Road (cut straight through the city for the funeral procession of Sun Yat-sen, that had caused a great deal of suffering and consequently of radicalism among the people whose property was taken and destroyed with very little compensation) looked like a good thing for the city, wide and straight and smooth, a real boon to traffic.

At the Old North Gate Bridge we got off and went over to the Methodist Girls' School, where there seemed to be business as usual, and the Hitt Residence, that had been lived in and partly spoiled by the soldiers who had been frightened off by the apparition of Miss Hitt, was clean and sweet and peaceful as though it hadn't been touched.

I walked over to the language school, and on the way was hailed by a rickshaw puller beaming with welcome. I had not seen him in four years, but he was pleased to see me and asked about many of the mission members as we walked across the fields to the Five Terrace Hill. That was truly depressing. Hillcrest, the American school, and many of the mission homes stood as empty wrecks, reminders of much worse horrors. Yet under the shadow of those wrecks, Chinese and missionaries lived and worked together in a bond that was stronger for the suffering they had shared.

At Shanghai there were errands, consular representatives to see, friends to meet, the P.& O. S.S. *Malwa* to catch to take me to India on the first leg of my journey home. The people who were to put my trunk on board and said, "Now lay down your heart and don't think of it again," somehow failed to get it on. Half-way down the coast I got a wireless saying it was aboard S.S. *President Lincoln* and I could get it in Hong Kong. Thereafter I looked after it myself.

In Lahore I had time to get into the act at Government Hospital, a real treat as I'd too long been the chief operating authority at Wuhu, with no chance to consult. There I met a very good British doctor who wanted to know what I was going to do while on furlough. I told him that I wanted to learn to do a bronchoscopy, as we had a child at Wuhu with a melon seed in her larynx, and no one knew how to get it out. When I said I'd probably go to Philadelphia for that, he said I should go to the source, and gave me the name of the Vienna surgeon who had invented the procedure. Mother joined me in India for the trip through Europe, and we stayed longest in Vienna where I was welcomed by the famous surgeon and worked with him.

Something I ate on the ship crossing the Atlantic went Bolshevik and knocked me out temporarily and upset family plans for our arrival. I stayed quiet at Spuyten Duyvil for a time, listening to the radio. It was past believing to hear the landing of the Graf Zepplin in Los Angeles, then the Mormon choir at Salt Lake City and the introduction of guests of honor at the banquet for women derby flyers at Cleveland. I felt like Rip Van Winkle come back, secretly glad for a few days to adjust myself. To see and hear things happen while they happened, was so far removed from China where news was well seasoned by the time we got it.

The Wonder of it All

1930-1931

In May 1930 Mother and I boarded the S.S. *President Jefferson* of the Robert Dollar Line in San Francisco to head back to China. The blue Pacific was in its loveliest mood, our good ship rolled on its way day after day through sparkling weather, its crew very patient with one passenger possessed of an insatiable curiosity. I picked up a cord weave and a knot I had wanted for years, and got acquainted with steam turbines. There were oil-fed fires under the great boilers, eliminating the fierce stoke-room heat that sent patients to us on the Yangtze.

Early one morning we looked out our porthole and saw the hilly shore of Japan. We were soon ashore driving over beautiful roads between wooded hills, past trim farms with fields of wheat ready for harvest and seedling rice ready to be transplanted. Everywhere were prosperous farmhouses with thick thatch roofs, well-fed oxen with straw sandals on their feet, beds of iris and early chrysanthemums in bloom, and contented-looking country people who looked well fed and well dressed, in no fear of civil war, bandits or famine. Nobody had yet learned to put earthquakes into the list of preventables, but nothing else seemed likely to disturb the peace of that countryside.

As a child I used to lie flat on the floor and pore over the pages of *Stoddard's Lectures,* and its picture of the big Buddha at Kamakura. I had always longed to see it, and finally there I was at its gateway reading the notice asking the stranger, whatever his creed might be, to enter in the spirit of reverence. And there was the

Buddha, of green weathered bronze, sitting upon the sacred lotus blossom, looking down in calm benevolence. A representation, not of Gautama but of the ideal Buddha, this statue was the center of worship of the Amida sect, whose emphasis was on salvation by faith, not works. I went inside the hollow image to a little shrine and climbed some steps where I found inside the head of the figure a gilt image of Kannon (China's Kuan-yin), the Goddess of Mercy, who holds a place in the hearts of Buddhists comparable to that of the Madonna for Catholics. How near this seemed to our own faith: a great figure representing our highest ideals harboring the spirit of mercy.

We left our car in a small seaside village where a long causeway led, across sands hidden at high tide, to the beautiful island of Enoshima. There we climbed steep stone steps through cool green groves to the temple of Bonto, the goddess of luck and patron of children. From the steps behind us came a great laughing and shouting, and a crowd of schoolchildren trooped up, fell silent as they formed in line by twos and marched up gravely to the simple shrine to bow low. Then away they went, their laughter floating back as we followed them on around to the delightful island shrines and tea houses and no end of small shops selling curios made of shells and other sea trophies.

In a grove near one shrine we found an archer teaching some students how to handle the long Japanese bow. Much longer above the grip than below, and with a curve in the larger part suggesting a cupid bow, it differed from ours. And the Japanese technique differed too: the arrow was laid at the right of the bowstring and both arms raised high above the head. Then with elbows bent, the arms were gradually brought down and separated, and finally the right elbow bent to let the string come back, not to the corner of the mouth as we do, but well back of the ear. Our shooting form is nothing compared to the elegance of this formal ceremony. The archer cut quite a figure, standing with his black silk kimono thrown off his left shoulder to get the big sleeve out of the way.

We walked across the island and down a long flight of steps to the rocky shore by the white-crested waves, around the rocky ledges and through a tunnel in a cliff to a cave where a famous old dragon once lived. We had expected to explore the cave, but the hour grew late, and we turned to something that looked more dangerous. The shortest way back to the mainland was to be rowed around in a tiny fishing boat that bobbed like a cockleshell, but looked seaworthy. We sat on matting in the bottom, and how she did ride. But our oarsmen were friends with the boat and the sea, and took us bobbing around into the lee of the island, and back to shore again.

One of the great joys of the day came as we pulled out of Yokohama harbor, when the haze over the hills thinned, and there, faint but unmistakable, gleamed the snows of the high slopes of Fujiyama; then the haze thickened and Fuji was gone.

All next morning we skirted the hilly shores of Japan and midafternoon crossed the breakwater into Kobe harbor where cargo was loaded into and out of hatches. The sturdy little winch engines shouted louder than the men that guided the cargo as it swung up out of the brightly lighted hatches, across the busy deck, and down into the dark to waiting lighters. Yet the racket and seeming chaos represented orderly transfer of bales of cotton from our southern states going ashore and bales of cotton cloth from Japanese factories coming on board; tires and auto parts going ashore, assembled cars swinging up out of the dark and into the hold. Down in the hold we could see bales of old newspapers going to Shanghai to be made into Chinese newspapers, for pulp-wood was not to be had in China, and somewhere out of sight were the silver bars like loaves of bread that were loaded in San Francisco to be made into "dollars Mex."

There came a day of beauty sailing through the Inland Sea, two last precious days aboard ship and then the water turned yellow and thick and we knew the old Yangtze had come out to meet us.

It did me good just to stand and look into Chinese faces when we reached Shanghai, where we stopped only long enough to visit friends, arrange our finances and scour Wing On's department store for powdered milk, shredded wheat, malted milk, honey, and, by order of family members, an eighteen inch electric fan which did wonders for our comfort.

Then up the winding old Yangtze on the S.S. *Poyang*, the water so high reeds stood almost submerged, the country a rich green and beautiful with willows, shores topped with temples and pagodas, thatch villages close to shore, a lovely region to come home to.

The hospital had about eighty patients, and I plunged straight back into a full surgical schedule, with one day a week at T'ieh fang-tzu, the outpatient clinic in the town, and a stop at the Episcopal Sisters' compound (Sister Constance's St. Lioba Mission) on my way home. I was operating Tuesday, Thursday and Saturday mornings, sometimes afternoons too, with fifty to sixty operations a month, among them a flood of appendix cases.

I'd have been glad never to see an appendix again; some patients were sailors from the gunboats, some were our hill people, others country people from far off. One was a boy of about fifteen with an appendix that had been acutely inflamed for ten days and had ruptured five days before he reached us. I asked his father why in the world he had waited so long before he brought the boy in, and he said, "At first I didn't know it was serious. Then I took him to a small hospital in a town not far from our village. The doctor there couldn't operate, so I started for Wuhu. It took five days to get here, and I was so afraid he would die on the way. Will he live?" If he had been an American, he wouldn't have, but being blessed with a good Chinese constitution, he did.

Among our patients was the Wuhu police chief who came in for recurring asthma attacks. He was also head of all the pickpockets and burglars, but as he was very fond of Dr. Brown and the hospital, he was a great help in keeping us from being robbed. Another was a Lamaist monk in the yellow robe and red hat of his order, who regaled us with tales from his years in Tibet. He came in with both feet gangrenous, and there was nothing for it but to take them off, which reduced his lot to that of a beggar. Two men were brought in by the police who were thought to be bandits. Both had gunshot wounds and one had to have about nine inches of damaged intestine removed. It seemed too bad to fix them up just to have them executed. They were very cooperative patients and we didn't believe they were bandits, and we rejoiced when they were able to stand trial and were found innocent.

We were short-handed, with one surgical intern who was unable to stay through the summer. That left me single-handed, so we found a new use for gunboats. There was a succession of British ship doctors in port for short periods eager to get in some surgical experience of which they had little aboard. They worked so hard and so steadily that people asked whether the British Navy had joined our mission.

Soon after our return a merit board was presented to the hospital. The "hot noise" of firecrackers began down at the gatehouse about ten in the morning. It was on the end of a long pole carried by two men in front of a procession led by a Chinese band playing "Glory, Glory Hallelujah!" and was elaborately made of painting on a mirror draped with scarlet silk with two ornaments waving at the top made of gilt paper and peacock feathers. It was framed to be hung in the hospital. Across the face of the mirror, which was bordered with flowers, were characters reading, "You lay on your hand, and spring arrives." But the board was presented by relatives of a man who had had a strangulated hernia for six days and had been eating opium to deaden the pain. I was laying on my hand again in a secondary repair operation, but he was a very sick man and there was little hope that spring would come again for him. I went down from the operating room to the chapel to receive the procession, and serve them tea and cakes. Our patient had had the hernia for twenty-four years, and lived near the hospital all that time. Again and again, as such cases came in, my heart lamented how my people perished for lack of knowledge. The wonder of it was that people who came to us for help brought with them so much beauty and good cheer.

Wuhu was as peaceful and lovely as one could wish. We felt no hostility anywhere, and when we smiled greetings to people they smiled and greeted us in return. Wounded soldiers had been moved from I-chi-shan to a military hospital miles away. But summer 1930 nearly everybody was still down in the Yangtze Valley as late as July as there were reports of fighting around Kiukiang and Kuling. It was very hot and everybody had prickly heat, often with a rise of temperature. Dr. Libby remained in Nanchang, off to the south of Lushan, but Lucile and their five children evacuated to us. We all celebrated the Fourth of July down at the Customs Club near the river where there were several acres of green grass, and a baseball team made up of men from the gunboats put up a good show against a team of Wuhu foreigners.

Life on our hill, down on the streets, and out on the river flowed back and forth that summer as though there had been no 1927. Among our many visitors was an image carried in a sedan chair. Someone who was ill went to a temple for advice and was told to go to I-chi-shan and gather herbs from the healing hill. So the image came out for an airing, her closed chair covered with a red cloth, and all who accompanied her gathered herbs.

Since furniture was not to be bought in Wuhu and it was standard practice to draw pictures of what was needed, Mother's and my favorite sport that summer was to get Ch'en Lao-pan, our hospital carpenter, to turn the crate from our Atlanta bed into three bookcases with glass doors to shut out summer dust and delay moulding in damp weather. Then he made a nest of four little tables, with lovely carving around the edge of each, and a bench with carved dragons for a seat in front of the fireplace. Later he made a neat little cupboard for the bathroom, to hold linens and my uniforms.

Ch'en Lao-pan brought his rheumatic shoulder to our clinic, but when we started to examine his shoulder we found something that was much more striking: scars, rows and rows of scars, extending down both arms from shoulder to wrist, and down his back between his shoulders like some fantastic design. How in the world could anyone be injured in such a way as to leave such scars? Later I did remember to treat his shoulder, but for the moment the scars took all my interest, and I asked how he had got them.

"It was for my mother that I ate that bitterness," he explained, then told us this story: "My father died when I was small, so as the only son I felt from childhood great responsibility for my family. When I was fifteen, my mother had typhoid fever. Day by day she grew worse. My sisters had already gone to their mothers-in-law, so I was the only one to care for her. I went to a coppersmith and had him make a lot of slender, very sharp knives. These I hid at home for a few days more, hoping my mother would turn back to me. But she grew worse, and I knew she would die unless I did something for her. So I asked my best friend to help me, to take the knives and put them through my skin. But he would not do it. I told him he must help me, at least pinch up the skin so that I could do it myself. So he did, and I put those knives through my skin two hundred and eighty times. Each wound left two marks, for the knife went in and came out again, piercing through the fold of skin my friend pinched up for me. Of course it hurt, but I did it for my mother. When I had finished as far as I could reach, we collected the blood into a cup and poured boiling water on it and gave it to my mother to drink. She turned back to this life and recovered. Did my mother know? Of course not! She would not have let me do it, and if she had known what was in the cup she would not have drunk it. She did not know, and she recovered!" Ch'en's face shone with the memory of that triumph.*

"Whether or not your method was right," I commented, "I cannot say, but I certainly admire your spirit. Did you ever hear that there once was a carpenter, like yourself, who ate great bitterness for us all, so great that he died of it?"

"Yes," said Ch'en, "I have heard of him. If he had not known that he was saving people," and there was a faraway look in Ch'en's eyes, "he could never have endured it."

The house at the top of the hill was to be for Mother and me and Culley when the Browns returned from furlough. We moved in, along with Culley's three canaries and all our new furniture and reveled in the fine views from our windows. From one in Mother's

---

* One of the traditional Confucian examples of filial piety was to feed one's flesh to a dying parent.

and my room we looked down on six pomegranate trees, all scarlet with fruit in season, and beyond them was a grassy bank and several Chinaberry trees, tung trees grown for oil, and mulberry trees all covered with wisteria. Our long view was way up the river along the shore where the boats landed, off to mountains beyond. From the other window we looked down on the tops of trees and shrubs and the brown river, across it a mile or so to the tree-fringed shore and mountains to the west. There were porches upstairs and down on two sides of the house, and it was well screened so that we did not have to use our mosquito nets. A large powlonia at one corner was full of buds.

We had two cats and a dog in our house and got fed up with opening the door all the time to let them in and out. So we fixed up a hanging panel at the back door that they could open themselves.

Culley and I were sitting upstairs one evening when we heard a terrible racket downstairs, a shrieking and screaming in several animal languages. Then something came up the stairs, along the hall and into the room where we were. Leading the procession was a *huang-shu-lang*, an animal the shape of a weasel but about the size of a woodchuck. *Huang-shu-lang* means yellow-rat-wolf. This creature was long and slim and came in top speed, followed by one of the cats, behind it the other cat and then the dog, all shrieking. They made a skidding loop through our room and back out and down the stairs with Culley and me in pursuit. Culley opened the front door to let the *huang-shu-lang* out, but he dove among some packing boxes in the space under the stairs. We got a long stick to encourage him and finally he shot out the door.

We thought it all rather funny, and next day when we went up to the hospital told our friends about it. They looked very serious.

"Wait a minute," they said, "that animal, are you sure it was a *huang-shu-lang*?" We said sure it was. "Did it have black across its face?" When we said it did they said, "That was no *huang-shu-lang*, that was a *hu-li ching*!"

Now the *hu-li ching* was the bad fairy that caused all the disasters that no one could account for otherwise, such as a house catching on fire. Some thought it was a *hu-li ching* that burnt down the old hospital.

We said, "Well, if it was a *hu-li ching*, what then?" They asked if we had killed or hurt it. We said no. "That's good," they said, "but something terrible will happen because you chased him."

After that, every day our friends asked, "Has it happened yet?" We were like people living in a haunted house to prove it isn't haunted. Every day we'd answer, "No, nothing's going to happen."

But it did. One of our cats found the electric transformer which was near where we lived, walked in and stepped on a live wire, and that was the end of the cat.

When our worried friends heard about that they said, "Good! Now it has happened. Nothing else will happen."

That was the end of our *hu-li ching*.

Dr. Brown arrived back from furlough one day, bringing along a Ford his church in America had given him. I was operating, but everybody else went down to watch as a derrick lifted the car off the steamer. I met them at the gate and rode up the winding road Dr. Brown had planned for cars but had until that moment been used only by rickshaws to bring in patients. How the nurses and attendants and such patients as could walk crowded around to see the strange sight.

September was beautiful, our I-chi-shan paths bordered with thousands of white lilies alternated with iris, our gardens full of the Kuling lily. Its stalk came up before the leaves, and the first thing you knew there was a stalk about fifteen inches high with a wonderful bunch of orange-red flowers with long curved stamens looking for all the world like a cluster of azalea blossoms. The *kuei-hua* blossomed, the honorable flower with leaves dark green like laurel and small yellow blossoms, fine and fragrant. Pomelos and persimmons were ripening and friends returning from the hills.

The Libby and Hayes families came back from the mountains, where they had finally gone to escape the heat, in spite of consular advice to the contrary. Walter Libby had been at Wuhu Hospital before I reached China, and had been sent to Nanchang to build a hospital there. With the countryside so unsettled around Nanchang, only Dr. Libby remained there while Lucile brought back to Wuhu their five children, her cook and other servants, and two white goats to furnish their milk. They moved in with Paul and Helen Hayes and their seven-year-old, Elsie, with whom I had lived when I first reached China.

There was a good American school at Kuling, but because of the troubles it moved to Shanghai for the winter of 1930-31. Helen Hayes always taught Elsie at home, and this year Lucile Libby and Virginia Huntington joined her to run a school for all the children. They took Grandma Watters onto the faculty, to teach nature study and the history of art, which gave Mother much pleasure.

After Dr. Brown returned and could relieve me, Mother and I had a short vacation, the first part spent unpacking and getting settled in our new home. Then we caught a downriver boat with indefinite plans. At Nanking we stopped off and engaged a very old victoria with a horse that was older still and a harness all tied up in strings, and traveled along cobbly roads which shook us almost to pieces. They had been the best roads in the city until recently, and we were much impressed by the fine auto road which had been cut through the heart of Nanking and from which there were several branches. But horses were not allowed on this wonderful road. We were also impressed with the new buildings for the Department of Justice, and other evidences that a city of a new age was being built over the old one. But there were many fine buildings that stood roofless with empty windows, ruin accomplished only three years earlier.

After visiting friends, we took a train to Chinkiang, to stay at the Lettie Mason Quine Hospital compound. We stayed longer than we had meant, and got plenty of sleep and time to read, and it was pleasant to feel the responsibilities of the hospital were not mine.

Dr. Kao, who had been at I-chi-shan, was our guide on a memorable hike. We started from the West Gate, not far from the Grand Canal, that piece of engineering that astonished Marco Polo, and followed a walk around the shoreline, under cliffs apparently of sandstone, to a hill projecting into the Yangtze downstream from the city. In a small cave temple full of incense smoke, a monk sat beside the altar reading the Buddhist scriptures, his concentration assisted by rhythmically beating a small wooden drum. Another monk lighted a smoky red candle and led us behind the shrine to a deeper part of the cave where we made out stone steps leading downward, the stone roof coming closer and closer to our heads as we cautiously descended.

Soon the tunnel came to an end, bricked up because of "snakes," said our monk, "and gasses." Then he told us that in the time of the Three Kingdoms, which was in the third century A.D., a general who had occupied Chinkiang was afraid he might be besieged and had this tunnel dug from his *yamen*, about a mile away, to the river's edge, a useful way to send spies out and get in supplies.

A climb up a steep road to the top of the hill brought us to the extensive Sweet Dew Temple with many stone inscriptions and a bronze incense burner built like a pagoda perhaps fifteen feet high, worn by the weather of centuries, but no images. This was a memorial to great men of the past. The temple was filled with wounded soldiers, and a notice pasted up on a wall told us that one of the officers had bought two pigs so that the men could have a feast, for it was the day of the Eighth Month Festival, when everyone in Chinkiang who possibly could manage it went home to feast with his family.

Our walk from Sweet Dew Temple to Golden Mountain Island took us the entire length of the city and more. The streets were gay with people in their best clothing, many carrying home food from the markets for their feast. Many children had their heads newly-shaved except for one lock of hair that stood straight up, wound with gay-colored silk, carrying a flower proudly at the top, five or six inches above the head. The incense stores were doing great business, selling bundles of incense that burned for hours under the light of the full moon. If it went out it was considered bad luck to relight it, but the incense was dried with great care so that rarely happened. All along the street were mooncakes, a pancake about a foot and a half in diameter, eaten only at this one day of the year, for the moon was associated with the festival. And since the Chinese saw a rabbit in the moon, as we see a man, there were lots of little toy fruits and vegetables made of plaster meant to be set out in the inner court of the homes as an offering for the moon-rabbit, perhaps more in fun and make-believe than in worship, judging by the attitude of the people toward them. The incense was not make-believe, though; we saw poor people carrying home great towers of it that must have meant a lot of skimped ricebowls.

Outside the city wall Golden Mountain Island, still an island at the time of the T'ai-p'ing Rebellion (1851-1864), had become a part of the mainland by a shift of the river channel. It is the site of an ancient and famous temple where in earlier times seven to eight hundred Buddhist monks lived. We found very few monks, and they were crowded by a great lot of wounded soldiers.

We climbed the pagoda, which was only seven stories high in place of the original fifteen, and from the top had a glorious view of the countryside. Little lights were set in the walls, bells hung from many uptilted roof corners and many gilded images sat in niches inside the tower. But when I asked Dr. Kao who they were, he shook his head sadly. It was always difficult to get an explanation of the temple images; a few were well known, but the legions of lesser ones had been largely forgotten.

In a cave below the pagoda was the gilded mummy of a holy monk who had lived and died there, not an unusual sight. Sitting up in an attitude of contemplation and protected by a glass case, he was there to inspire the devout. Behind his shrine was the opening of another tunnel that led out under the river to Silver Mountain Island, about three miles away.

Among the many connecting temple buildings we found the guest room, and in response to Dr. Kao's card a monk came to lead us to the temple treasures. He was a most intelligent and learned man, with a spiritual and kindly mien. He led us through rooms inhabited by wounded soldiers to the temple library, and there showed us five Buddhas of white alabaster brought from India; then through various courtyards and past several shrines, including one where worshippers had hung up many paper eyes in hope of healing their own diseased eyes, up through the monks' dining room where the long tables were neatly laid with bowls and chopsticks for the next meal, to another guest room. There he showed us a bronze drum, beautifully engraved, and an incense burner, dating back to long before the time of Christ. While we sipped delicious tea, he explained an ancient white jade belt that was graven with poems by a famous poet who had composed both words and music of the song about the four classes of men— farmer, fisherman, fuel-gatherer and scholar.

At last we thanked the monk and bowed our way out, I with an increased interest in this old temple of which Marco Polo told stories that Venetians would not believe. He must have come to it often, for Yangchow, the city he governed for three years under the Great Khan, was just across the river.

How glad we were of a chance to visit old Chinkiang before heading on down to Shanghai and Wing On's department store to stock up on kitchenware. Failing Woolworth's, which had not reached China, we favored Wing On's, which means Eternal Peace. We were also on the track of a Russian folk song we had heard in Vienna and were referred to a Russian music store in Harbin. There were a great many White Russians in China at that time, in most cases very poor, doing anything to keep alive. For a while we had a man at I-chi-shan tinkering machinery who had played in the Moscow orchestra. He had stayed with us until the Southern Army with its Red Russian advisors arrived, and then fled again, to Shanghai.

Back in Wuhu we found many letters from home asking about the unsettled conditions. We were quite out of the picture, but Kiukiang had been on the edge of it for some time, and Nanchang in the thick of it.

We found on our return a new operating table, a beauty and a great improvement over the one we had been using, which was retired to the smaller operating room. One of the first patients to use it was a man who had told some soldiers about two bandits, information that had led to the arrest of one of them. The other bandit vowed to kill this man and his whole family. He tried to satisfy the bandit and to save his family by cutting his throat, but he had failed to study anatomy and made a poor job of it. He arrived in pretty bad shape, but recovered and had to move to Wuhu and find work in the city, for he knew if he returned to his old home the bandit would carry out his threat.

Another man was badly bitten by a tiger that had killed three people in his small village about twelve miles from Wuhu. He was one of twenty-two men who went out to rid the village of this menace, and unluckily stumbled on the huge yellow cat with black stripes hiding in some bushes. His friends shot the tiger, but not before it had badly mangled one arm. The tiger was so large it took four men to carry him, and they sold him for several hundred dollars. I saw pieces of the ankle bones, which had been carefully cut off to be made into medicine, and by the looks of those it was a very large animal. The man who had been mauled had waited six days before coming into the hospital and had a bad case of blood poisoning. We managed to save him and his arm.

Several years earlier we had had an interesting woman as patient who had been a bandit victim from across the river. She was with us for several months while her leg healed. Grandmother Hsu had made a lot of braided napkin rings while her daughter embroidered needlebooks to help pay expenses, and they had been drawn into the life of the hospital. While she was with us there had also been a three-year-old boy, so pale and thin and lifeless that no one expected to see him well again. His crib was moved to the sunniest corner of the women's ward, and week by week a change was noticed. The nurses began to call him Yao ch'ih, because when anyone came by his crib he could point with his thin little hand to a box of crackers on his table and say, *Yao ch'ih,* which means, "I want to eat." When he went home, after many weeks, his cheeks were round and rosy and he was full of fun, the pet of the whole hospital.

Grandmother Hsu remembered Yao ch'ih, and came to see us again, bringing with her her daughter's six-year-old son, a living skeleton from malnutrition and disease. His name, T'ien-pao, which means "Heavenly Package," did not seem very appropriate as he lay unconscious on the examining table. His mother was feeding him opium and Grandmother Hsu and a circle of aunts and uncles stood around him as I came into the room. He was a few sticks of bone, just nineteen pounds, and someone remarked gravely that he looked like the bone doll, as they called the skeleton in the nurses' classroom. T'ien-pao had been sick for six months and had lived chiefly on opium for the last month. His father was dead, and he and his mother lived with his father's father in Wuhu. Grandmother Hsu and the other relatives lived north of the river and were farmers, the ladies in black head-cloths, wadded black coats, and black trousers tied down around the legs and ankles, with a blue apron tied around the waist. We think of women as having some touch of beauty about their clothing, but these women had none. We were glad to see Grandmother Hsu again, for we cared a lot for her; and she fell on our necks and wept for joy to see us again and called Mother her elder sister.

Day by day as new life began to flow in Tien-pao's veins, he proved, to everyone's dismay, to be a spoiled little tyrant. The nurses did not like him, but not all patients can be likeable, and they were kind and patient. When after many weeks he left us, he could walk and talk and had doubled his weight. Perhaps more important, he had learned something about living with other people and respecting their rights.

Then we had a twelve-year-old girl with a broken arm. No amount of splinting or application of casts held it in place, so when Dr. Libby was down from Nanchang briefly, he and I opened the arm and put the two ends of the bone together and sewed them fast with sinews from the tail of a kangaroo. The bones knit and the child recovered and could have gone home to her in-laws, but didn't want to. The mother-in-law refused my offer to put her into our I-chi-shan school, because the family wanted her to work. Little Cunning Cloud had a hard life before her, and we hoped that when she was older she would bear a son and be in great favor.

Little Tiger came to us writhing and screaming with pain from a bladder stone, as he had for seven long years. He looked like a little old man and scratched anyone who came near him. His family told us he had a devil, and we agreed with them, for that devil was indeed the terrible devil Pain. He was half crazed by it, and because he did not act like a human child his family was afraid of him and had often beaten him cruelly. They were glad to leave him with us and agreed not to come back until we sent for them.

It took several people to do anything for him, one to hold him and keep him from biting and scratching the others. It was quite a fight to get his dangerous claws trimmed to a semblance of human fingernails. The one cheering thing about it was that we knew we could relieve his pain with surgery; but we wondered how we should manage his post-operative care. When we showed him the rough stone that had caused his pain, he didn't believe for a moment that it wouldn't return and waited, sometimes in his bed and sometimes about the hospital in defiance of orders, for the pain to come back.

Gradually it began to dawn on him that what we said was true. Then began the most marvelous transformation. Starved for affection for seven years, he changed into an affectionate child. In fact, he became quite a problem, for he would greet us with a glad shout and run to throw his arms around us whenever he saw us, and whatever we might be doing. He learned where the hospital office was, and often ran in and embraced the office force too, to their amazement and not altogether their pleasure.

When his family returned for him, they couldn't believe this sunny, loving child was the wild creature they had brought in. We never heard how they made out, but felt sure no one could resist the joyous child who had been Little Tiger.

Another small boy picked up a strange thing by the side of the road where men were working, and used the stick of dynamite to pound some rocks. It blew up knocking him unconscious, and mangled his left hand almost beyond recognition. Chan Sen was quickly loaded onto a cot, wrapped in a blue and white quilt, and the cot was slung by ropes under a long pole which four neighbors took turns carrying down to the river onto a small sailboat and brought to our hospital landing. In the examining room, his father urged us to cut off the hand altogether. "*Ai-ya*, my son!" wailed the mother, "He is useless; he can never be anything but a beggar!" But I said the little finger looked hopeful, and one little finger would be better than none at all.

Sometimes when a neighbor's boat came to town with a load of vegetables or pigs for market, one of his parents would come along and bring him sweet cakes or preserved duck eggs. One day, instead of greeting him as usual, his mother sat down and wailed, "*Ai-ya*! Where is he who was my son?" Puzzled, the boy replied, "I am here, Mother. Why do you wail now that my hand is getting well?" But she could not be comforted. She had gone to a temple to burn incense to the idol and a priest had told her the explosion had frightened away the child's soul and an evil spirit had taken its place. In vain the boy protested and the nurses comforted; she went mournfully away, saying she would not dare to take a devil to her home. "Even if he were still my son," she said, "he could only be a beggar, for his hand is useless."

Long before the last bandages were off, I took the boy up to see two convalescent British sailors who found time hanging heavy on their hands. He could speak no English, they no Chinese, but they rose to the challenge and taught him to tie all kinds of knots, how to use a pencil, and by the time the second sailor returned to his ship the boy no longer needed hospital care. He went to live with the hospital pastor, and it was arranged for him to go to our school. The ability to read and write and do simple figuring made him more valuable to his family than before the accident, so that at the year's end his parents, fears forgotten, gladly took him home.

Those two British sailors were especially delightful patients. Old salts, with a cockney accent, when they came in they began talking to each other across the hall before they had seen each other. When Gale was able to sit up he was wheeled into Woods' room. He looked at Woods and said, "I say, Jack, you'd make an 'andsome corpse!" When Woods improved, he had a great time playing an accordion up on the roof where he wouldn't disturb anybody, but we could hear his music floating out over the compound. Soon both men were up and looking scrumptious in their white uniforms.

Another youngster tangled with a stick of dynamite and lost one eye and three fingers on one hand. When Ti-ti, Little Brother, came out of the "dream medicine," he saw the nurses in white around him and thought they must be funeral mourners, and that since he felt so strange he was probably dead. Then he heard his mother asking, "Do you suppose the explosion frightened away his soul? He will look so dreadful with only one eye and what can he do without three fingers?" We reassured her that he could learn to do a lot with the fingers he had left, and that we'd get him a glass eye.

During his days on the ward Ti-ti made friends with older children there, including "Hoppity Skip," a boy in the next bed who had had a bone disease in one foot, so bad that the foot had to be amputated. But he went cheerily about on one foot and a crutch, which earned him his nickname.

As Ti-ti's strength returned and he began to run about, we called him in to try out three glass eyes. He found one that fit comfortably and we handed him a mirror. Ti-ti was speechless when he saw himself with two eyes just like before. As his hand healed, Ti-ti wore the glass eye to get used to the feel of it, and every morning the nurses took it out and washed it and replaced it. They taught his mother to do the same, and someone else was watching the process too. Later, when they were playing alone, Hoppity Skip said, "Ti-ti, let's take out your glass eye and see what it looks like on the back. I know just how to do it." So out it came and the two boys examined it, but alas, suddenly it slipped and broke into two pieces on the floor.

Resourceful Hoppity Skip fit the two pieces together and managed to slip the eye back into place. Next morning when the nurses took the eye out to wash it the accident was discovered, and Hoppity Skip had his crutch taken away for a day. As for Ti-ti, his misery was complete, for there was not another eye in Wuhu that would do, and his mother was ready to take him home. They couldn't wait around for the two to three weeks it would take to get a new one from Shanghai. And there was no way to send mail to their village.

But we thought of a method. The broken eye was sent to Shanghai with an order for another like it, and Ti-ti and his mother were instructed to go in one month's time to the village where a Bible Woman* lived; it would be sent to her. And so it came to pass.

One day down at the clinic a most attractive baby came in, carried by his father. I was puzzled, as not many babies were brought in by their fathers. And some, indeed, had more toes or fingers than ordinarily allotted by an all wise Chinese Providence; but when did one ever see a tiny foot minus a little toe? The crowd of patients had to wait while this absent toe was called on to explain itself. Absences do not usually have voices, but this one had, the rather gentle voice of the father. "Quite right," he said, "there is no little toe on the right foot. It was there when he was born, a perfect baby to look at and play with." The father's weather-beaten face broke into a wry smile, "And so we were afraid; all our friends said we'd never keep him, as evil spirits would take him just as they have taken every one of our six other babies. Could we hope to keep this one, the most attractive of them all? What could we do?

"We began to inquire of many people how to foil those prowling evil spirits. Some people said one thing, some said another. We burned incense in the local temple and said prayers there. We put a silver chain around his neck to hold him to us. We clothed him with special garments to fool the spirits, and hid him in dark places when he took his naps. Finally a wandering magician came by our village and he told us the thing to do. It was a hard thing, and his mother thought about it for several days before she could get up her courage to do it. Then the baby fell sick, and in desperation she carried out the magician's advice. The baby got well quickly, and his mother died, as was expected. But now he is

---

* Bible Women were women trained and paid by each denominational mission to minister to people hard to reach in other ways.

ill again, and I beg you to save him."

"And what was the magician's advice?" The father hesitated, then answered, "Yes, she bit off the baby's toe and ate it to save him." We saved him, too, but in a different way.

A woman came in to us with one foot dangling, its ankle joint wide open, for it had been half pulled off by a running rope. We found most of the chief blood vessels intact, and decided to try to sew the foot back on, telling each other, "Doubtless it will have to come off later, but at least we'll have tried."

Next day, when the woman was feeling better, we tried to find out what had happened. Her husband was captain of a junk, she told us, and the offending rope was its towing hawser. But how she had been hurt was not easy to understand. To clear up the mystery, we sketched a tugboat, identifiable by clouds of smoke pouring from its funnel, and behind that the hull of a junk. "How many masts has your ship?" we asked. "None," she said, "the mast was down and we were being towed." Asked to point out where she was at the time of the accident, she startled us by pointing between the ships. But when marks were made to indicate a figure on the hawser, she laughed and shook her head.

So we put down two hospital charts on her bed saying, "Look, this is the tug, and this is your ship. Now just where were you?" "Give me something for a rope," she demanded, and quickly fastened a piece of bandage to the two sides of the bow of her junk, then tied a loop in the middle and tossed that to the tug, calling out realistically, "Make it fast!" While that was done she coiled down the slack rope on her deck. We handed her a fountain pen. "Look. This is you. Where were you standing?"

"Astern at the helm, usually," she replied, "but this time my husband and the deckhand were both busy in the cabin when the tug suddenly appeared in a great hurry to be off. As I was standing here by the coils of rope, I threw the hawser-loop. Start that ship!" she instructed us, and when the chart representing the tug made a sudden start, it yanked the bandage, which in uncoiling actually caught the fountain pen in its loop and threw it "overboard."

But we didn't see charts and bandage and fountain pen, we

saw a puffing tug and a palm-fiber rope, and a woman disappearing into the muddy Yangtze under the blunt bow of a junk already underway.

"Here I am," she cried, "under the ship. The rope is still around my foot, and I am holding that rope and pulling myself along it with my hands—like this. But I can't get free, and my husband doesn't know where I am. He is hunting frantically for me, worried to death!"

"And the men in the tug?" we asked anxiously, "surely they see you?" "Oh yes, they see me. So they cast off the tow, and shout, 'The responsibility isn't ours! You sent for us, you know, we didn't offer of ourselves to tow you!' And they steam away very fast. A man in a sampan sees me, but of course he doesn't dare pull me out but only points to where I am until my husband shouts, 'Save her! I promise not to blame you, the responsibility is on me!' "*

"So the man gets hold of me and my husband pulls me up on deck. My foot is still caught in the rope and bleeds but my soul is not there; some devil from the river makes everything black in front of me. My husband calls me, using my name, which he knows I love to hear, and at last I hear him. My soul comes back, but my foot is still caught in the rope and bleeds.

"My husband turns over a bamboo bed and lays me on it and he and the deckhand carry me to the Catholic mission. They tell me I must come here, and some of them help carry me as our deckhand has gone back to the ship. You see, the army is catching carriers, and he didn't dare be on the street. Why did he go that far? Well, it is really no further from the shore to the Catholic mission than your eye is from your nose. And so I have come to the hospital, and you have NOT taken off my foot. Will it get well?"

That question we could not answer. But day after day as we watched and dressed that foot, it steadily improved. The woman's

---

* Another reason river people hesitated to save a drowning person was the belief that the water devil, cheated of his prey, would soon take the rescuer instead. A water devil was believed to be the spirit or ghost of a previously drowned person who was on the lookout for a substitute to take his place in the nether world so that he could be reincarnated.

good constitution gradually overcame the infection Yangtze mud had carried into the joint. One day, with the help of crutches, she stood beside her bed. The foot was still swollen and clumsy, but it was her own foot and still improving, and she was content.

A man came into the hospital as a casualty after a bandit raid, and none of us, seeing his cruel face, had any doubt that he had been on the wrong side of that fray. He was seriously injured. A slashing blow from a "big knife" had sliced away the side of his head so that his brain was partly exposed, while the tissues that should have covered it, including some of his skull and part of an ear, hung down on his shoulder. While we cleansed the wound and replaced and sutured the flap, we discussed the man. "He won't live. There will be one less bandit in the Yangtze Valley, and a good thing, too." Our hearts were sick with the suffering of those who came to us burned and broken and tortured at the hands of that brotherhood. Yet our duty was to save life, and day by day we worked with this silent, hard-faced man used to inflicting pain and bearing it stoically himself. After weeks of effort we saw to our amazement that he was going to recover, and one day on rounds agreed he was out of danger.

"Congratulations!" we told him, "when you came in, we thought you would surely die, but you are getting well instead." No flicker of pleasure lighted his face. He looked up with weary eyes and made no reply. So we tried again. "Aren't you glad that you are getting well?" To our astonishment, he replied with an unqualified "No!" Thinking we must have misunderstood, we had one of the Chinese nurses ask him again, "Wouldn't you rather be well than die?" But again he gave an emphatic "No!"

Puzzled, we asked why he would rather die, and he answered simply, "Because I have sinned." It was quite obvious he had sinned, and grievously. His bodily hurt was healing, but had we no help for a far deeper hurt?

"You have heard," we reminded him, "while you have been here about a heavenly Father who loves us earth-people and has thought out a method about sin so that you don't have to carry the burden of your sins all your life. When you are sorry for them, he is

willing to forgive them. Did you know that?" No, he hadn't understood that. So we sent for our wise Pastor Liu, and while we went on
to other sick folk, Pastor Liu talked with this unhappy man until
slowly the meaning of the old, incredibly joyous truth dawned and
the hard-bitten look disappeared. There went out from the hospital one day a new man, and there was truly one less bandit in the
Yangtze Valley.

Mother was welcomed back after furlough as a beloved elder,
someone to whom Chinese and foreigners alike could take their
troubles. She never stopped studying Chinese, and used it every
day with the servants and on the hospital wards where she enjoyed
visiting, but her heart was not strong, and the Yangtze Valley
climate weighed on her, so that she spent more and more time
watching the ever-changing panorama from the windows of our
room.

There she could look out over the broad river to the green
hills beyond the swelling flood, as she liked to speak of them, and
the mountains beyond. Sometimes the river could be very quiet,
enough air stirring to move some of the big bat-winged sails of the
southern junks, quiet enough so that we could hear the shrill voice
of some sailor calling up the wind to help him along a little faster,
while down by the river's edge the fisherman threw their great nets
from the rocks that defined I-chi-shan, and several water buffaloes
might be all under water, except the tips of their noses and a bit of
their backs, to escape the heat.

More often the river was busy and noisy with more than a
hundred watercraft of every description, from the round wooden
washtubs paddled across the dangerous current without hesitation
by women bound for the opposite shore, to the enormous battle-
ships that occasionally sailed majestically past, and the great
lumber rafts with more than a hundred men living on board,
floating their produce to market. Sampans and junks of all sorts and
sizes, steamers of the Jardine, Butterfield & Swire, San Puh, China
Merchants and Japanese lines, launches that made the run to
Nanking or upriver, and of course the gunboats, all contributed to a

fascinating and changing scene. Old ship hulks, used as docks for the steamers, rocked by the bund; freighters from all over the world anchored midstream to unload their wares; a Japanese gunboat was always docked along the bund, a British gunboat anchored midstream, and U.S. warships were on constant patrol.

On 23 December 1930, Wuhu became a port of call for the Shanghai to Hankow airplane. It also stopped at Kiukiang, and the twenty-five hour boat trip Dr. Perkins took to come down and look after our eyes was reduced to two hours by plane. It carried six passengers and the mail, and had been doing so for some time. The airplane was a great advantage when we needed supplies from Shanghai in a hurry, and this we did quite soon, as a sailor named Cotterell came in from H.M.S. Gnat. He needed oxygen and was very sick. Cotterell was with us until the end of May, when he went home to England on the H.M.S. *Vindictive*, but he left behind a special gift for us and the people of Wuhu.

It all started with the work of bandits across the Yangtze. One of their victims was a chubby boy of nine with a bullet in his abdomen. His father also had been shot, and it was his grandmother who, having learned of the distant hospital, twenty-six miles away, engineered his journey to us. It had taken a day and a night to reach our hill, part of the way by sampan, part carried in a crude stretcher made by turning a bamboo bench upside down, and finally by sailboat. He needed operation, immediately. It was already late at night, the surgery would be serious work, far better handled if we could get one more surgeon to help out. There was a good one, Dr. Warmolts, on the American destroyer U.S.S. *Stewart* anchored far out in the river, but how were we to get word to him? The hospital car was sent down to the landing with a letter to be carried across to the ship, but there probably would not be a boat at the landing to take it.

Then I thought of Cotterell. He was a radio man. He'd been with us some months already and had just had another minor operation so probably would not feel much like signaling the ship. But we asked him, and he was eager to try. He selected a suitable light from several we brought him, then up to the roof went Cotterell on a stretcher.

"Since the port is comparatively peaceful now," he said, "there may not be a lookout on duty, but I'll try, and if I don't get them perhaps I can get the British ship and get a message from there."

"S-T-E-W-A-R-T" went the dots and dashes flashing out over the water, and he had hardly finished when two bright masthead lights gleamed out with startling suddenness high above the ship. We heard a gleeful chuckle from Cotterell as he settled down to work he hadn't been able to do for months: PLEASE ASK YOUR DOCTOR COME HOSPITAL AT ONCE EMERGENCY OPERATION CAR WAITING BUTTERFIELD HULK.

The flashes stopped and Cotterell lay back to rest while we watched. Presently came the put-put-put of a motor boat, and we watched its red port light as it steadily brought Dr. Warmolts to shore. Then the auto headlights flashed on and we heard the familiar honk of its horn. By the time we got our tired but happy telegraphist back to bed, Dr. Warmolts was studying the x-ray, and a few minutes later we were at work. That night a British telegraphist, an American Navy surgeon, our Chinese and American hospital staff, and the little Ford car saved the life of one little Chinese boy.

Cotterell was none the worse for his trip to the roof and after recovering completely signed on for another ten years in the Royal Navy. But before he left us Mother said, "Why depend on having a sick telegraphist in the hospital? Why not learn to do it yourself?" So Cotterell taught me to signal in Morse with a light, and to use signal flags to wig wag messages to the ships.

Signaling, except for the curious disinterest of our young interns, became a popular pastime for everyone on our hill. One time Dottie and Elsie were practicing on the hospital roof and in fun they signaled an S.O.S. to each other. Before we knew it, a British gunboat had landed an armed party to rescue us, and it took the representatives of several nations to straighten that out.

That was a cold winter; we had a lot of unusual snow in February, and everyone seemed to be on the sick list while our households all bulged with extras. Nat Marmot, a young Jewish man in the egg business who had come to us in 1928 with smallpox, had stayed on to become a part of the Brown family. Gladys Harmon, our second American nurse, had been with the Hayeses for some time and their home was used by many other people as a way-station going up or down the river. Then the U.S.S. *Edsall* came into port and four officers' wives wanted to find homes among Americans. We thought their lives must be very difficult, moving around so much, and took them in.

Our old friend from across the river, Grandmother Hsu, T'ien-pao's grandmother, turned up one day with ten red eggs for us to celebrate the birth of a new grandson, and ten white eggs to celebrate a new daughter-in-law-to-be. We presented her with the traditional one dollar wrapped in red paper for the grandson and two dollars for the new daughter. Grandmother Hsu was full of news about her village, quite pleased that the bandits who had shot her and ten other villagers had been executed and their heads put up on poles in the village.

But she also had some bad news. Her daughter, T'ien-pao's mother, a comely woman, was a widow, so she was the property of her father-in-law. He wanted to sell her for the $300 he could get for her and to keep T'ien-pao himself. We found her a position at Sister Constance's True Light Industry where she could sew and make some money and put off the day of sale. But there was no legal escape for her if her father-in-law decided to sell her anyway.

As buds swelled on the willows and the parson crows gathered twigs to build their nests, Paul Hayes was out on the district to close down some of the smaller village churches. The Depression in America was seriously threatening all our work and we were already taking salary cuts while members of a fact-finding group from America studied the situation. They made a practical, money-saving plan, but it was never carried out because of the war that was almost upon us.

Gathering Storms

1931-1936

The summer of 1931 was very dry at Wuhu, but further west heavy rains sent an unusual flood of water downriver. Practically all of the farmland around Wuhu was flat rice land lying at a lower level than the very changeable river, and as the waves swirled nearer to the top of the outer dyke, watchmen were posted with big gongs to warn of danger. By day farmers worked frantically to reinforce the dykes, and at night waited in dread for the sound we at last heard—the persistent beating of gongs and the shout, "Run for your lives!"

At first only the wash from passing ships pushed over the dykes and into the fields where the rice was beginning to form its precious heads; then the pounding waves found a weak spot and swept over the city leaving I-chi-shan an island in a river 150 miles wide. Thousands of Wuhu families fled as their mud huts crumbled, to say nothing of the drowned-out families who had refugeed down from north of the river bringing with them their pigs and chickens to sell at Wuhu. We knew there would be lots of sickness and banditry by fall and winter, and I needed my rest to get ready for it.

Early August I got up to Kuling where Mother had been laid up for some weeks after a fall. Housebound, she spent her time in the dining room where she could look out on the steep hillside covered with scrub chestnuts, thick with weigelia and deutzia and azalea. There were many immense boulders that looked as though they might roll downhill, scattered pine trees and yellow daylilies

blooming wherever they could get a foothold. Neighbor bungalows, built of the valley stone, were all around and below ours, and
around the shoulder from us was the Gap, the business center of
the town of Kuling.

Some of the town activities appeared at our door. A silver man
would come with all sorts of trinkets: puzzle rings, pagoda pepper
boxes, napkin rings, spoons. The shoe man, the lace man, the dish
man with yellow and blue china and the famous Thousand Flower
pattern, the man with sheets of silk wadding for bed spreads, light
as a feather; the barber, fruit man, and the flower man. Some
mornings there was a bazaar in the dining room since Brownie was
filling a chest for her son soon to be married, and Mother could not
resist the flowers. For about three cents she could buy a large
bouquet of Easter lilies, or yellow lilies, or red ones with narrow
petals and long curved stamens, or lovely tiger lilies that were
white spotted with red. There were great bunches of purple platy-
codon, flame colored lychnis, huge blue hydrangeas.

Soon it began to rain, as only it knew how to rain on Lushan,
and a gale blew down through our valley making the bungalows
shake on their foundations. The word "typhoon" is a Chinese word
taken over into English; in the northern dialect "ta-fen" literally
means "big wind," which it is. There were many storms in the
Yangtze Valley that summer, and floods. One of our Hankow
friends said that the water was sixteen feet deep in her house; the
first storey completely sunk along with all her books and
furnishings.

Dottie hadn't been well, and Brownie decided to take her
back down to Wuhu, but when they reached Kiukiang they found
their boat was at Hankow to help with evacuation from the flood.
Brownie was able to buy deck space on another boat, and after
reaching Wuhu wired back to us advising us to be in no hurry to
return.

So we stayed on longer into September and enjoyed the quiet
and peace and coolness of the mountains, and learned some of the
Lushan stories. If you go over to the little village and turn to the left
as though you were going to go downhill, you will find a small

shrine to a man who lived there long ago. Some people hanging around the shrine told us he had gotten from the Fire God a sword to cut through all troubles and a flyswisher to swish them away. He spent his life helping troubled people. Finally one day word came that he was to go to heaven because he was such a good person. Up in heaven he couldn't help but go out each day and look down over the battlements to where he could see someone in trouble, and he would jump down and help that person. For two hundred years he kept returning to earth, but finally word came that he must stay put in heaven.

One day we went for a picnic at the small brook below the Temple of the Three Trees. To get there you had to go along a small stream down a gulley with narrow rock walls on both sides, and a waterfall. Carved into rock were the words, *T'ing An,* "Listen Quietly."

Down beyond that was another stream that had carved on the stone behind it, "Let all creation rejoice together." The beauty of those mountains was enough to make everyone rejoice.

As we were having our picnic, there came a sudden rain and flash flood, and we scrambled out of the stream and went soaking wet back up to the temple, where we asked the fine old abbot if we could hire a room with a charcoal brazier to dry off, and meantime, would they make up a meal for us, as temples did to raise money.

After I got dry I went rambling around, and in a corner I found a little shrine with a beautiful, evidently very old, bronze Buddha head. It wasn't any Buddha I had ever met, so I asked the abbot who he was.

"P'i-lo," said the abbot. I asked him to tell me about P'i-lo. "If you ever," said the abbot, "through deep meditation and prayer, over a long time, get to know the inwardness of your own heart, you will find P'i-lo there."

"Yes," I nodded, "we know P'i-lo. We call him the Holy Spirit."

Another time when we were on a hike we saw a little hill called Crying Tiger Hill. I knew there must be a story to that. "Yes," said a friend, "there's a good story. Throughout Chinese history there have been a lot of terrible wars. For each war there have been thousands of refugees, and children often got separated from their parents."

In this particular story, one small boy got lost from his family on Lushan. A mother tiger heard him crying. She took a liking to him, took him home to her den and brought him up with her cubs. She taught him the things a tiger should know: to hunt, to hide, to find food and avoid traps.

Then one day she said to him, "You may have noticed that you don't look the same as your brothers. That is because you aren't a tiger at all, you are a man. Now you are grown up, and it is time you went to live as a man. You must go down to the plain and go over to that city of Kiukiang and learn about clothes and how to talk like a man and to handle fire."

His tiger mother finally persuaded him and he went over to where the trail begins and walked down the mountain and across the plain to Kiukiang, where he learned all the things his mother wanted him to learn. Gradually he was taken into the affairs of people. He was clever and had been well brought up and could think clearly, so he was given more and more responsibility until finally he became Kiukiang's chief magistrate, a position he held for many years. Everyone liked him and the decisions he made, but finally one day when something particularly unfair happened that he could do nothing about, he said, "I declare, it is better to be a tiger."

He resigned his position, walked back across the plain to the mountain, climbed the mountain and looked for his mother. He couldn't find her, although he hunted every day, so he settled down in the little village we know as the Gap. One evening he was playing mah jong with some friends when suddenly they heard a tiger crying outside. He jumped up and said, "That's my mother! She's calling me!" And he rushed out the door into the darkness and they never saw him again.

In September there were baskets to pack and the house to clean, and off we started down the mountain in a pouring rain. The fog came thick around us and shut off the view so that we couldn't

162

see the thousands of steps we were descending, the hairpin turns. But the chair carriers splashed along in perfect safety, and in about two hours we were at the foot of the hill, crowded into a bus where rain dripped through cracks in the roof and ran down our faces like tears. At last we came to the flooded plain where flat-bottomed boats were waiting for us. Mother was unsteady on her feet, but there were helping hands, and we got her safely to Kiukiang. There many buildings were standing in water.

For hundreds of miles along the river the little mud villages at the water's edge, with their mud walls and straw roofs and their green rice fields, had disappeared. There were only tree tops, and now and then a straw roof, and miles and miles of water. We landed from our steamer at Wuhu into a flat-bottomed boat and were rowed to the hospital gate where a welcoming crowd was gathered. Our old friend Grandmother Hsu was there, and T'ien-pao and his mother. North of the river, where they had lived, the low wheat fields were not dotted with hills as were the rice fields on our side of the river. The Hsu family had gathered everything they could and escaped to higher ground at Wuhu. Many others drowned before they could get away, or when boats they were in, most of them overloaded, capsized. But the Hsu family came safely to shore and set up housekeeping on the road against the wall of our compound. Their new home was a lean-to of reed mats, with the poles and straw roof they had brought along. But it was home. The pigs and chickens and the crib for the baby were evidence of that, and all eleven people who dwelt there beamed good cheer, for were they not all alive?

From the hospital roof we could see that all the beautiful fields where the people had worked so diligently through the spring were gone. A few roofs and trees showed above water, and a big boat sailed along where the people had lived. Coffins floated by as well, some from the fields where they had been left to await an auspicious burial day, some from a coffin shop across the street from our gatehouse. The whole shop was washed away. Wherever the land was a few inches above water, hundreds of mat shelters were built as thick as they could stand. Next day, T'ien-pao's mother came to tell us that the water was rising in front of their lean-to, and we invited them to join others who had moved inside the gate. Into our household we took two orphaned boys, Patrick and Jimmy Hu.

The old Ark was turned into a school for refugee children, where each morning each child got a big bowl of multipurpose food, for most of them their only meal of the day. The Ark was surrounded by water, but a boardwalk to the door made it all the more fun. When the children gathered on opening day, there was T'ien-pao in white jacket and pink trousers and a shining face.

One man was fairly well off because he had a small fishing boat with four cormorants, each anchored by an ankle to the gunnel. He would carry this on his shoulders, and as he stepped along the cormorants' heads would bob up and down with the rhythm. Each morning he went fishing with his birds. They had rings around their throats so that they could swallow only small fish. Big fish they took back to the boat. He would let them fish for a while, then take off their collars and let them swallow anything they caught.

There was a story about a man, oh, a horrible tale! He was cruel to his birds and wouldn't take their collars off. His birds could swallow the little minnows, but not enough to satisfy their hunger. So one day, when he wouldn't let the birds fish for themselves, those four birds, their ankles tied to the boat, spread their wings and flew away and they, the man and the boat were never seen again!

Green vegetables were hard to get, but chickens, ducks and geese were plentiful. In contrast to the water everywhere was the dry ground, drier than we had ever seen it, with the earth cracked and plants shriveled. The chief cause of the flood, we learned, was the political turmoil for so many years when no one saw to the annual dredging of the Yangtze or Yellow rivers or the Grand Canal.

Children fared poorly. Evidence of infanticide was everywhere. How could the tiny ones be cared for? And there were many more babies to come. One mother tried to give Dr. Brown her baby, but he arranged to give her a dollar each week so that she could keep and feed him herself. Another man sold his eight-year-old daughter to a richer family who could afford to pay the twenty dollars he asked and would be able to feed his child. Twenty dollars was enough money to feed the rest of the family for many weeks, but when he got back to his shack he threw down the money and wept bitterly.

This was hardly a sporting time for Japan to hit China another blow in Manchuria,* and feeling ran higher against the Japanese, much to the concern of a Japanese patient we had who was assistant to the Japanese consul. He had tuberculosis and was very nervous until Dr. K. B. Liu had a talk with him. Long afterwards Dr. Liu received a letter from Mr. Yamoto who wanted him to know that the way he had been treated at Wuhu hospital had led him to become a Christian.

When I went over to Sister Constance's compound to tend the sick there, we took a sampan at our gate and went straight across the flooded fields to land in her back yard. Of the little weaving village where we used to hear the clacking of looms day and night, more than twenty houses were gone.

Wherever small pieces of land rose a few inches above the water they swarmed with people and their possessions: farm implements and wooden looms, tables, baskets and cradles, fine silk fishing-nets and long bamboo perches of cormorants. Feeble old people sat amid the assemblage and children and babies romped about. Here and there we saw a familiar face and received a cheery greeting.

I-chi-shan walls were all standing in water, but the Sisters'

---

* Japan had a long history of involvement in Manchuria, where by 1931 more than a million Japanese subjects lived, most foreign investment was Japanese and nearly half of Japan's trade with China was located. The area was viewed as a buffer against Russian attack, and as compensation for 100,000 Japanese lives lost in the Russo-Japanese War (1904–1905). An appearance of Chinese sovereignity was maintained under a puppet warlord until rising Chinese nationalism after 1928 challenged the Japanese position in Manchuria. The explosion of a bomb on the railway north of Mukden (Mukden Incident), planned by Japanese army officers, led to Japanese conquest of all Manchuria by early 1932. Pu-yi, the last Ch'in boy emperor, was proclaimed emperor of the state of Manchukuo ("Manchu-land").

wall, and that of the main Episcopal mission across the road, bordered a dry road and formed the back walls for hundreds of mat shelters. Such a lane of misery. Where the people were well they were full of good cheer; but they were not always well. About forty-five were in the little hospital Sister Constance had set up. She also ran a small school and a nursery, and had put a lot of the women to work sewing. Among them we found T'ien-pao's mother making beautifully embroidered scissors cases, handkerchiefs, table linens and many other things to sell to support the mission.

The Chinese doctors and nurses in our hospital formed a "Pity the Neighbors Society," with a committee to investigate and help refugees. Many gave up their own food and worked long hours without pay to help out, and we who had enough to eat in our high, dry, comfortable houses, found that we too had to share what we had.

At I-chi-shan relief work went on day and night; wholesale vaccinations were underway. Dr. Brown was made chairman of a relief committee appointed by the Chinese national relief society and told to organize however seemed best. He went to Hankow to see how they were doing it and I was health officer in his absence.

A cholera patient was brought in from a river boat, and we had to quarantine the boat, then vaccinate the seven hundred people on board. The captain, who was the only foreigner aboard, turned out to be Captain Edwards whose steamer I had stowed away on in 1928. He must have been sorely tried to have his ship delayed while I wired the health board in Shanghai for instructions, but was very patient and accepted the inevitable.*

Brownie organized a sewing group for women to make children's clothing, for which they were paid by the hour. With cold weather ahead, food and clothing and warm houses would be needed; and when the water went down the unsanitary conditions

---

* A year later Captain Edwards left China. His ship went aground and couldn't be got off, so the company sold her and she was broken up. The *Ngankin* had been running on the Yangtze for fifty years.

would be fully exposed. There was plenty of dysentery among those who did not or could not take precautions, although we waged a merciless war on flies.

We expected to have a lot of cholera that summer, but whole-sale vaccinations were effective. Squads went out from the hospital most afternoons into the refugee camps and various parts of the city, carrying the precious vaccine, a combination of typhoid and cholera, and the people flocked to get it. You would never have thought that there had ever been any fear of foreigners or foreign ideas. City police cooperated beautifully, assembling the people and explaining to them what was to be done, and kept the crowds moving.

We got our Shanghai newspapers two days late, but world news was radioed to the gunboats each day, and when I signaled them each evening with surgery schedules, they passed the news on to us. That way we learned that China was to have some of America's surplus wheat, and then that the Lindberghs were nearby. They had flown to Nanking on one leg of their trip that Anne Lindbergh later described in her book, *North to the Orient.* When they saw the flood they placed themselves and their plane at the service of the Chinese government. So in the midst of that flood came one of our bright spots: a visit from Colonel Charles and Anne Lindbergh.

After circling our hill they settled down way beyond some hills near the city. I signaled the H.M.S. *Gnat* that as soon as we knew where they were we would dip our flag three times, and they could send their launch over.

Presently along came Dr. Borcic, a Yugoslavian epidemic expert who had flown up with the Lindberghs. It had taken him two hours to come from the plane by sampan, rickshaw, and on foot. He gave us the plane location and we signaled the *Gnat*, and off we went in their launch up the river to the pagoda, then up the creek jammed with sailboats and sampans, much further than I had ever gone before, across flooded fields. At last we changed into a sampan on the far side of a dyke, and there was the plane. Colonel and Anne Lindbergh greeted us as genially as though they had not been waiting for hours. Immediately there happened what happened to everybody the world over who met them: we felt as though we had always known them, and liked them tremendously.

We persuaded them that we had just as attractive flooded fields nearer the hospital, and that we could get a Chinese guard for the plane. By the time we reached I-chi-shan, they were waiting on a field nearby.

They stayed overnight, visited the hospital and many of the patients, and were particularly interested in the flood refugee patients and those injured by bandits. The Lindberghs were certainly messengers of goodwill, and his famous smile under that tousled hair needed no translating. The only possible way for anyone to look so winsome was to be that kind of person.

The Nanking Government Flood Survey, based on those made by the Lindberghs and by the Nanking University School of Agricultural Economics, found that the central China area had been hardest hit by the floods and had suffered more damages than average, with the Wuhu area hardest hit of all. When all the flood damages were finally assessed, a staggering hundred and fifty thousand people were found to have been drowned, with millions more left homeless and eight and a half million acres of farmland flooded.

By October the water had receded from its high of 31'6" and some roads appeared. By November sampans laden with people, furniture, pigs and bags of seed made their ways back across the river, and new houses started to spring up in place of the dreadful wrecks left by receding water. The courage of the people was amazing, and it was astonishing with what joy they set to work to build new homes. They knew, and we knew, that the hardest times were yet ahead. Winter approached, yet they had few supplies stored up and nothing with which to buy more. Their weakened bodies, chilled by cold winds, would be unable to withstand sickness. The number of girl babies discarded by their parents was a grim indication of the hard struggle ahead. One daughter-in-law of about fifteen, who by custom was living in the home of her parents-in-law to be, was driven out and found crouching against a wall of our compound. Her own parents, when they were found, begged us to keep her until there was a harvest.

An elderly man fell at a food distribution and was trampled. Thinking him dead, his wife sold her pots and pans and their mat shelter, all that was left of their family possessions, to get him a coffin. When he was in it she saw his leg move, and for a number of days he lay there not quite dead. One of our hospital workers found him and tried to get him to come to the hospital, but it was warm and comfortable in the coffin and he refused. So Dr. Brown had him brought in, coffin and all, and we kept him as comfortable as we could his few remaining days.

All stories are continued stories, and we followed that of Grandmother Hsu and her family with much affection. One day Mother went into our kitchen and found Grandmother Hsu there wiping away many silent tears. Our amah and cook and several neighbors were also there, arguing and sympathizing. T'ien-pao's mother, Mrs. Ho, a bright-faced and attractive widow whom we had once before saved from being sold by her father-in-law, was again in danger. He had decided to sell her for $260 to an old man with a long white beard. The money urge was on the father-in-law again, and what could she do? And she would have to leave T'ien-pao behind.

I was incensed. "Who bore the child?" I asked. Our amah said quickly, "It is the custom of our country. The father bore the child." "No indeed," I argued, "that never happened, either in this country or in any other!" Everybody was very sorry for Mrs. Ho, but no one seemed to understand that a woman had any rights or that nature gives her any claim to herself or her children. Then there came a way out. The man in charge of the hospital laundry asked to marry her and was able to pay $110 for her. She was willing, and the father-in-law was talked round, and with the marriage he had no further claim.

The winter of 1931-32 was a mild one, a great mercy for the refugees, but I went into dry dock with fever before the end of the year. I thought I'd be getting up steam on all boilers again soon, and enjoyed a restful vacation, watching the ships on the river to my heart's content. But the weeks went by and it was May before the strange fever was diagnosed. Malaria it was, tertian malaria, not the most devastating kind, but the most stubborn to fight, and malaria with something added. That something, suspected for some time to be tuberculosis, turned out to be undulant fever, a far better diagnosis.

While I was laid up for so many months, the rest of the country wasn't faring quite so peacefully. Japan took further advantage of China's woes to attack Shanghai 29 January 1932. They bombed the Chinese city within Shanghai and used Hongkew, the Japanese section, as a base to attack Chapei. Chinese troops threw up barricades of sandbags and barbed wire, but had no defense against bombs, which demolished the North Railway Station, the Oriental Library that housed some of the rarest volumes in China, the Commercial Press, and vast areas of private property.

Our Wuhu foreign community gingerly celebrated the February birthday of the Japanese Emperor. H.M.S. *Cockchafer*, U.S.S. *Edsall* and the Japanese warship in port were all dressed in flags, and the foreign community gathered at the Japanese consulate for an elaborate party, where clanking swords, gold braid and long gowns prevailed.

After a week of fighting in Shanghai, Wuhu was still peaceful, but the Japanese consul and Mr. Sudo, Commissioner of Customs, were advised to leave by a hurried meeting of Chinese civil and military officials, who immediately set guards around their property to prevent looting.

After two weeks of heavy bombardment and infantry charges at Shanghai by the Japanese, they were prevented from moving inland by the Chinese who then with the help of U.S. Marines, British, French and Italian troops, held them off the International Settlement.

It was the middle of June before I got back into the game, but I filled in only briefly before taking off for Tsingtao June 1932. After a two-day quiet boat journey from Wuhu, we were out on deck early in the morning to see the ruin which had been wrought in Shanghai by the Japanese. Chapei had been most heavily damaged by bombardment, but we saw enough and more than enough along the Whangpoo, the river that leads from the mouth of the Yangtze to Shanghai: houses torn to kindling, holes in the sea wall, general ruin and destruction. Gunboats from Japan and other nations lay in the river, but their guns were quiet, and Shanghai, the beautiful cosmopolitan city with wide, tree-shaded streets and gracious homes, was peaceful.

Work at the Wuhu hospital moved along about as usual through 1933, with triumphs and disappointments. People sometimes insisted on going home when going home meant failure, while staying a few more days success. A broken leg, for instance, that failed to unite, could have been helped by wiring the bones together. But then again some critical case would make a fine recovery and everybody rejoiced.

One of these was a sixteen-year-old girl whose father had a shop where he sold some Japanese goods. Someone threw a bomb that exploded in front of the store, and a piece of the shell went through one of her eyes and carried a piece of bone with it into her brain. The one who threw the bomb wrote her a letter of profound apology and said the bomb was never meant for her. After surgery and many days of confusion, she came along alright.

I was glad to be able to put in a full day's work again, and add a part of the night to it if necessary. One day I had eleven operations, and then about midnight pumped opium out of a would-be suicide. There were fewer cases from banditry than usual, but many surgical cases were coming in, and a great boon was our new fluoroscope, a great help during hunts for bullets.

One day while I was operating we had a big blow. I finished up in a hurry and dashed down through the falling trees to be with Mother and saw the roof sail off our house. When I got there I found the wind had come straight off the river through our open windows, lifted the ceiling so that the curtains flew up and were caught flapping outdoors when the ceiling settled back down. The chimney fell, landing on our bed beside where Mother was sitting, but she wasn't hurt.

We were considerably worried as we watched the Yangtze rise again during the spring. The beautiful, long straight rows of vegetables on the island farm downshore from the hospital, over which the farmer and his family had labored so carefully, disappeared, and the willows on our waterfront stood in water, but none of our local dykes broke. Fortunately the flood of the year before had enriched the soil, and the fields along both sides of the river were green, the rice harvest exceptionally good. Even Grandmother Hsu's fields across the river had a bumper crop, but a lot of that was promised to pay ransom to a group of bandits who carried off two of her grandsons and returned them for an I.O.U. based on the coming harvest. She had first paid a hundred dollars Mex to a woman who claimed to be the mother of the bandits, but she was the mother of the wrong bandits, so that was a loss.

Of more trouble to the farmers was the construction of an airfield about five miles from I-chi-shan. Thousands were conscripted by the government to build it, and were taken just when the wheat and mustard were to be harvested and the rice transplanted into the flooded fields.

Such progress in Chiang Kai-shek's programs for China seemed to appear almost daily. One day we saw a cargo-boat go by with a locomotive on board for a new railroad under construction. Then a freighter anchored upriver to unload something like a hundred thousand railroad ties. 24 June the new auto road from Wuhu to Nanking was opened with great ceremony. Busses ran regularly to Nanking, and we began to hear the honk of a strange car from time to time.

A huge red neon cross for the roof of the hospital was sent by a church in Michigan in 1933, a strange and wonderful gift. Ten feet high and six feet across, it rotated three times a minute and served as a beacon to river traffic and to people traveling the new roads as well.

The 1933 highlight for Mother and me was a visit from my sister, Sally, her husband, Clyde Stuntz, and their four children, enroute from India to America for their furlough. Clyde went forty-five miles upriver with some of the men of our mission on a Customs launch to inspect dykes. They met a number of well-to-do gentlemen and Clyde said they had no disposition to speak out against Japan; it was almost as if they had made up their minds to bow to the blast of the Japanese, should it come, and as in the past begin the task of assimilating their conquerors.

But no one expected more trouble once Japan got what she wanted beyond the Great Wall. We didn't realize when Japan took Jehol that she was looking for an excuse to cross the Great Wall and take Peking and Tientsin,* that the only thing delaying her was the increasingly unfriendly attitude of the rest of the world. Jehol was nearly a thousand miles from us, and Chinese students were noticeably silent, their furious and melodramatic demands of their government, their attacks on government ministers of a year earlier, noticeably lacking. Apparently they had lost some of their violent patriotism when they had to face Japanese guns and troops around Shanghai.

For us the depression in mission finances was a greater worry than the Japanese. Paul Hayes, our Central China Mission Secretary/Treasurer, had to cut down or out both programs and people that were not absolutely essential. We all had salary cuts from time to time, and the Board reminded us that we were lucky to have homes and a small income. Anyone who could find work from some other source was urged to do so, and people sent home on furlough were not returning.

In October I got down to Shanghai to the first medical conference held by the new Chinese Medical Association, which had been formed by the amalgamation of the China Medical Associa-

---

* Japan invested heavily in Manchukuo, which increased her interest in further expansion into North China, and a demilitarized zone was created between Peiping and Tientsin with a Chinese puppet regime in control. In 1935 North China was made a neutral zone by agreement, but an effort by Japanese officers to promote a separatist movement for the five northern provinces collapsed with Peiping student demonstrations. Peking, "Northern Capitol," was then known as Peiping, "Northern Peace," while Nanking, "Sourthern Capital," served as Chiang's seat of government.

tion (the old missionary group) with the National Medical Association, composed of Chinese doctors trained in Western methods. Work had been underway for years to join the two societies, and we were glad it had finally been accomplished.

Such a conference is a great time for meeting friends, old and new, from as far away as Korea, as far south as Manila, from the border of Siam and from all parts of China. It was a great experience with all kinds of reports and papers, medical movies, demonstrations and no end of exhibits on the diagnosis and prevention of disease in China, on the distribution of various diseases, and on education of the people. Quite a point was made about preventing malaria, and we were introduced to some mosquito-larva-eating fish that had been imported from Manila. They were to be used to stock ponds and rice fields, and I carried two buckets of fish back to Wuhu. One was a paradise fish, which normally has beautiful colors but was bleached out by chlorine in the Shanghai water. The other was *Cambusia affinis,* and was viviparous, the small fish being born alive.

What a procession we made down to the Shanghai bund to our ship: first Mother in a rickshaw with various bundles; then another rickshaw with an organ which we had bought for a friend; then I came along in a third with the two buckets of fish. The ship's water was cleared with alum, so we got one of the sailors to haul up some water out of the river for our fish. It was muddy, and I'd have thought it would stick in their throats, but they seemed much cheered and went chasing about, probably catching small insects.

Our group of doctors grew the summer of 1934. I had two Chinese surgeons working with me while Dr. Brown was on furlough, and we added a Chinese-Indian from London University Medical College, and a Chinese doctor on the medical side. Dr. Lorenzo Morgan, a corking surgeon of thirty years' experience in Huichow with the Presbyterian Church South also came to us. Loren Morgan, as he was known, supervised two other Chinese doctors on the medical side and worked with us on surgery, where he had a special gift for bone work. He also had a dental outfit with him and knew how to use it. His wife, Dr. Ruth Morgan, was a great addition to Out Patient work with women and children.

Work at the hospital increased continually because of the families being brought to work on the new railroad which was under contract with us for medical care. People began to come with small ailments before they could become serious, whereas those not under contract worried along, often until their complaint got past help. Obstetrical work also picked up, and at one time we had three Caesarian cases in at one time. They went so well that the next normal case demanded a Caesarian and we had a hard time refusing it.

Among our challenges was a woman who came in with a 64½ pound tumor. What a plum to pull out! Another was what to do about a man who pulled a private rickshaw for one of the foreign men in port. He had no nearby relatives, but after he died of heat stroke his friends produced an old mother who was dependent on this only son and needed a large compensation. If it were not forthcoming, the corpse was to be parked in the office of the company where the man's employer worked, and not removed until the demands were satisfied—a threat not to be lightly disregarded in our weather.

Joe Wharton, of the American Advent Mission Society, was pinch-hitting for Dr. Brown and was called in as middleman in a big palaver. Thanks be, there was no raid on our morgue and Joe was able to straighten things out and the man was buried.

There was always the problem of how to keep some patients in the hospital long enough for them to heal. One of my surgical patients thought he had to go home because he could no longer pay the small daily fee. I didn't want him to leave, so I told his wife I wanted some centipedes and would look after his fee if she could find some for me. This request came about because the H.M.S. *Mantis* captain said he had never seen a mantis, so I supplied him with one. Much interested was one of the ship's officers who had hundreds of butterflies in cases, and wanted a mantis as well as some of our poisonous red-headed centipedes. Several people joined in a successful centipede hunt, and we later saw them mounted in the officer's collection.

One of our big events the summer of 1934 was the visit of an Italian cruiser, the *Quarto*, with its band. All hands gathered for a concert at the Recreation Club where each piece ended with our applause and a Fascisti salute from the bandleader. Such a treat could not leave port without being enjoyed to the utmost, so the Asiatic Petroleum Company got them to play at a garden party over on their hill and combined it with a swimming party, for they had a small outdoor tank fed by their artesian well. Some of us splashed and the band played and the rest of us watched and listened and enjoyed the fun and marveled at two band concerts on two successive days in our little port.

The Yangtze Valley was so hot that summer that we were thankful to get away to Japan for a holiday. We reached Shanghai in time to see Culley off for furlough in the *Trier* of the Nord Deutsche Lloyd, a German band playing, *Nur am Rhine will ich leben*. It sounded stirring, but we wondered what would happen in Germany and Austria that summer. We remembered Vienna as such a quiet, friendly, delightful old city, and hated to think of the state of things there.

When I got back from Japan in August, I was in time to deliver Helen Priscilla Stam, whose parents, John and Betty Stam, were on their first assignment with the China Inland Mission. We enjoyed this good-humored young couple, who were in their twenties, and were sorry to see them leave for their small Chinese home within the walled city of Tsingteh, about one hundred miles south of us in a beautiful valley.

We were also a little apprehensive for them, for they were not far from the region where Chinese Reds were besieged by General Chiang's forces,* and we knew of too many missionaries who had

---

* Chiang Kai-shek's first four extermination campaigns against the Communists, in the mountainous Ching-kang-shan area on the Hunan-Kiangsi border, were checked by guerrilla tactics that drew Kuomintang forces into ambushes. In late 1933-1934, a systematic blockade (a German-devised strategy of encirclement along a line of blockhouses) became a greater threat to the Reds, and as a result 100,000 of them broke out of the encirclement in October 1934 and set out on the legendary Long

been caught in the paths of Red armies. Only the previous May Howard and Gertrude Smith of the Christian and Missionary Alliance in Penhui, Szechuan, were captured by the Red General, Ho Lung, when he took the city. Gertrude's cousin and her brother had both lost their lives to the Reds the year before, and some fifty missionaries had been besieged, taken captive or killed in 1934 already. Gertrude, who was pregnant, and two-year-old Ray, were sent downriver with a $3,000 ransom note, while Howard was marched off into the mountains with 5,000 Red troops. After fifty day's march, Howard managed to escape when his young guard dozed off. Within moments the alarm was sounded, but he evaded capture. Snatching grain from the fields and begging raw eggs from farmers, he made it back to safety, and to I-chi-shan, where Gertrude and Ray were staying with the Hayes family while awaiting the birth of Anne.

John and Betty Stam did not escape. In December 1934, a Red army swooped down on Tsingteh where they killed most of the officials and well-to-do citizens and marched the rest off to Miaoshou about fifteen miles away to hold them for ransom. Among them were John and Betty and Helen Priscilla. Next morning they were led out to a small hill and the shocked villagers were summoned to witness the execution of the running dogs of imperialism, the enemies of Communism and slaves of Chiang Kai-shek. After debating the fate of the baby and sparing her life when a townsman stepped out of the crowd and offered his life for hers, they killed him, then John and Betty.

For a day and a half Helen Priscilla cried alone in a deserted house, unfed, uncared for, unharmed, but no one dared go near. A colporteur named Lo, had also been taken, then released when the townspeople assured the Reds he was an outsider. Mr. and Mrs. Lo and their own small son fled to the hills where they hid for two days and two nights until their child became sick from exposure. They returned to the village, learned of the deaths and of Helen

---

March. One year and six thousand miles later, on foot and fighting all the way, less than 20,000 reached northern Shensi.

Priscilla, gathered up the broken bodies and the baby and made their anxious way to Wuhu. We found Helen Priscilla healthy and unharmed and buried her parents in our small cemetery.

Howard and Gertrude Smith were evacuated back to I-chi-shan to stay with the Hayes family again. Other missionaries were evacuated to Wuhu and a representative of the Chinese Ministry of Foreign Affairs, our American Legation Secretary George Atcheson, Jr., and various gunboats all descended on us. Large numbers of government troops passed through Wuhu southbound in pursuit of the Reds, the countryside was an armed camp, businesses dead, and the gunboats prepared to take us out.

But that was not necessary. The Communists went off in another direction, followed by Chiang's forces, and in their legendary Long March, fighting all the way, reached northern Shensi on foot a year later, their numbers decimated.

Wuhu was peaceful in 1935, our chief worry the falling off of funds that shortened the line of our workers. We were also threatened once again by the possibility of floods. Some of the Wuhu streets were adrift by July, and the water was nearly to the top of our bund, having long since gone over the Kiukiang bund. The ships went by I-chi-shan standing high up, and it was strange to look up to the landing hulks instead of down as was usual. But the dykes seemed to be holding, and Grandmother Hsu stopped by and said that the dykes across the river were holding too. T'ien-pao trotted around after her, happy to have his grandmother visit.

The hospital had received a gift of $4,000 to build and equip a new children's ward. Its walls were rising, the second storey windows appeared, and luckily the money for the new wing was safe, for it was not in any of the American banks that failed. Personally, we did not lose either, but a good many missionaries lost their savings.

To benefit the nursing school and the coolies' evening school, the hospital crew put on two plays. The nurses dramatized scenes from the life of Florence Nightingale in Chinese. The second play, put on in English by the Chinese doctors and upper staff, was an incident from ancient Chinese history.* It showed how an empty city with neither population nor guard defeated a besieging army by the simple ruse of leaving the gates wide open. The strategist sat on top of the main gate playing a lute, and invited the besiegers to come in, while two old men with brooms swept the pavement in front of the gate. The besiegers, led by an able general, suspected a trap, and after a most amusing exchange of courtesies with the wily strategist on top of the wall, they marched away.

Stage conventions were those of the old Chinese stage, and the besieging general, Ssu-ma I, in the most imposing regalia, advanced in great dignity with a tasseled wand representing the horse he was supposed to be riding. As he looked up and saw the strategist playing his lute, he remarked to his aide-de-camp, "Well, I'll be blowed. There sits Chu-ke Liang on the wall playing a lute!" The group who got it up had promised us some laughs, and certainly made good their promise.

The hospital was full most of the time with every one of the eighty-eight beds (and some extra ones) taken. In October we had a record number of ninety-nine, the greatest number we had had except in time of war or cholera. One patient was a woman whose husband cropped her ears to wreck her beauty and so discourage the attentions of a rival. The rim of the left ear was completely gone. The top half of the right one was almost cut off, but not quite severed. We sewed it up again, and it healed. The hospital crew were all interested in her, and one ward coolie was so smitten that he asked for a few days' leave and went home to collect forty-four dollars to buy her from her husband. It was a complicated romance, for while he was away, someone else offered fifty-six, and won the lady. In any case, she was probably glad to change husbands, and everybody was happy except our ward coolie.

T'ien-pao's mother had a third child and T'ien-pao was living

---

* This is a famous story taken from *The Legend of the Three Kingdoms*. It is also rendered into many forms of opera, the Peking Opera version being the best known. Chu-ke Liang, the strategist, is a household word and is commonly considered the embodiment of wisdom, loyalty and goodness, something like the Biblical Solomon.

with her and attending school at I-chi-shan. Grandmother Hsu came over from across the river to visit them, and reported that there were no bandits left over there. The local militia shot all they could catch and the rest stopped their activities.

One day when some of us were walking in the fields outside I-chi-shan, we met a woman coming along who appeared to have two heads. I thought, "That isn't possible!" But the second one was there, somewhat flopping around, lying on her shoulder. When she came closer I could see that it was some kind of growth. She had had it for many years. When I suggested that she come up to the hospital so that we could take it off, she came very happily.

We got her ready and took her into the operating room, and I began to wonder whether I had taken on more than I should have. But I thought, "The stem of this thing is quite small, I should be able to take it off quite easily with a local." I said to her, "Now you lie perfectly still until we get through with this," and she said, "Alright." And we put in the novocain.

Then I started cutting. I found the roots of it were quite a lot deeper than I had thought. They were way down among the important things in her neck. We gave her plenty of local anaesthesia and went deeper and deeper until we got down to where the neck of it was very short. But the foundation of it was resting in such a way that there wasn't any chance to tie blood vessels, and there were lots of blood vessels. We cut, and put on all the hemostats we had prepared, and got more ready.

The further we went the more we needed, and we got out and autoclaved all the hemostats we hadn't used in a long time. I kept telling her, "You're doing very well, you're doing fine, just lie still." She lay perfectly still until we moved the growth away from her. Then she moved her head a little bit, found it different, and suddenly sat up and said, "So light and free!"

Hemostats flew and blood spouted in every direction. It was a horrible scene. I said, "Lie down! Lie down!" But she kept repeating, "It's so light and free!" We finally got her to lie down. The hemostats had been gathered up and were being boiled, but they weren't ready to use yet. We'd used everything we had in the house, and there was nothing for it but to hope for the best. Finally they had stewed long enough and we got them out, clamped them on and started tying. We didn't take time to connect anything, just started tying. I was terrified, but she was very pleased. I was sure she was going to die. But she didn't. The tumor was not malignant, and just the same size as her head. Fortunately, we got rid of the right head. The lady was very cheerful about it all.

One of our patients went wild after his operation, jumped out of a first-floor window, ran down the hill across the snow, climbed over the wall and leaped into the river. Most people died if they were in the water more than a few minutes that time of year. And once in, this patient decided he wanted to live after all and swam as best he could against the terrible current.

A ward coolie saw the man go and followed him, calling others as he went, and Ch'en, our reformed pirate, did a brilliant piece of driving down the slippery, muddy-slushy, very narrow dyke in the Ford. Some fishermen in a sampan off the Japanese iron-loading wharf a half mile downstream hauled him out of the water, and our coolie took off some of his own clothing to put on the man while others of us fought the man into submission and held him in the car while Ch'en navigated back over the dyke, a difficulty that had to be seen to be appreciated. The patient fractured a wrist when he went over the wall, and it took several men to hold him down while I set it.

But a couple of weeks later, while he was still in the ward recovering from his original ailment, another discouraged man said, "I'm going to jump into the river." This man immediately jumped up and shouted, "Don't do it! I tried that, and it is COLD!" He finally went home, apparently sane, well, and with his wrist healing.

A more difficult situation was that of an attractive young bride who cut her own throat because of family trouble. The throat healed, except for some nerve fibers so that she couldn't speak above a hoarse whisper. Eventually she had to go back to the same family, and we all wondered how she would make it. Then there was an affianced daughter-in-law whose husband-to-be made a partially successful attempt to hack off her leg with an axe because he discovered a rival on hand. She was shortly to be married to this axe-wielding youth. Fortunately she was very fond of her mother-in-law to be.

A poor little girl came in nearly exsanguinated from the bleeding from a wound in her head. The people who brought her claimed she had been knocked down by a rickshaw, but our Chinese doctors found out that she was a slave child and had been beaten over the head with an opium pipe. When she was finally up and around she was a sweet little helper on the ward and we hated to have to let her go back to the place she had come from, as was too often the case.

Another girl, in her early teens, was rescued from an infamous place in Hankow, where she had been since the age of eleven. She was like a caged animal, in terror of everybody, and we had a big job winning her confidence enough to let us look down her throat or take her temperature. She became sunny and beamingly happy, her smile shining through the door of the room where she was quarantined with whooping cough, which was the least of her troubles. She had been rescued by her sister, who sold herself to a man with a couple of wives to the good already, on condition that the money be used to buy her sister out.

Then came a telegram from Anking that Dr. Harry B. Taylor, the head physician there, was critically ill with pneumonia. "Please send a doctor and oxygen." I took the afternoon boat and arrived at four in the morning. Landing was quite an experience. Everyone who traveled the Yangtze ships looked down over the side sometimes to watch the noisy scramble of passengers getting on and off from barges in mid-river at "boat-stations" at ports where the ship did not go alongside a hulk as at Wuhu.

It was an appalling performance, even in daytime. A little barge somewhat like an oversized rowboat came out from shore, a rope would be thrown from the moving ship and made fast to a cleat in its bow deck, and the barge would swing around to the ship's side and be made fast. Then an awful scramble ensued, people shoving and pushing up and down a small ladder which was let down from the ship and ended in midair above the barge. Everybody would yell and haul bundles and beddingrolls, and heaven help anybody who wasn't able-bodied and agile. It was a wonder people didn't drown and barges overturn frequently instead of occasionally.

Well, picture all that in the black of a winter's night under a searchlight trained down the ship's side, and you can imagine the scene off Anking. The purser assured me that the ship would wait, and had my luggage and the precious oxygen tank sent down into the boat for me. After the scrambling and yelling subsided, I grabbed the ropes at the side, but slid the last few feet through space, landing on beddingrolls. After locating my stuff I waved goodbye to the purser, and then the searchlight was out and the ship disappeared into the dark as the boatman swept his big oar to start us toward shore.

A voice beside me asked if I were Hua I-sheng, Dr. Watters. When we reached shore, the servant who had been sent to welcome me was hailed by another voice, and there was Robin Ch'en who used to be a neighbor of ours in Wuhu and was then acting dean of the Anking Cathedral. The guards at the city gate, which of course was shut, shied at the oxygen tank, which looked to them like a torpedo, but let us by with Robin Ch'en's assurance that it was something to help Tai I-sheng, whom everybody there loved and knew was very ill. I was there four days, and Dr. Taylor pulled through.

Mother was seventy-four in 1936. We had had another visit from the Stuntz family enroute back to India, another holiday in Nijiri and my furlough was long past due. It was six years since we had last been home to Tupper, years of brave efforts to unify China, and of growing disaster.

Dr. Paul Sommerfreund, 1938 (courtesy, *Stella Sommerfreund*)

Florence Sayles, Frances Culley with Peggy, Hyla Doc with Darby and Joan, her pet pigeons, and Ada S. Watters, late 1930s.

Col. Charles A. Lindbergh and Anne Lindbergh visit Wuhu General hospital in 1931. Hyla Doc and Dr. Robert E. Brown to the right of Anne Lindbergh. Back row: Frances E. Culley, Helen Hayes, Gladys Harmon, Ada S. Watters. *(Paul G. Hayes)*

Dr. Ruth Morgan, Dr. Loren Morgan (courtesy, *Carrel Morgan*)

Dr. Stella Sommerfreund, Frances E. Culley, Hyla Doc, Dr. Loren S. Morgan, 1938.
(courtesy, *Stella Sommerfreund*)

Bombing of the British steamer, S.S. Tuckwo, December 1937, by the Japanese.
Photo taken from Ichishan. (courtesy, *Carrel Morgan*)

Mr. Tao, after his ears were laid flat, and the son he wanted
to give Hyla Doc, 1940.

Staying on Under the Japanese

1937-1939

M other and I were on the Danish freighter, *Peter Maersk*, in the Caribbean, August 1937, booked for Shanghai from New York after a great furlough, when we heard Japan had attacked Shanghai.* People were being evacuated as fast as they could be got out, and there was no place for us to land. There was still a month before we were due to arrive, but the captain said that, unless things changed a good deal, the ship would probably unload at Hong Kong, then stop in Japan and Manila.

The Board found me a place at the Mary Johnston Hospital in Manila, where we waited through the terrible days of the Japanese march inland, their infamous Rape of Nanking† followed by brutal occupation of Wuhu, and it wasn't until April 1938 that I finally made it back. I tried to rein in my impatience to be in the thick of things by brushing up on Chinese and Spanish and studying Japanese, which I thought might come in handy.

Culley, Florence Sayles, Dr. Brown and Brownie, Dr. Loren

---

* Japan attacked China in 1937, first near Peiping in July, then at Shanghai in August. After the fall of Nanking, when the Chinese did not acquiesce to Japanese demands to recognize the importance of north China to the security of Japan's economic empire on the continent, full-scale war against China was launched. This was really the start of World War Two. For four years the Chinese fought on alone while the West was preoccupied with the Great Depression and the rise of Stalin and Hitler.

† Nanking was captured in December 1937. As capitol of the nation and a center of anti-Japanese agitation, it was punished by Japanese commanders through brutal slaughter that shocked the world.

Morgan and Dr. Ruth Morgan carried on as best they could. The American ambassador and consuls urged all Americans, over and over again, to leave. But ninety-five percent of the missionaries all over China chose to stay on. In Wuhu the U.S.S. *Oahu* arrived just before the Japanese, to once more urge Americans to leave, but everyone signed the papers absolving the U.S. government of responsibility for their lives. The Chinese Red Cross and Chinese medical practitioners of Wuhu had left on the great westward trek; how could our people have abandoned the several thousand refugees who had fled to I-chi-shan for safety, the sick and wounded and frightened yet to come? They were glad to stay, and would have been ashamed not to.

The hospital carried on normally up to three months after the outbreak of war in July 1937. All the river ports except Wuhu, which seemed unimportant, had been bombed. When Nanking was about to be bombed, the German Ambassador and his wife, on advice of the Japanese, moved quietly to Wuhu and stayed at I-chi-shan for a few days. But war conditions gradually became more apparent as wounded Chinese soldiers, officers and airmen came in groups to be operated on, treated and sent on upriver. Air raid signals became more frequent, and a big American flag and a white cross superimposed on a red background, were painted on the hospital roof.

An air base south of Nanking was lost, then a Japanese detachment attacked a town about forty miles south of Wuhu and the city burst into excited activity. People became panicky to leave. The rail service was suspended and river traffic jammed as tickets sold out weeks ahead. Fearing overcrowding, river boats called without docking. Those people who could afford it moved westward in autos, carriages, trucks or steam launches; others in carts or junks, or on foot carrying bundles and baskets.

Day and night unnerved crowds went by, husbands losing their wives, women losing their luggage or their children, children crying in fright, many pregnant women dragging their tots through the streets trying to get on a boat, the old and crippled struggling with their loads, moving—where to? Nobody knew. Many had moved from one war zone to another, hoping each next place would be safer.

Chinese military base hospitals that had come west to Wuhu started to move further west. Chinese soldiers commandeered junks to ship military supplies upriver, and what they could not take away they burned. By withdrawing from Wuhu without fighting it was hoped that civilians might be saved from slaughter. Buildings, bridges and railway equipment which could be of use to the Japanese were destroyed. Fire raced through the railroad area, the banks, post office, the entire business section.

I-chi-shan people watched from the hospital roof as a small airfield about three miles from the city was the first target of air attack. Then came indiscriminate bombings of Wuhu 5 December. Pamphlets were scattered from the planes telling the Chinese people that the Japanese Army was their friend, come to help drive out the Communists. But there were no Communists. The first bombings came suddenly, and before anyone knew what had happened, one British steamer, the *Tuckwo*, was on fire, and another, the *Tatung*, disabled, with hundreds of people injured or killed.

Scores of dead were lying in the streets when members of our staff went out to collect the wounded. The Asiatic Petroleum Company man brought in wounded in his car, while student stretcher-bearers, organized by Joe Wharton, formed a cavalcade to the hospital. The staff worked until midnight to patch up the maimed—intestines gaped out of abdominal wounds, arms hung on bleeding skin tags, faces were contused and battered beyond recognition, extremities amputated showing bare bone stumps, lungs flapped through open chest wounds. Those treated first had a better chance. Others were given relief for their pain and left to die. Casualties included men, women and children; only one carried firearms, and he was a railway guard.

The second day the Japanese chose the business center of the city to bomb. The same scenes were reenacted in the hospital. The planes returned a third day. With planes hovering overhead, power-diving, dropping bombs nearby, Dr. Brown, Dr. Morgan and the rest tried with shaking hands and trembling hearts to patch up the human wrecks, knowing they might be the next victims.

The Japanese marched into a deserted city: few people, no police, no post office, no telephone, no telegraph; dead people and animals dumped by the roadsides; fields planted but not tended; garments, even comforters dropped on the road and left there; doors open to the mud huts, their contents turned upside down and strewn about. The city of some 200,000 residents was reduced to about 3,000 crowded into I-chi-shan, or left wandering among the ruins.

Everybody actually hoped for early Japanese occupation so that unnecessary bloodshed would cease. To their amazement, a ruthless reign of terror began. No one had believed the stories of Japanese cruelty in Korea, Manchuria and elsewhere in China, but now saw with their own eyes that such stories were not half as bad as the cold reality. Civilians, including aged merchants and scholars, were made to carry like beasts of burden. There was wanton destruction of property left standing, unlimited systematic and thorough looting and incendiarism, unbridled violation of women, old and young, and cruel killing. When there was nothing left worth looting, a command forbidding looting and destruction was posted. Even a month after the occupation, refugees on I-chi-shan dared not return to their homes, in spite of assurances of protection, as they could see wounded victims daily brought in for treatment.

A dying man was brought in one morning with a gunshot wound of his abdomen. He had tried to shield his wife from the soldiers. Another died on the operating table from three sabre cuts to his face and neck, nearly severing his head from his body. Any of these cuts penetrating a little deeper would have killed him outright, but he died a slow death. He said it was because he opened his door too slowly when the Japanese soldiers were on a woman-hunt. Another man was slashed with a bayonet because he failed to find young women for the soldiers, after he had carried a load for them for more than seventy-five miles. Another was a woman who was caught in a fire started by four soldiers. When she rushed to her house she was stopped by another Japanese looking for a woman. She knelt down immediately and pled, motioning to her hair and gesticulating that she was old. The soldier turned her face to the bright flame. Disgusted because she was old, he repeatedly stabbed and slashed, then abandoned her and caught a younger woman. The old lady crawled out into the darkness to safety, her body saved by her wadded garment but her scalp lacerated so that it took an hour to clean and treat.

The Wuhu representative of the Associated and United Press and Dr. Robert E. Brown made successive tours of the city following its fall. They found corpses everywhere. In one section of the city there were dead in every house.

Some miles north, in Hohsien, the U.S.S. *Panay* and three Standard Oil steamers were bombed and machine-gunned from the air, the survivors fired at by surface craft and from the shore. The *Panay* sank within an hour. Three American survivors, including Jim Marshall of *Colliers Weekly*, and many Chinese were picked up and sent to I-chi-shan for treatment. All were convinced the Japanese knew the ship to be American. Some suggested the incident was premeditated to test the strength of those who advocated "peace at all cost" in the United States. Sensing the stiffening of the American attitude, the Japanese diplomats made the usual rounds to explain and apologize. Some actually arrived at I-chi-shan with a box of chocolates to "comfort" the wounded Americans.

There were other indignities to third parties. An American flag was thrown from the hospital junk into the river. The safe in an American mission school was cracked open. American missionary homes were broken into and looted, and an American lady was threatened with a bayonet. When protests were made, profuse apologies were like a conditioned reflex.

The sudden shelling of the British gunboats, *Ladybird* and *Bee*, one bright Sunday morning, left I-chi-shan dazed. Shells whizzed over our compound and exploded precariously close. The British commander had called on the Japanese commander the day before and informed him of the location of the Wuhu ships and the sites of British and American properties in Wuhu. One British sailor was killed, another wounded. Then came the usual official explanation and apology to Great Britain that it was a foggy day and the British boats were mistaken for Chinese.

The panic caused by the approaching Japanese forces had depleted the hospital staff, and volunteers filled in on routine procedures. During the first few days medications and meals were often delayed, but rarely missed. A high school boy assisted with therapeutic pneumothorax treatments for over forty tuberculosis patients; when they dwindled to eight he won promotion as a full-fledged substitute nurse. Other boys and girls initiated into the nursing profession in like manner also did well.

Dr. Brown was loaned to the Government at the outset of war to head an army hospital. His place was capably filled by Dr. George L. Hagman, who arrived after his hospital in Tung-chou, Kiangsu, was demolished by the Japanese 17 August. Among those killed were two doctors and three nurses while they were operating, five patients and seven workers. Many more were injured.

Refugees continued to come into our compound after Japanese occupation. They came with bundles and children, climbing over the walls in their panic. Huts sprang up overnight all over I-chi-shan like mushrooms, and campfires were used for cooking. Soon there were more than three thousand, with twenty-seven trades represented among them. Pigs, cows and plowing buffaloes, chickens, ducks and domestic pets were among our refugees too, for the Japanese soldiers used them for rifle practice. Each refugee volunteered some service. When the hospital light plant was out of order, mechanics restored it. Teachers started a school to keep the children occupied. The butcher killed a pig every day for the hospital, while tailors and shoemakers plied their trades, the barber carried on a flourishing business and British sailors came by for their haircuts.

Christmas came in the midst of Japanese bombers' constant hum, intermittent machine-gun fire and shelling. The traditional candle march through the wards was held, an impromptu choir caroled throughout the compound, a tree was put up for the children. There was nothing to be bought, and the hospital was thankful to have plenty of rice on hand. Food was rationed, meals simple.

These same refugees, who had lost so much, spontaneously suggested that a memorial should be erected on I-chi-shan where they had found refuge. Many wanted to make a pledge toward a tuberculosis sanatorium, that had been an urgent need, as a token of gratitude. Nothing could then be done, and it was hoped the project might someday be realized. But it was never possible.

New Year 1938 came and went. Chinese raiders bombed Wuhu. Five Japanese airplanes were reported destroyed, and two gunboats sunk. It was the turn of the Japanese soldiers, with pale frightened faces, to run for cover during Chinese raids.

When the Japanese first entered Wuhu and Dr. Brown watched them hunting down civilians like rabbits in the fields behind I-chi-shan, he went to the Japanese commander to ask protection for our hill, and this was promised. During that winter and spring of 1938, not one of the three thousand people who entrusted their lives to Wuhu Hospital was harmed, although time and again soldiers climbed over the walls demanding women and loot and had to be escorted out of the compound. Dr. Brown and Dr. Morgan spent many weary hours at the gate fending off squads of soldiers with leveled bayonets.

In Manila I was perishing to get back to Wuhu. My job and my heart were there, and by January 1938 word from Shanghai sounded promising for my return. Mother was game to return with me, but the war zone was no place for a person in her state of health or her difficulty in getting around. I took her to Sally in India and planned to fetch her later, when China was peaceful once more.

When I got back to Shanghai, I got passage upriver on the Japanese line. I found the hospital quiet, with about 110 patients, desperately wounded civilians arriving every day. We had to take them in and were glad to do so, but they were penniless. That was a real problem, and without help from the American Red Cross we would have been sunk.

Dr. Brown was back as skipper, and liaison with military authorities. Dr. Wesley Mei was doing tuberculosis work, Dr. Loren Morgan the medical, and Dr. Hagman had been at I-chi-shan six months on surgery. Dr. Hagman was an excellent general surgeon, his specialty bone surgery in which he had done wonders. In spite of a return of pulmonary tuberculosis and sprue, he felt better working than not, but he was glad for relief and I stepped back into my old job, while he stayed with bonework. We had two good interns, Thomas Yü and Edith Huang, working all services, and sometimes we could relieve Dr. Hagman on the bone jobs while he stood by to direct. He had very good judgment and taught us many fine things, among them how to make and fit artificial legs, as quite a few patients had need of them. How we wished artificial arms could be made as simply. Dr. Hagman was much beloved, and we were all relieved, for his sake, when he returned home in July 1938 to cure at Saranac.

After the U.S.S. *Panay* was bombed below Wuhu in December 1937, the U.S.S. *Oahu* was the only U.S. ship for a time with a regular run on the lower Yangtze. There were no steamers left, and railroad box or open cars were our only way to get to Nanking or Shanghai, or to get supplies. There was no railroad above Wuhu, and it wasn't long until the rail lines between Wuhu and Shanghai were cut. So all through the Japanese occupation we relied heavily on the help of our friends in both British and American navies. I-chi-shan hospital could not have survived without them. The American and British naval vessels became liner/cargo ships, sometimes their decks so full of food and medical supplies for us upriver people that the crew could hardly get around. The U.S.S. *Guam* and *Luzon*, occasionally the destroyer the U.S.S. *Stewart* or yacht *Isabel*, gave us all the help they could. But it was the British navy we depended on most, and the rollcall of their names sounds a distinguished note in the story of those days: H.M.S. *Aphis*, *Cockchafer*, *Cricket*, *Gannet*, *Gnat*, *Ladybird*, *Mantis*, *Petrel*, *Scarab*, *Widgeon*, and H.M.S. *Bee*, Flagship of the British Yangtze Squadron.

When I arrived in April, the Wuhu postal service was slowly

awakening from its long slumber, and it was remarkable what care the postal people had taken of the mail they hadn't been able to deliver. It was unpredictable whether any particular letter we wrote would get out by way of the British or U.S. navy, a route we preferred to avoid Japanese censorship, and we fell into the habit of indirection. It was not expedient to say all that passed in our minds if we wished to be allowed to stay on; we heard of some who wrote not wisely but too much, and whose words rolled too far and whose names were MUD.

The white house between I-chi-shan and Sister Constance's compound belonged to the railroad. During 1927, three hundred soldiers had been quartered in it at one time; since it was only an ordinary-sized foreign-style house, it must have nearly burst at the seams. As the Japanese approached Wuhu in 1937, it was to be destroyed in the scorched earth policy, and Dr. Brown was invited to take from it all the paper he could use, as there was no way of salvaging it. So our storeroom had a good supply of paper of all colors, shapes and sizes, quite fascinating for our reports and letters, and we made our own envelopes. The remnants of the house still standing in 1938 were fast disintegrating, with hardly one brick left on another, and I finally understood that expression. The original cataclysm destroys a building as a building, and the populace do the rest until literally not one brick remains on another, although the bricks are used in some other building, wall or roadway.

Dr. Ruth Morgan scoured trunks and closets for anything that could be made up into bandages or diapers for the babies, and a great clothing exchange was underway. Dr. Ruth herself had a light tan coat Sister Constance insisted she have in return for so many clothes cut up for the babies. One of our doctors wore a sweater that belonged to the Morgan's daughter, and a pair of Dr. Brown's shoes. Everybody seemed to be wearing somebody else's underwear, shirts or shoes. In other words, everybody managed nicely.

But Wuhu was a hard place to stick it. Brownie's health worsened, and she went back down to Shanghai. The Brown family later got out to West China. Culley was sent off for a rest in Hong

Kong, then Shanghai where she helped at the Chinese National Children's Welfare babies' nursery. But she got back to Wuhu and stayed until the Board evacuated her in 1941. Dr. Ruth had a bad heart and her days at the clinic were limited to four half days each week. Her health deteriorated, but she too remained until 1941.

Sister Constance had thirty orphan babies as well as her school and women's sewing group. One of her orphans was a baby about to be thrown away that a Japanese sentry insisted the father take to Sister Constance instead. Perhaps he had a baby at home the same age. She had so many more people to look after than usual, and so much less sale for the goods her women made, that she put on a special sale June 1938. We all laid in some of her products and she made enough money to keep going a while longer. Then the gunboat crew saw some of the fine things and clamored for a sale for themselves, and kept her going even longer.

Wu Shih-fu, our old cook, who had refugeed across the river, heard we were back and, what with the place he was staying getting pretty hot with the fighting, came back to work for us. We found T'ien-pao at Brownie's little school, which now had two teachers and more applicants than it could manage, but Grandmother Hsu had died the year before. Her daughter said she was peaceful in her heart and clear in her mind, all through her illness.

It was amazing, but no foreigner in Wuhu had been killed with all the bombing and fighting, no one on I-chi-shan injured except for Ch'en our pirate and one other man, who both recovered. Chang Shih-fu, the engineer, was still on the job, and I found a very nice Swiss lady, Mrs. Hao, and her two children, living in our dining room.

The Japanese issued us passes and we could get around the city once more. It was again possible to buy all the vegetables and eggs we wanted, and I took a liking to duck eggs, much larger and cheaper than chicken eggs, and reveled in *pi-chi*, the water chestnuts. Our rose and calendula beds alongside the front porch had lettuce and onions among the flowers because there were so many refugees on the hill and the sanitation was so hard to control that we didn't dare eat raw vegetables from the garden. But we didn't suffer for food. Ducks and geese were again to be bought, and sometimes fish. The Spanish Fathers had fresh milk for sale, and the Browns bought it every day but we preferred tinned milk, less likely to be contaminated. Pork was the only meat, but we preferred poultry to four-footed meat even in peaceful times.

There was nothing monotonous about living behind the lines. We heard big guns and anti-aircraft guns frequently, and the Chinese pilots came in to bomb. The rest of the crowd had had quite a bit of the bombing before I got back, and my first experience came during chapel. Suddenly blasts went off all around, with the windows rattling more than they did for the big guns. Then the rapid fire of the anti-aircraft guns nearby added to the row, and we went out to see what was happening. The objective of the raid was the air field to the northeast of us about a mile away. The Chinese bombers flew so high we couldn't hear them until the bombing started. After the bombing was over planes droned above us, and Japanese pursuit planes were up and after the bombers. Presently Japanese bombing planes were up too, and they and the pursuit planes went off like a great flock of birds.

Japanese planes appeared after each bombing like a swarm of hornets, their number growing as more arrived from other places, and took off to the west. I-chi-shan was their favorite spot to make up formation, sometimes forty at a time, and we realized that they were the ones that made the retaliatory raids on Hankow.

We had a huge American flag on the hospital roof until Pearl Harbor. The Chinese planes knew I-chi-shan was a hospital and didn't aim for it, but did try to get a ship just off the hill loading iron ore to take back to Japan, and got a direct hit. It was so close to us that all the windows of the hospital blew out, including all the big plateglass windows of the operating rooms which were our pride and joy. There was never enough money to replace those windows, even after the war.

It would have been convenient for us to keep on signaling the gunboats, and we did a few times before we were told to stop. One evening we were talking over our cases, when in walked a Japanese officer. He said to me, "You were signaling, weren't you?" I said that yes, we were sending the ship doctor a list of the next day's operations. He said, "Come up on the roof and signal for me." I didn't much like that. It was a cold night and I didn't have a warm coat. He told me to get my signal light, but I wasn't going to show him my fine light with a lovely trigger handle that had been made by one of the gunboat engineers. So I got an ordinary flashlight and went up on the roof with him.

He told me to signal in a certain direction, and when I asked what to signal, said anything would do. So I did the alphabet, and when I got to the end he took my flashlight and signaled in Japanese. From the Japanese headquarters over on another hill came an answer, and they signaled back and forth for quite a while. Finally he said, "We go down." He didn't know that for the first time in my life I was so peeved I was tempted to push him off the roof.

Anyway, we went back down. He came over the next day and said, "Someone is sending radio messages from your hospital. Who is it?" He knew it wasn't me because my signals didn't match the hand of the signaler they had caught on to. I insisted that no one was sending radio messages because no one knew how to. They searched the hospital, but found no trace of a radio.

The time came after Pearl Harbor when the Japanese took us away under guard, and it was still a mystery. But a few days before we went our engineer said, "What do you think I have found! A radio-sending station! Do you want to see it?" I said, "No! I do not! I want to be able to say truly that I never saw it." Chang wanted to get it through the lines to Free China, but somebody might have been killed in the process and I thought the best thing to do was to smash it to bits and sink it in the pond. He agreed, and did it.

Those same boys who years before had supposedly got bored with Morse code had been far from bored. Every time the Japanese bombing planes went over us on their way to Hankow, our boys signaled Hankow and Chinese planes would be up waiting for them. When I went back to Wuhu in 1980, I said to an elderly doctor who had been one of the young men, "I'm glad you didn't tell me about it." And he said, "No, we didn't tell you because you are not a good liar."

There was one Japanese officer who was particularly obnoxious. I decided to get rid of him if I could, so every time I saw him I would look concerned and inquire, "What is wrong with you? You don't look at all well today." Others joined my conspiracy, and after several months of this he went to the Japanese military hospital for a checkup, where they told him he was fine. But we kept telling him how ill he looked, and how doctors could be wrong, and finally he asked for a transfer.

We were no longer getting any wounded soldiers in the hospital, for there were no Chinese soldiers in the area and the Japanese took care of their own. But we got civilian casualties from the scattered fighting in the countryside about us. All sorts and conditions of people came in, usually too long after injury because of difficulties in transportation.

One day several of us spent a good half day trying to put Humpty Dumpty together again. That was our nickname for a tailor who managed to stop a bullet that hit him in the back of his shoulder and came out his face, opening it out like a flower. He looked like nothing human when he arrived, but was mighty game and took it marvelously as we struggled to reassemble the jig-saw puzzle that was his face. Because his throat and jaw were in bad shape, I was afraid to give him much ether; but we did give him some as we sewed the remnants of his tongue together. Eight days later he looked human again, even fairly presentable, but wasn't able to speak intelligibly. We had a bad time trying to keep his lower jaw in line because there wasn't much upstairs left to fasten the downstairs to, and he couldn't stick pressure of a strap under his jaw. He got his meals through a nasal tube, and looked eagerly to the day when his hard-hearted doctor would let him take some food in the ordinary way. He wasn't interested in further beautification of his face, although we were doing a bit of plastic surgery, but went home with at least parts back in the general direction of where they belonged.

One afternoon, the operating room orderly asked to show me something. He said, "It's in that basket, over there on the table." So I went over and lifted the cloth that was on top, and there was a bomb. It was about twenty-three inches long and had a three-fluted tail. One was bent a little. Evidently it had landed a bit crooked and hadn't gone off.

I said, "Where did you find that?"

"It was right out here under the window, close to the hospital."

"Well," I said, "thank God it didn't go off. But what do you expect to do with it?"

He looked hopeful, "I don't know. Maybe put it in the splint room?"

"Certainly not in the splint room. Someone will go in and pull out a splint and that would be the end of us all."

"Well," he said, "that was my idea. Now you have to think of a place."

"You could bury it somewhere."

"No! People are always digging holes. If we take off a leg and bury it somewhere, sometimes the man digs it up again."

That was a fact. For the Chinese it was important to present your whole body to your ancestors after you die. We couldn't think where to put that bomb and it was late and we were all hungry. So I said, "Well, there are only three of us, you and Dr. Yü and I, who have keys to the splint room. Put it in there on the floor, and I'll tell Dr. Yü. The three of us will exercise great care when we go into that room until we think of a better answer."

So I went home to lunch and he put the bomb in the splint room and we all racked our brains as to what to do.

The next day I went over to call on some friends at the Episcopal Mission and while we were drinking tea suddenly there was a great explosion. I jumped and said, "There goes the hospital!" But it wasn't. We never did find out what exploded. We had to think of a better place for that bomb.

Finally I said to the orderly who had found it, "I'll give you some money. Put the bomb in a basket and put some stuff on top of the bomb and hire a sampan. Then when you reach the middle of the river you put the bomb carefully over the side of the sampan and tell that man to row just as hard as he can away from that place."

Later in the day I met the orderly and asked, "Where's the bomb?"

He said, "At the bottom of the river."

I said, "Good! How far out?"

And he said, "Oh, far, far out."

I said, "As far as half way across the river?"

He said, "No, I couldn't throw it that far, could I?"

I said, "The junks always lower an anchor as they go around the point, and someday a junk will lower an anchor on it." But he said he thought he'd thrown it further out than that.

Our clinic was not approved by the power in authority, and they tried in various ways to stop it, even to the extent of taking Dr. Morgan off by force one day to military headquarters. He returned, after a lengthy and useless discussion, and the incident was reported along with all the others through our consul at Nanking to Washington, and word came back from Tokyo to keep the clinic open and for the military people to apologize.

Returning to I-chi-shan from our clinic, I'd pass the Japanese sentries on my bicycle. One time as I approached a sentry he said something like, "Uur, up!" And I thought to myself, "That has nothing to do with me," and kept on going. He got up and came stamping after me, grabbed the upright bar under the saddle of the bike, and yanked backwards. I lit on my feet, fortunately.

He said, "I talk 'Stop!' You stop!"

I said, "You talk 'Stop!' I stop. You talk 'Uur, up,' I no stop!" I got on my bike and went on, and left him standing there with his mouth open.

Another time, on my way home from the clinic the sentry asked for my army pass and I reached for it but didn't have it. He told me, "Wait." When it was time for him to go off duty he'd take me down to Japanese headquarters. I didn't like that idea. Along came one of the young men helping in the clinic, and he wanted to know why I was standing there, got on his bike and went top speed to the hospital and got Dr. Morgan to get my pass and bargain for my release.

We had plenty to eat and drink and to put on, and did not live in expectation of anything violent happening to us, but for our Chinese neighbors outside the compound I could not say the same. We got no end of atrocity victims, men patients who had had bayonets poked into them for not handing over their womenfolk, women raped and mutilated. One woman finally reached us after she had hid in an attic four months in a house occupied by the Japanese, sneaking down for food when they went out to drill. She managed successfully, but we had no end of them that didn't.

Of course there are good and bad in all groups, and we met and talked with some of the invading army who were thoroughly sick of the whole wretched business but helpless in the grip of it.

By August 1938 we were well behind the lines, but with troop movements going on constantly. Several mornings we counted nearly thirty reconditioned freighters and tankers serving as transports in the river off I-chi-shan. The harbor was busy day after day with small boats loading and unloading men and horses and supplies. Some days the bund was full of artillery, other days with cavalry. And on our way down to the city clinic, sometimes the streets were full of troops, ranks of hot and weary men in heavy khaki uniforms unsuited to a Yangtze Valley summer. No wonder that when they had a chance to get out of a uniform they went primitive.

The number of 1938 patients was less than in 1937, but patient days were greatly increased due to the prolonged stay required for the many surgical patients who had desperate shrapnel wounds. Actually, we had at times as many as 180 patients. Malignant malaria was an outstanding feature of the year. We were able to save nearly all our hospital cases, but in the city and country nearby thousands of people died of it.

By the end of the year we were lucky to add Paul and Stella Sommerfreund to our staff. Paul specialized in internal medicine and Stella in eye diseases. They were refugees from Vienna, graduates of Vienna University, recently married in Shanghai. I held a lingering hope that by spring Mother could come back to Wuhu, but travel was still difficult, passes upcountry from Shanghai hard to get, and the countryside about us was still far from peaceful.

Surgery picked up during January 1939, even more than at the height of hostilities, and curiously, we had almost an epidemic of alveolar abscesses and osteomyelitis of jawbones from toothrot.*

We were asked to do many difficult things, but the most difficult was after we had operated on a man and found a complete mesenteric thrombosis with the whole intestinal tract destroyed. There was nothing to do but close up. "We can't possibly cure him," I explained to a relative, "because his intestines are destroyed." And she asked, "Can't you exchange them for new ones?"

The variety of our cases changed at different times. Sometimes we had a lot of malaria, as the summer before, when the shifting population brought in the malignant malaria that had not previously been common in Wuhu. During 1939 we got a lot of new cases of bone tuberculosis in adults. Malnutrition and general low resistance as a result of the conditions were the determining factors. We also got an abnormal number of complete personality breakdowns, which was not surprising. The milder ones could be salvaged with good care, but we were at a loss for total breaks. In many other cases tension, while not at the breaking point, intensified and complicated the physical picture.

A very worried man came in to the Second Street Clinic one day, his back all over humps after a friend had told him that a good cure for scabies was to drink pollywogs. He caught a lot of them, put them into clean water, added sugar, and drank several hundred. The scabies improved, but a few days later humps appeared all over his back and he was properly worried he might be turning into a frog. When I first saw him I must confess I wondered whether any chemical in the skin of so many pollywogs might possibly induce a similar condition in the person swallowing them. But presently it dawned that we were dealing with a bilateral case of herpes zoster (shingles) which had nothing to do with his unusual lunch. The man was greatly reassured when we told him he would be alright if he didn't develop dysentery from

---

* Alveolar: relating to part of the jaw where teeth arise; osteomyelitis: inflammatory disease.

the germs on and in the tadpoles.

One afternoon a patient appeared with outstanding ears. They really stood out like ears of a deer. He asked, "Are you Hua I-sheng?" I said "Yes," and he said, "I've come to see if you would operate on my ears and lay them flat alongside my head."

I said, "Yes, we can do that. There's not much going on today; I'll operate on one this afternoon." As I started in I asked, "How did you know to come here to get this done? And why did you want to have it done?"

He said, "We are four brothers and we work very hard, but we never get rich. I came to town and asked a fortune-teller why we never get rich. He said, 'Because your ears are standing in your way.' I asked him, 'What can I do about that?' And he told me to get them made flat. But when I asked him where that could be done he didn't know. So I walked down the street and asked people where I could get them made flat, and someone told me to go to the clinic on Second Street.

"So I went to the clinic and registered, and they gave me a stick with a number on it and told me to sit down until my number was called. I sat down and waited. Quite a number of people were waiting. They were talking about Jesus and told me I must believe in Jesus. I said, 'Sure, that's alright, I'll believe in Jesus.' So when my number was called I went into another room and Jesus was standing there. He was a tall man (Dr. Loren Morgan), a foreigner, but he had a mouthful of Chinese words, so I asked him if he could operate on my ears and make them flat. He said, 'You go up to I-chi-shan Hospital to Hua I-sheng, and she'll make them flat for you.'"

I asked him, "Did you know anything about Jesus before?"

He said, "No, but he's a good man, he told me to come here."

So I sent for the Bible Woman and said, "Mrs. Chao, I'm operating on this man, and he wants to know about Jesus. Just talk with him while I'm working." So she did, and she told him a lot about Adam and Eve, which I wouldn't have done.

When he came back after a week I took out the stitches and started on the other ear, and he said, "Please make this one much flatter than the first one." So I did. And when he came back to have those stitches out he said, "Please do the first one over again to make it as flat as this one." So I made the first as flat as the other.

I don't think he ever got rich, but he was very grateful to have his ears where they belonged. He came back often, and one day he brought his wife with him and their nine-year-old son. I had heard him speak of his son and knew he thought a great deal of him. He said to me, "My wife and I are very grateful to you, and we have brought our boy to be your boy. Where you live, he will live. Where you go, he will go." I tried to think how I would get along with a nine-year-old boy to look after. I said, "You know, I work in the hospital every day, and how would I ever be able to take care of a boy? Besides, there is a proverb you have that says a child should grow up before the face of his father and mother. I think the proverb is right, and the best thing for him is to stay with you. I appreciate the honor, but truly I think you had better keep the boy yourselves." They were very pleased and went off with broad smiles taking the boy with them. Someone suggested that the Bible Woman may have told him the story of Abraham sacrificing Isaac.

Later on the man came one day and said, "I want to talk with you where no one else will hear." I took him into a separate room where he said, "I have come with a message from the troops in Free China. They would like to send over some men with guns to lead you and the rest of your missionary group through the lines into Free China where you can work in hospitals that have not been taken over by the Japanese, and you can contact the rest of your mission."

We wanted very much to take him up on that offer. It would have meant that we could go on being of use to the people and to the country. But the more we thought it over the more we were sure we must not, because the Japanese would then clamp down on all the missionaries up and down the Yangtze. They had been strict enough with us, but they could have been much more so. Also they would have punished our Chinese friends for letting us go. So I told him we were honored by the offer from him and the troops in Free China but we couldn't accept because of the trouble it would make for other people.

The front line had advanced almost to Kiukiang. But the conquered territory was only a strip along the river, and from the hill we could look across the port to nearby hills that were as Chinese as ever. We frequently heard bombing and cannon fire, and got in lots of civilian casualties. Making general rounds one day we checked out the causes of illness of fourteen women patients in one ward, and every one of them was directly or indirectly the result of the war: gunshot, fracture, shrapnel, malnutrition, but we realized the actual battle-wounds were the least of the damage; some of the women would never get over what they had been through, and we were more than thankful to be able to do our bit to relieve some of the horror of it, help them relax on the hill.

One of our hospital patients was a very attractive Japanese lady, the lady friend of a local high official. She had been very pleasant, and the crew liked her. Some weeks earlier another Japanese lady had been afraid to come to the hospital as a patient for fear something might happen to her. So it pleased me very much when I looked out the window and saw this lady sitting on a mat on the lawn with a group of the nurses, trying to converse. I did not know of a single case of any of our crew being unkind or rude to a Japanese patient, and I marveled at their good spirit. I remarked about it to one of our nurses, and she laughed and said, "But this lady has been very polite to us; why shouldn't we be nice to her?" That's the right spirit, but I remember some Germans in America in 1918 who weren't so kindly treated.

The sentries were keen about making sure no one came into or went out of our gate they thought shouldn't, and sometimes it was hard to be patient with them. One time three of our group walked past a sentry, and without provocation he slapped each of them in the face, so hard that the marks showed hours later.

Another time Dr. Brown had invited the crew of a French gunboat in port to come up to I-chi-shan and enjoy our swimming pool. This had been built to bring relief during the hot season since we could no longer go to the mountains. One pass had been issued for the group, and the sentries at our gate insisted that each man had to have his own pass. The skipper was not on the hill, and until he came back I didn't want to send the men away. So I had tables set up for them and gave them my game of pickup sticks to play until Dr. Brown got back. He decided that the ground just outside the gate where the men were was hospital property, insisted the men had already been admitted to I-chi-shan and that they should come in and have their swim. The sentries were furious, while we all took it as something of a joke. This made the Japanese even angrier and they insisted we had insulted the Emperor himself.

Dr. Brown reported all incidents to the U.S. Consul in Shanghai who relayed them to Washington. Bad publicity was created, and was responsible for Japanese harassment taking subtler forms. They refused to grant travel permits, blocked our supplies whenever they could, refused permission to give vaccinations or inoculations, until our work was brought almost to a standstill. But we were not about to give up.

Things got so bad that Dr. Brown's value diminished a great deal, and he accepted the invitation of the National Christian Council and the Chinese Medical Association to coordinate the work of the 268 mission hospitals with that of the Chinese Red Cross, the army medical service, the International Red Cross and American-British Relief. For distinguished service, particularly for his part in diminishing malaria along the Burma Road, Dr. Brown was later decorated by Chiang Kai-shek.

Meantime, our numbers were fewer and Dr. Loren Morgan was now skipper. Our troubles from the Japanese were also fewer, and they lessened September 1939 when the sentries were taken from our gate and away from the various crossroads and sent to the upriver drive.

As conditions grew more stable, people started to return. We met long lines of them on the road, sometimes walking, carrying bundles of possessions hung from carrying poles across their shoulders. The women carried babies. But it was chiefly, and wisely, men who were mostly returning. We could tell who were refugees because they lacked the identification tags everybody was obliged to wear fastened to the front of their clothing. Often one person with a tag led a party without them.

One day we met a group of Buddhist nuns returning to their convent. Their temple had been very much occupied until a few days before, and would need no end of repair, as one corner had been knocked off to widen a turn in the road for trucks, and there was a big hole in the wall as well. The nuns had a look of gladness to be returning, but we wondered if they weren't a bit premature. One said, "We escaped when the fighting came here, and we have been far away in the country. We have eaten a great deal of bitterness. But we've come back!" I wonder whether the Jews who came back after captivity to rebuild Jerusalem had that same look in their eyes.

People were also returning from across the river which was Chinese territory again. Our Ling Shih-fu came back, scrubbed the house and washed windows, and the weeds began to vanish out of our garden.

Forecast Impossible

1939-1942

Around seven in the evening of 3 September 1939, we gathered around the Brown's radio to listen to the news, and what we heard was, "A state of war now exists between Great Britain and Germany."

No one could speak for awhile, then Dr. Loren and Dr. Ruth Morgan, Dr. Paul and Dr. Stella Sommerfreund, two convalescing Royal Navy patients, West and Hallet, and I sat down to supper, where we were joined by Mrs. Biermann and her son Max, two German Jews, and Mrs. Berta Hao, a Swiss. We listened to various reports and conjectures from Manila and San Francisco, and there was a lull as we waited for the late news from England via Hong Kong.

We were all talking rather vehemently about and against Hitler, when Dr. Paul said, "It is hard for you to realize how we feel. I thank Hitler that I shall not now have to fight for the 'honor of Germany.'" He was very bitter, and I had to admit that we couldn't imagine how it felt to have no country and to hate the one in which there was everything we held dear.

Dr. Stella, sitting on a floor cushion near the radio, stood up looking agitated and went over to the settee to lie down, with difficulty restraining herself from breaking down. The atmosphere was strained, so I fetched some newspaper and a pair of scissors, and gave a strip of paper to each person. The one I kept I folded into a pattern, and in a couple of minutes everybody was copying my movements. Nobody said anything, as we each tried to assimi-

late the fact that what we had dreaded had come to pass. We cut out
Jacob's Ladders, and when we were finished the tension broke.
Later we heard a resumé of the day's events and Mr. Chamberlain's
speech.

Hallet and West had been helping us in the hospital. After we
broke up for the night they packed ready to leave if signaled by the
H.M.S. *Cockchafer,* but no signal came for several days. Dr. Rowsell
of the *Cockchafer* had been at the hospital seeing a patient on
whom he had operated, and was making rounds with Dr. Paul and
Dr. Stella, and had just come into the admitting room where Hallet
was helping me when suddenly the postman from the *Cockchafer*
came in all breathless. "The Captain says," he blurted out, "will you
please come back to the ship at once, Sir, as he's received sailing
orders." Instantly Hallet sprang to his feet, laid down his pen, and
dashed off to get West, who was typing letters for Dr. Morgan.

The military passes for these two men had been carried off in
their own ship, the *Gnat,* and the *Cockchafer* had no passes that
they could use. How were they to get past the sentry on the bund?
There was no time to waste. It was decided that the *Cockchafer*'s
motor launch would come to the hospital landing, where Hallet
and West would be waiting inside the Water Gate. Dr. Rowsell and
the postman hurried back to the ship and we all went over to our
house where four officers from U.S.S. *Guam* had arrived for lunch.
There we watched for the launch, as our house was just above the
Water Gate.

Then a new difficulty arose. The gate had not been used for
months, and the key was not to be found. There was no time to get
a ladder. Our house-boy carried down a sawhorse. When the two
men ran down from the house and discovered me on top of the
wall they exclaimed, "What are you doing there?" But I just
laughed and said, "What do you think?" and disappeared down the
other side. Our house-boy dropped their gear to me on the road
while they scaled the wall. We all ran down the road and down the
stone steps to the bank where the bow of the launch touched
shore, and with only time for "Goodbye—God bless!" they were
off.

The *Cockchafer* was already underway downriver, and stopped off the hospital to pick up the launch. This gave me time to go top speed up the hill to the hospital roof. There stood Paul Sommerfreund, an Austrian Jew exiled by Hitler, on the top of a Christian hospital in China, dipping an American flag to a British gunboat on her way downriver under orders in the war against Hitler Germany. At our house the group there was waving farewell, and one of the *Guam* officers semaphored a cheer-up message and I made another from the hospital roof. Hand-flags in the *Cockchafer* replied, and they were gone.

That night I had a dream. I dreamed that the hospital was down on the rocky point near the river. One day we were out in front on the rocks and saw an enormous tidal wave approaching. We rushed into the hospital, double bolted the doors, then hustled everybody up out of the first floor. The wave struck the hospital a terrible blow, came in all the cracks and filled the lower floor to the ceiling. Then it died down and no other wave followed.

There were a lot of people in the hospital, and they were hungry. So I went up and down the wet corridors shouting, "Ma T'ai! Ma T'ai!" After awhile Ma T'ai answered and I told him the people were hungry and asked if we had any food. He said, "Yes, we've got plenty of food."

"Have you really got enough to feed all these people?" I asked. And he said, "Yes, would you like me to cook a meal for them?" I said that would be fine, and when he asked what time we would want it, I asked if four o'clock would be alright. He said it could be ready by then, so I told all the people that Ma T'ai had plenty of food and would have a good meal ready for us at four o'clock.

That was a vivid dream. We didn't have a cook named Ma T'ai, but that was the Chinese name for Matthew. Perhaps the hospital stood for the hospital, and the tidal wave the war that threatened us all. Matthew had what all the people needed, and plenty for all. I puzzled and puzzled over it and finally got out my Bible and looked up Matthew the fourth chapter, fourth verse: "It is written, man shall not live by bread alone but by every word that proceeds from the mouth of God."

I don't remember much else about 1939, a year of sorrow. Mother died at Landour, India, in August, and the war in Europe made all personal griefs seem a part of the great sorrow and misery in which "the whole world groaneth and travaileth together."

Night by night we gathered around the radio and wondered what new awfulness was in store. We listened to news of the sinking of the H.M.S. *Courageous,* in which many of our Royal Navy friends had served, and wondered which of them were on it at the time. We watched to learn what Russia would do, and how long, we wondered, could America stay out.

January 1940 was Christmas-card-picture winter in Wuhu, with plenty of snow. The river turned a slatey gray, and the refugees made straw shoes lined with chicken-feathers woven into the straw to keep from freezing. Pneumonia was our most popular diagnosis, but brilliant results came from intromuscular Dagenon, a British variant of sulfanilamide. Unfortunately, we didn't have but a few doses on hand, and great difficulty getting more.It had one dangerous feature: in about two days the fever came down and patients felt so much better that a lot of them insisted on going home, where too many relapsed and died. It would have been a real kindness and life-saver to give them something to make them feel rotten in the interval.

I went down with malaria again. It began with what Mother called an "every-other-dayness," then showed its hand in chills and fever, so we started with atabrine, which gave me a Little Buttercup complexion, and with intravenous tartar emetic. This was a new method of treatment which made the miserable parasites turn up their toes and quit. Dr. Paul and Dr. Stella were in Shanghai, Dr. Yü, my right-hand man, was down with paratyphoid, and for a couple of days Dr. Chen was out too. All three of us surgeons had 103° temperatures simultaneously one afternoon. That left Dr. Morgan and Dr. Riego, a Philippine who had finally got upriver, and the two medical interns to carry the whole service and the city clinic. Dr. Morgan carried on, with the slogan we adopted from 1914, "Are we downhearted? NO!"

Things were humming on the surgical side. We treated as

out-patients those not extremely urgent, and at that we had more patients than we could properly care for. One unbelievable case came in, a man with a gunshot wound in the back of his right shoulder and evidence of damage to his lung. His right lung didn't sound clear on percussion, and he was spitting blood. The bullet was still in, somewhere. But his abdomen was soft and his chest bad so we kept him quiet, deferring x-ray until he should feel better. Two or three days later, to our surprise we found the bullet in the lower quadrant of his abdomen. It moved up and down with respiration, and we could roll it back and forth with palpitation. There was no tenderness, no sign of abdominal complication, so we deferred operation to give his chest a chance to improve. About a week later, preparing for surgery, we took him up for x-ray to make sure we didn't go hunting for it in the wrong place, but though we hunted high and low there was no bullet to be found. There had been no question of it before.

Then we learned that for the few days after his injury it had hurt to swallow, and a couple of days after injury he had passed blood, and later something hard. How had that bullet got from his chest to his abdomen without doing damage? Now was all explained. The bullet went through his lung into his esophagus. The wound in the esophagus healed, and the bullet slid quietly along the whole gastro-intestinal tract and was expelled. The lung cleared, and the man went home well and happy.

April 1940 was once more golden with mustard bloom, the air sweet with the scent of it. But we were startled to hear shooting and saw smoke out in the mustard fields one day. From the hospital roof we saw men running through the fields, shooting and dropping down, a near group in uniforms and those further away apparently farmers. I tried to think how we could handle a new lot of casualties with our wards more than full, when the farmers came out from shelter and we learned it was a practice battle. With Chinese regulars only seven miles away and real fighting now heard every day, it was not surprising we took it seriously.

Alarms took various forms. One night about midnight neighbors called me downstairs to tell me that they had heard that seventy or eighty bandits were coming to rob our hill, and they wanted me to be ready. Just what I was to do by way of getting ready wasn't clear, but by all means I was not to sleep soundly. On questioning, it developed that the bandits weren't necessarily to come that night, but some time soon. Whereupon I said I thought the best thing we could do was to get some sleep, and they laughed and agreed.

There had been no holiday for me through 1938 and 1939, except for Annual Conference week* and while I was down with malaria. In May 1940 I managed a week away from the hill, and stayed at the Episcopal compound. Six of us took time out to sight-see in Wuhu. We began with a potter, a genial old soul living in a thatch-roofed mud-walled house outside East Gate, where small children gathered about to watch. He sat on his bench alongside a thick wheel which turned on a vertical axis like a top when he kicked it or spun it with a stick much like stirring porridge. It was magic to see the lump of clay rise up and spread itself out and hollow itself under his wet hands until it became a bowl or vase or jug or flower pot. The apprentice was putting handles and spouts on teapots. When the potter finished each piece he cut it off from the rest of the clay lump by pulling a thread under it. When the children crowded too close, he shook his wet muddy hands at them with extended fingers spattering brown wetness. The children squealed with glee and backed off a few inches; they knew him.

From the potter we went to see cloth being woven on wooden looms, the warp threads separated by a set of frames that the weaver worked with his feet like the big notes of an organ, the shuttle racing back and forth between the parted threads. The weaver tripped the shuttle with one hand and shifted in shuttles of different colors with the other hand for the pattern, in a smooth rhythm so automatic that he could do a complicated plaid yet talk about it at the same time.

---

* Annual Conference week was the gathering of missionaries and Chinese co-workers to report the work of the past year and plan for the next.

We visited a coppersmith hammering out bowls and samo-vars, very noisy. The pewter-making shop was quieter, its floor strewn with silvery shining cuttings and filings. Even quieter was the shop where the quills of Wuhu's white geese were made into fans. The shop where high-geared sewing machines were stitching woven straw braid into hats was not quiet at all, nor the one where pieces of iron were being ground down into razor blades.

Then we visited the Confucian temple, which had been so important in the life of the city, and where we once saw the ceremony in honor of the great sage held in the night "at the moment when spring arrives." The great hall with its red tablets lettered in gold stood empty. In the dust of the incense-burner before the chief tablet we saw a strange thing: a handful of ripe wheat stalks, heavy heads toward the tablet, and beside this a bamboo cross that stood up in the ashes. We asked the caretaker about it, but all he said was, "Yes, I know it means that God ate bitterness because of the sins of men."

We also went back to see the big Hell Temple. One devil was the one that carried off small babies when they died. Imagine mothers that had lost small children seeing that. Another was the smallpox god, to whom children were taken for protection against the disease, or for healing when they had it. One huge figure carried an umbrella; he was the one sent to get adults when they died, and the umbrella meant that if you died on a rainy day he got you just the same.

The temple was badly hurt by bombs, but none of the images had been damaged; they were gods, said the caretaker, so of course could not be hurt. On the ends of the roof were compli-cated structures with many points that the caretaker explained were protection against lightning. There didn't seem to be any ground connection, but the idea was that the points stuck out so that the dragon flying through the air would not dare claw at the temple.

Soon after that I was called to Kiukiang where Dr. Walter Libby had gone to substitute for Dr. Perkins, called back to America by the illness of Georgie's mother. Dr. Libby suddenly came down

213

with appendicitis. Complications which nobody could have foreseen or prevented developed, and Dr. Libby died. He was one of our very best men, a good friend to us all, and his death left Kiukiang with no surgeon. Fortunately, in view of the emergency the Japanese rushed through my military pass, and I went upriver third class in a Japanese ship with two graduate nurses.

It was fine to have the new Water of Life Hospital, that I hadn't seen before, in active use. It had established traditions and esprit de corps. Like our I-chi-shan hospital, it was set on a hill with trees and green grass around it, but was too far from the river bank for the kind of view we had. Instead, there was the marvelous view of Lushan standing up out of the plain a few miles to the south.

Surgery ran rather light. One reason was the absence of gunfire such as we had at Wuhu, and equally weighty was the absence of Dr. Perkins, the known quantity. As it was, we had plenty to do, and knew non-urgent surgery would swarm in on his return.

American gunboats didn't anchor at Kiukiang as often as at Wuhu, only about once in four month intervals, and then it was difficult to get passes down to their anchorage at the Socony Installation. But the *Luzon* arrived a few days after I did, and permission was obtained for all Americans to go down, with an escort of *Luzon* officers and Japanese military, as guests of Rear Admiral William A. Glassford. A most delectable pass-around supper was served us on the upper deck, where I was particularly glad to see Dr. O'Neil, as this was his last trip up the Yangtze. At Wuhu we had learned long before that it did not do to mention in his hearing the fact that we lacked any particular thing, for he would certainly produce it from the ship or bring it on his next trip. Coffee or bacon or Fowler's solution or sulfanilamide all came our way. He was a special comfort to Dr. Paul and Dr. Stella, because he took their families in under his wing throughout their struggle from being refugees to becoming Shanghai business people.

Dr. Perkins returned to Kiukiang, and a letter from Dr. Morgan directed that instead of returning to Wuhu I should go up to Kuling for a rest, where I stayed with Lucile Libby and two of her children.

Kuling wasn't much like its former self, with very few people present and a lot of its few trees cut down for fuel. But the quiet of the hills and the life-giving keenness of bracing mountain air and the inspiration of the play of light and shadows across the hills and plains seemed to mean more than before.

Hikes were limited to short ones, to the fine botanical gardens a few miles away, and to the Yellow Dragon Temple near the Three Trees. We built a fire and had a picnic by the side of the stream below the temple, a lovely place, with steep green hillsides rising both sides of us, and the sound of water running over the rocks. Because it was an "open and shut" kind of day, we kept an eye on the stream, one that sometimes rose suddenly, swollen with rain-water, with dire consequences.

Just as we were enjoying baked beans and sausage hot from the fire, Don Libby suddenly put up a shout, "Hey! The stream is rising!" In a moment water covered a rock that was inches out of water. We grabbed our things and scooted out of the brook bed while the water put out our fire and carried away the burnt sticks.

We went back to the temple, where a special annual service was going on, in which representatives were present from all through the hills. Ordinarily we were welcome to watch their services, but I remembered from years gone by that they didn't care to have visitors at this one. The old priest, a scholarly and charming old gentleman, invited us to their guest room, where we waited while rain pelted down outside. Our host remarked that Christians had many different denominations. We replied that unfortunately that was true, but differed chiefly in minor things, the important ones being the same. He smiled and said, "Yes, it is so with us, too." He mentioned several branches of Buddhism, and that "We have minor differences, but in the big things we are alike." Then he went on, "And there are many things in which your religion and ours are alike. I have read about Jesus. He was a righteous man and taught righteousness. Gautama also was a righteous man and taught righteousness. Peoples of different nations are also more alike than is supposed. Our languages are different. But the human body differs little, and the human spirit is

215

the same in all countries." We reminded him of the old Chinese proverb, "Under Heaven, one household. All mankind are brothers of one family."

Most impressive to me at Kuling was an elderly lady doing the doctoring that summer. Little and frail and thin, she and her husband had reached the age for retirement and decided Kuling was the place to spend their remaining years. Then came the war, and with Kuling anything but a peaceful retiring place, they stayed. She had an ailment that meant her days were numbered, and the number not great, and an ailment that would make most people sit down and feel sorry for themselves. But this plucky little old lady ran the medical work of the community hospital and did a splendid job. Nobody who saw her going about briskly and cheerfully guessed what it cost her.

Going back downriver I traveled second class, instead of our usual third, which meant half a cabin with a Russian lady and her beautiful cat instead of being one of sixteen people sleeping on the same shelf.

It was a very hot summer back down in the valley, that sent us in more malignant malaria patients than we could take care of, and raised normal temperatures because of the humidity and knocked down the less resistant of our crew when they tried to carry on the extra work. As a result, we took in only the most serious cases, turning away people who in ordinary times would have been taken in without question, and sent home post-operatives much earlier than they should have gone. Even so we hardly kept even with the work. But in the thick of the terrible rush, someone said, "Aren't we the fools. Look at the way we're working, without proper time to eat or sleep . . . and not one of us would swap our job for anything else in the world!"

"It might have been," may be sad words at times, but they can also be exceedingly joyous ones. The most appreciated birthday present I had October 1940 was a pathological report on tissue Dr. Morgan dug out from between two of my lumbar vertebral spines. It read "chronic inflammatory tissue, perhaps ganglionitis of a spinal nerve," so much less appalling than some of the things it might have been. That "bit of gristle" explained the awful pain. The next best gift was a visit from two of our ships, our flagship, U.S.S. *Luzon*, and Admiral T.C. Hart's yacht, the *Isabel*.

Admiral Glassford of the *Luzon* once came to a waffle breakfast with a tin of Log Cabin syrup under his arm, to us a real luxury. He was a most understanding person, and we all liked him immensely. The *Luzon* came in to the Butterfield pontoon, where some of us had lunch with him, and where stores he brought from Shanghai were unloaded, and their inspection by the authorities carried on. Then the ship was moved down to the Standard Oil Installation, and he invited me to ride on the *Luzon* bridge. And did I accept! It was less than a mile, but with getting away broadside into the wind and later making a landing alongside the *Isabel* with the wind driving us on, it was exceedingly interesting and perfectly done. That evening most of the foreign community assembled aboard the *Luzon* for buffet supper on the upper deck and a movie. The new *Luzon* doctor came and got into the game with us at the hospital.

There was another installment to the Hsu Family saga when T'ien-pao's step-father brought him around to me one day dressed up in a new blue gown of the sort that students wore, and told me T'ien-pao's uncle had appeared and offered to send the boy through the rest of grammar and middle school. So he was off on a new chapter of his life, and we all wished him well.

Our foreign community grew smaller by the day, and we wondered how long it would be until America entered the war. The British-American Tobacco Company had had no agent in Wuhu since the last one joined the British forces, and three agents from the Asiatic Petroleum Company did the same. That was the last business firm to have a foreign representative in Wuhu. As to the missionary community, several were evacuated. Nobody left as a matter of personal safety, and every one of them hated to go. Culley's furlough was due, and the evacuation plan merely hastened it a few months.

When Dr. Morgan took Dr. Ruth down to Shanghai to see her off to America, I was the only Methodist left in the city. Dr. Paul, Dr.

Stella, Max Biermann, who was now our bookkeeper, his mother, and Berta Hao with her two children were still with us, as the evacuation plan didn't affect them. Dr. Morgan and I planned to stay on as long as possible, not that our work was greater than that of the others who had to go, only that our work couldn't so well be interrupted and begun again later on. We followed Father's old instructions, "Sit still in the boat," and remembered that bit of wisdom, "Nobody knows what'll the day fetch."

Supplies were difficult and often impossible to obtain. As a substitute for cotton and gauze we used soft Chinese absorbent paper made of mulberry bark. For many skin diseases and for burns, we found ordinary diesel oil both effective and economical. Chinese bean oil frequently replaced olive oil. The fuel shortage having put our steam instrument sterilizer out of commission, we improvised small boilers heated by coal-dust balls or brickettes. With little or no heat in the hospital, we added layers of clothing and protected our patients during operations with quilts and hot-water bottles.

There were a few days during the transition from steam when we ironed surgical towels up in the operating room to sterilize them. It was fun thinking up ways to meet problems as they came along, and most cheering to see how our crew used their heads to get around difficulties without sacrificing surgical sterility.

In spite of the abnormal conditions, our ten doctors and seventy-seven nurses were busier through 1940 than ever before, caring for nearly 4,000 patients and giving 62,000 outpatients treatment. Over forty percent of this was charity work.

We began to hear of the loss of old friends. Captain Foyn of the *T'ai Shan,* the freighter that took us home last time, was one of the war casualties. Then the *Lillian Möller,* the collier that once brought Mother and me down the coast from Peitaiho, and gave me my first instruction in scientific navigation, was lost in the Atlantic, probably carrying British supplies. She had formerly been a transport for Russian immigrants from Odessa, and still had an Odessa piano on board when we sailed on her. Two good friends who were captains on Royal Navy gunboats were lost. Then we heard that the *Ladybird* and the *Aphis* helped capture Bardiyah. There were some casualties in the *Aphis.*

Apropos of the *Aphis*, having not yielded to the entreaties of Tao of the flattened ears to adopt his son, I suddenly found myself with a small boy on my hands after all. He was the adopted son of one of the Chinese in the *Aphis,* and had been on our hill for years as one of the waifs and strays that seemed to accumulate with us. He attended the small I-chi-shan school, and made cotton-sticks after school by way of helping to pay his way. Some of the crew discovered that somebody had been knocking him about rather badly, and kept him terrified with ridiculous and awful threats. He took it with his chin up, but some of the crew brought him around and begged me to "think of a method" to help protect him from further abuse.

So he was in our house to help our cook, and played happily with our two half-Swiss refugee children; their mother and our cook taught him many things. He brought me his report card, and his marks were fine. Half a dozen of the waifs and strays always brought me their cards to sign. We were working on the problem of getting some relatives to assume responsibility for eleven-year-old Yü-t'ang, "Jade Hall," a name that didn't seem to fit, and the crew called him Flat Head, which did.

Some months later Flat Head's father came home from the Battle of the Mediterranean. He had been officers' cook on the *Aphis,* and was in the Bardiyah bombardment. He said the ship was badly damaged and went into Alexandria for repairs, and about a dozen of the crew were killed. We were glad Flat Head had a home of his own once again; for too long he had been nobody's boy.

Another time when the *Luzon* was in, several of us went aboard while she was at the Butterfield pontoon unloading supplies, and were invited to ride along down to the Socony dock. As we passed the hospital, suddenly a bell sounded and the crew rushed out in their tin hats and appeared to shell the hospital, but it was a drill. They went through the motions of defending us every time they came into port, only the problem was different each time.

As we touched at the Socony Installation, the crew dashed ashore and mounted guns on top of the big oil tanks. One man jumped up by the guns with hand-flags and signaled that some of the crew were wounded. The "casualties" had first aid and were helped back to the ship. Afterward one of the officers told us the "game" that day was to suppose that coming downriver they got word all the Wuhu foreigners were in great danger. As they neared the hospital the captain told the crew I was standing on the hospital roof signaling that all the foreign community were at the hospital but we were being attacked from the inland side. So what they did was not to shell the hospital, but drop shells over it on the "enemy troops" beyond. From the Socony tanks they again fired on those troops. An actual airplane overhead during the maneuvers added to the realism, but the stunts looked pretty convincing. We always asked at the end of such a day whether we had been successfully defended, and always got the answer that we had.

The Japanese occupying Wuhu planted poppies in all the fields that had been mustard, and paid the Chinese working for them in opium. There was some land left for growing vegetables, and these the Chinese sold to them. But the Japanese didn't always have the best of it. One group camped in a poison sumac grove and got an awful dose. Another group of soldiers burst into the home of a Chinese family about to sit down to supper, and ate it while the family fled. What they didn't know was that the family had made a suicide pact, and had poisoned the last meal they were to have together. The officers died and the family returned home and canceled their pact.

A ceremony of great satisfaction the spring of 1941 was when our seven nursing students received their diplomas. We had wondered whether we would be able to carry on long enough for them to graduate. Eighteen new nurses who had finished their probation time appeared at the same ceremony in their new blue uniforms and were capped. The following morning we were all startled by a sudden outbreak of staccato noise. It turned out to be firecrackers, not shooting. There was a long bamboo pole out of the third floor window of the nursing office of the west wing, and from this hung an eight-foot string of firecrackers, each as big as a finger. This was the way one of the patients had taken to thank and congratulate the nurse in charge of the ward, who was one of the graduates.

For us it was forecast impossible. All we knew was that we intended to stay on or head for some other part of China. If it came to war for our country, we knew it wouldn't do anybody any good if we were interned, and that wasn't part of our plan.

Of course the Japanese would have been pleased to see us go earlier. Hence obstacles arose in buying enough rice to feed the hospital, enough drugs to treat the sick. The game being played was an attempt to make us lose patience, get fed up, and quit. But the rice could be spliced out with wheat, which was in part locally obtained and in part through the Red Cross. As for drugs, Uncle Sam's ships brought orders from Shanghai about once a month, and a few things could be obtained from the local branch of the International Dispensary, a drug company in China.

We had gone off the steam standard back to running a small sterilizer over charcoal and having boiled water poured over our hands from a pitcher as we scrubbed, as in the early days of the mission. Laundry was done without benefit of the steam-run machinery and the steam-heated boiling tub. As for fuel for cooking and boiling water, with the river as high as it was, and the small streams too, sailboats brought wood from out in the country. We hated to think of trees being cut to supply it, but we even had to cut down some of the trees on our own hill for fuel, chiefly diseased trees, and always replaced with small ones.

Meantime we had more than two hundred in-patients in our 160-bed hospital. That was more than ever before, barring cholera and nearby battles. This was just the usual run of sick people. Some we put on the floor, some we sent home days before they ought to have gone, some we pushed out against their will, but still they came. I had to keep combing the surgical wards, for my crew staggered on their feet. Dr. Yü was ill again, but fortunately the *Oahu* was in port with Dr. Creeman, who was keen on surgery and

221

good at it. Two of the non-medical men were also interested, and we "scrubbed them in" on operations too. The Chief Executive Officer helped me amputate a leg, and at the critical moment I handed him the saw, so it was really Chief Officer Berkeley who took it off. If it came to war, it might be valuable for several of them to have had experience of this sort. This officer had also repaired all our radios, putting us in direct touch again with the world, and the ship supplied us with distilled water in the interval between losing steam and getting re-rigged to run our still with alcohol.

The *Oahu* was with us longer than usual, about seven weeks, during the mercifully cool summer of 1941. We spent many evenings down on the *Oahu* deck at the movies and while we suspected the crew were fed up with being at Wuhu so long, we enjoyed them.

Dr. Morgan and I were over at the Spanish Sisters' frequently because their orphan babies had a lot of illness. We had to learn a good bit of Spanish on each visit since Madre Piedad, who had the babies in charge, knew neither English nor Chinese, and smilingly demanded that we say things in Spanish, patiently saying phrases over until we learned them.

The *Oahu* left for Shanghai just long enough to get refueled. While they were gone in September we learned that, beginning in October, foreigners would not be allowed to travel to or from Wuhu for an indefinite time. One day I was about to get on my bike to take off for the convent when the cry was raised that the *Oahu* had returned. There she was, already tied up at the Socony pontoon. Her arrival, even though she was gone for only short periods now, was always an event. Everybody who could get away hustled down to welcome her. Goodness knows how many cases of supplies she brought for us, for Sister Constance's dispensary and for the Spanish mission. Of course Japanese inspectors checked the cargo, marvelous cases from the American Red Cross and China Relief filled with gauze, surgical dressings, bandages, quinine, ether, sulfanilamide. We kept exclaiming with joy and wished those women at home who sat around tables long afternoons folding gauze and rolling bandages could have seen them welcomed. When I used to pay Red Cross dues I never knew how it would feel to be on the other end.

We hoped the winter would be as mild as the summer had been, for there was no coal at all to be had. B.W. Lanphear arrived back from his furlough bringing two tins of yeast, a huge tin of Borden's malted milk, real butter, some margarine and cheese. It was like an early Christmas. Dr. Morgan pointed to the yeast ads in *Life* magazine to show the sort of pep that would be expected of us.

The Kiangsi Methodists came up to Wuhu for December Annual Conference. There were seventeen people present. Bishop Ralph A. Ward planned to get us all across the lines into Free China, but we all thought we had some days before we got into the war and could finish Conference first. We missed our guess on that. Some of the Chinese were also trying to get us out. Everyone miscalculated.

At breakfast on 8 December (which was 7 December in America) we had the radio on listening to the news, when suddenly we heard: "Pearl Harbor in the Hawaiian Islands has been bombed by the Japanese. The *Arizona* and another ship were sunk. America is at war. We are no longer nonpartisan, but enemy aliens. Americans, please stay off the streets in Shanghai."

We looked up, and there at our window stood a Japanese soldier with a rifle and fixed bayonet. Someone murmured, "Thou preparest a table before me in the presence of mine enemies."

We were confined to I-chi-shan 8 December 1941 until March 1942, three months during which it was our job to close the hospital and send home all the patients, well or dying, so that the Japanese could use it as a military hospital.

We had sneaked a lot of our hospital equipment out over the wall past the Japanese sentries down into the city and hidden it in the homes of Chinese Christians. Dr. Francis Lum, a Hawaiian-American of Cantonese ancestry who had been with us for a while, asked, "Would you be willing to let those medical and surgical

223

supplies be taken through the lines into Free China?" We said we certainly would, because if the Japanese were to find them in the homes, those people would be in plenty of trouble. And besides, they were needed in Free China. He organized a group of people, including some Chinese who were puppet Japanese troops, and they got every bit of that material into Free China.

One of the first things Dr. Lum did after Pearl Harbor was to burn his American passport. We were shocked, but he said he could get another. It so happened that he had a Chinese face and could pass as a Chinese and didn't want to be interned with the rest of us. He thought he could do more as a free man.

Bishop Ward wanted very much to send word to Methodist headquarters in Chungking to let them know who was in Wuhu and that we were safe. Dr. Lum volunteered to carry the message through the lines. So Bishop Ward got his secretary to type his message on Kleenex. Chinese women took out some of the stitching on Dr. Lum's padded gown, put the message between the layers of the gown and stitched it up again. It didn't rustle, and couldn't be felt. One of the women who knew the country very well said to Dr. Lum, "I'll take you through the lines, but keep your mouth shut! Your face is Chinese, but your tongue is American!" They got through and back safely.

On a fake Chinese travel pass, Dr. Lum also got past the sentries and down to Shanghai where his fiancée, Dr. Yin-yin Wang, who had just graduated from medical school, joined him, and he brought her back to Wuhu. Then the two of them went together through the lines to Free China and were married there.

One of the first things the Japanese did was to take down our red neon cross from the hospital roof. So I looked in my Japanese dictionary and worked out some Japanese sentences, and went to the Commandant. He was about to have his lunch, and I remembered what Kipling said, "If you want to accomplish anything with a person, let him have his dinner first." So I waited until he'd had his lunch, then asked, "You want cross?"

He said, "No."

So I came to my second sentence, "Will you give it to us?"

He said, "Yes."

I said, "Good. Thank you."

We got it from where it had been left on the ground and carried it down to my house. The Spanish Sisters had sent us a note saying that they would be glad to store things for us, so we took up their kind offer and along with our dining room table and chairs and some other furniture, we sent over the cross. We told them to use whatever they could, but a lot of it went into the far end of their attic, where they had a brick partition built across the end.

The Japanese Commandant wanted me to give him my police dog, Toby. I knew I couldn't keep him with me in an internment camp, but neither did I want the Japanese to have him, and regretfully put him down instead.

On March first, 1942, our Annual Conference guests who had come for a week in December and had been confined to the hospital compound with us, were escorted back to their own towns under guard. Dr. Paul and Dr. Stella were not enemy aliens and were given Hobson's choice as to a job and taken on the staff of a Japanese civilian hospital. Of our Chinese staff, Chang, our chief engineer, and the gardener were kept and the rest sent away. Dr. Yü went to Maolin, Chinhsien, to open a small hospital, and was accompanied by many of the nurses and by Chou the laundryman. But most went over into Free China, about ten miles off then.

About the middle of April we Americans were confined to St. Lioba, Sister Constance's compound: Sister Constance and Laura Clark of the St. Lioba mission, Bishop Lloyd R. Craighill and B.W. Lanphear of the Episcopal mission, Dr. Morgan and myself. Joe Wharton was Irish and free to move about. Left behind on I-chi-shan were Max Biermann and his mother and Mrs. Hao and her two children. Mrs. Hao hadn't heard for more than two years from her Chinese husband who was in the army. They had plenty to eat and were being helped by the International Red Cross, but we worried about them for the winter as fuel was gone.

When the Japanese ordered the American flag that flew over St. Lioba's gate taken down, Sister Constance sawed down the flagpole herself so they couldn't run up their own flag in its place.

225

Her small clinic and ward remained open, but the industrial work was stopped and Chinese smuggled out about $2,000 worth of her materials. Our radios were taken, we were not permitted to leave the compound and could write only postcards that were censored, but our Chinese friends were allowed to visit us.

We were well and not mistreated, and I "broke jail" only twice, once when a child half-drowned in a nearby pond, and again in June when three of us went to the Japanese headquarters to find out whether we were to leave for Shanghai the following day as rumors had it.

But it was not until August that we were finally transferred to Shanghai. Sister Constance and B.W. Lanphear were both seriously ill by then, and Dr. Loren Morgan and Laura Clark were permitted to stay behind with them until they were well enough to travel.

Prisoner of War

1942-1943

We were taken down to Shanghai under guard by train. A Chinese gentleman in our boxcar gave me a card with his name and address on it and said to come to him for help if I needed it, but I never did, as we didn't want to get Chinese friends into trouble. When we reached Shanghai the internment camp was not ready for us so we were scattered about and I stayed at McTyeire School, a fine school of the Methodist Church South. We were permitted to go about the streets because all exits from the city were carefully watched, but we had to wear a red flannel armband with an A on it for American, and our individual number. We were all supposed to be very much ashamed of that letter A, and to wear it on the outside of our left coatsleeves, especially when we were on the streets.

It was a pity not to be useful, so I found clinic work and chased about on a bicycle. Every morning I went to the clinic and infirmary of the American Relief Center, located in what was left of the former Shanghai American School (S.A.S.) after most of it was taken over for a gendarmerie.

Living at the Relief Center was a varied collection of all sorts and conditions of more or less stranded Americans, some very worthwhile citizens, others a tough lot. I was on call for the patients there, and streaked across town pretty fast on some of the calls. Afternoons there was also interesting work to be done in two clinics run by the Moore Memorial Church, one in the crowded quarters to which the church moved when their beautiful big new building was taken over by the Japanese, and the other in a slum alley.

When some people were brought in from Manila, I took some of them over to the slum clinic to help. One was a dentist, and he had quite a few of his instruments with him. One day he was working in one corner of the building and I was seeing medical and surgical patients in another corner. I finished first and thought, "Well, I'll go down the street and see if I can drum up some more work for the dentist." I had taken off my coat that warm afternoon, and never thought to put it back on again. Just as I realized I had forgotten it, and the armband I was never to be without, a Chinese man wearing an armband that identified him as member of an organization set up by the Japanese to regulate something or other, came toward me with a very determined look on his face.

To divert him from my lack of an armband, I quickly asked, "Do you by any chance have a toothache or any trouble with your teeth? We've got a dentist up here in this building. If you've got any dental work to be done, go on up and see him."

He said, "Please, I want to ask you . . ." and I thought, "Oh no, brother, you don't want to get into that!" And I immediately interrupted him, "What about the people on this street? Do you know them since you are on duty here? Do you know anybody in trouble with his teeth? Better take him up to see the dentist."

He waited for me to stop, then began again, "Ch'ing wen . . . Please, may I ask you . . ." and I thought, "Oh goodness, I'd better think of something else." So I said, "There's an apartment house over there and a lot of people living in it. Maybe some of them have toothaches. Do you know anything about that?"

"No," he said, "and I want to ask you . . ."

I kept him going as long as I could, but he couldn't be switched off that idea he had, so finally I thought, "Well, I'm in for it. There's no help," and said, "Yes, what is it you want to ask me?"

He looked very solemn and said, "Please, may I ask you, are you a male person or a female person?" So I satisfied his curiosity and beat it back up the stairs to get my armband on. Thus conscience doth make cowards of us all!

I had to go to Wing On's department store one day to get something I needed. The streets were crowded, and there was a great parade going on with no way to get across Nanking Road. The parade had been arranged by the Japanese and people marched along carrying signs that said things like, "Death to the Foreigners!" and "Down with America!" I joined the procession in order to make my way slowly across the street, and everybody was very kind and polite to me, cheerful too.

Bob Johnson was one of those prisoners brought up from Manila on the ship we called the *Cockroach Maru*. Bob Johnson was lost, strayed and stolen, but I didn't know that. I only knew that he was sick, very sick, with cerebral malaria, and that he had been lucky the *Cockroach Maru* had even reached Shanghai as some of those Japanese transports coming up the coast, carrying some of our own people, were sunk by our American bombers.

His temperature was 105°, and first I used quinine, then atabrine, but they didn't help. I knew that in South America they often gave salvarsan for malaria that did not give way to other treatment. So I tried that on him. I said, "Now Bob, this is not quinine. This is salvarsan, which is used for syphilis. But we are going to try it for your malaria." I stuck a good-sized dose in his vein and that started his fever down.

Realizing he was very sick, Bob kept trying to tell me who he really was, but each time I stopped him. "Now wait a minute," I'd say, "when the war is over, Bob, I'll be glad to know who you are, but for heaven's sake don't tell me now as there are ears in every direction and some of them shouldn't know." And he'd say, "Oh yes, that's so." For about fifteen minutes he'd keep still, then start all over again. And I would shut him up again. In a few days he was well enough to not want to let me know who he was.

He got to be an active and lively person and in the internment camp signed up to do lab work where he thought he might sneak a look at his own blood slides once in a while to see how active his malaria was. Some people suspected he was a deserter from the armed forces, and one of the regular lab people said to him one day, "Bob, which one of the armed forces did you desert?" To her amazement, and mine, he wept, "I never deserted from anything in my life!" She immediately apologized, and said she was very sorry she had asked the question.

"But it's true!" he insisted, "I never deserted from anything. I was in the Philippines where my uncle sent me as a mining employee."

It was true that Uncle Sam had sent him to the Philippines, but as a B-17 navigator, and he reached Clark Field just before it was destroyed by the Japanese. He evaded capture at the fall of Bataan by fleeing in a rowboat to Corregidor, where he was caught in the surrender of The Rock. Escaping, he swam eight hours through shark-infested waters in the dark to the mainland, struggled for weeks through snake-infested jungle and sailed at night down the heavily-patrolled coast. Finally he was caught again, and had to make a split-second decision.

To give his rank and serial number meant execution as a military prisoner who had escaped, torture for his friends in the crowded stinking cells of Fort Santiago, and death for the loyal Philippines who had fed and sheltered him in his attempts to escape.

"I am Robert Fred Johnson, mining employee," he said.

About four years after I returned to America, I got an invitation to the graduation of Edgar Whitcomb from law school. I had no idea who Edgar Whitcomb was, but soon learned he was our Bob Johnson, and for the first time heard his real story.* Later he ran for Governor of Indiana. During his campaign I had occasion to stay overnight in his home and before I left he said, "If I should be elected, would you offer the invocation at my inauguration?" He was elected, and I did.

---

* Edgar D. Whitcomb, a Lieutenant Colonel in the Air Force, served five years during World War Two. Caught in the defense of the Philippines as a young navigator, Edgar Whitcomb wrote an account of his remarkable escape from the Japanese and subsequent capture in *Escape from Corregidor* (Henry Regnery Company, Chicago 1958). He became a lawyer and Assistant U.S. Attorney for the Southern District of Indiana, was a member of the Indiana State Senate, and 1968–1972 was Governor of Indiana.

Prisoner of War

Our freedom to roam Shanghai streets came to an end February 1943. I was assigned to the internment camp on the campus of a Chinese university in Chapei, a camp for women, children and sick people. The men, interned before we were, were in a number of different places, and for a while I went into some of their camps to work in their infirmaries. Two of us would go together and separate when we got there, one to sit alongside the guard, the other to deal with the patient. The one of us with the patient would say, "I want to listen to your chest," and take the patient over to a little sofa. Sometimes the guard came over, but when he didn't we passed messages back and forth between families that way. We memorized the messages, and stood with our backs toward the guard and said them all over as fast as we could in a very low voice while theoretically listening to his chest. We were never overheard.

I was in the Chapei camp about seven and one half months. There were 1500 of us, the majority Americans, but also some British and Dutch, all living in two large university buildings left standing after the 1937 bombing. One had been a dormitory and the other a classroom building. I lived in a classroom with twenty-seven roommates. Our camp wasn't too bad; by comparison with others we got on fairly well. We had plenty of water, with showers and plumbing. Nor were we treated as badly as were the prisoners in the Philippines, or in Hong Kong, which was the worst.

Our camp was a rather pretty one, with grass and trees and room for baseball, and a stream running under willow trees just outside the barbed wire on one side. The place had been bombed and repaired with cement that never dried so that seeds blown in took root and attractive green vines hung out of all our walls. We called our camp the Hanging Gardens of Chapei.

But it wasn't a picnic. The campus had been used earlier by Japanese troops, but so many of them died of malaria that it was condemned for the troops and vacated for us.

We got four things to eat each day. One was either rice or cracked wheat, the wheat from the American Red Cross and not much of that. It was done up in bags with GIFT OF THE AMERICAN

231

PEOPLE in big letters across them. As soon as a bag was empty, somebody made it up into an apron with those big letters right side up across the front.

The rice was the sweepings, what was left on the floors of Shanghai storehouses that people had tramped over, all broken, mixed with pebbles and weevils and just plain dirt. It had to be sorted carefully, and our biggest work group, made up of the elderly and not very active, sat at tables for long hours picking out what was edible. It was cooked by another work group. The second food was a vegetable, cabbage or turnip, and the third one raw egg that we got from the Red Cross and hung in a bag in boiling water to cook, then pulled it out with a string. The last was a small piece of bony fish. I had seen that fish in the Shanghai market, but didn't know what it was. It was shaped like a snake but wasn't either snake or eel, and had a funny face.

Sometimes we had soup. And that soup caused a sad accident. It was boiling hot and somebody was carrying a bucket of it when he collided with a small boy. The boy was terribly burned, but recovered. From then on, anybody carrying anything hot kept hollering, "Hot stuff! Hot stuff!" as he walked along.

Another child was also badly burned. His mother got a bucket of hot water to give him a bath, put it down beside his crib and went off to get cold water to cool it. For the first time, the child climbed over the side of the crib and fell straight into the near-boiling water. His older brother saw him fall, tried to grab him but burned his fingers and the child fell back in. Then the older boy very bravely grabbed again, right into the hot water, and pulled the baby out. It was hard work, but we saved him.

When we got our food in camp we stood in line to have it ladled into a bowl or mug that we had to supply ourselves. Some had foresight and took dishes and utensils with them, others used a tin can and ate with their fingers, but we swapped things around to help each other out. We each washed our own dishes and stood in line to do it, each stooped over. Whenever word came that someone was to be repatriated, you could see the line straighten up.

Our diet was short of calcium, so we got everybody to save their eggshells, which we ground up in a stone mill and fed to the children and others who needed it most. We counted on the hydrochloric acid in our stomachs to dissolve the stuff. The dentist we had said, "Don't grind the shells down quite to powder and we can also use it to scrub teeth. Better than powdered pumice."

I got Bob Johnson assigned to our camp because of his malaria, and in the lab he and some of the Catholic sisters helped grind up egg shells. Those sisters didn't stay with us the whole time as they were transferred to another camp, but we got to like them a lot while they were there.

A very elderly Sister had a toe that had become infected and ulcerated from a thorn. It was so painful that someone got me to take a look at it. I said, "Sister, if I were you, I'd get that toe taken off."

She said, "How can I?"

I said, "I haven't any surgical instruments with me, but I'll see what I can borrow."

So going around on inspection tours, I found one man who had a small pruning scissors. I borrowed them, and while I didn't have an autoclave, you can sterilize pretty well by boiling 5-10 minutes on each of three days. When they were sterile, I took off that dear lady's toe. We had no anaesthetic, but she was a wonderful patient.

We medical people weighed every one of our 1500 people every month. Everyone lost weight. One man, no taller than I, and that's *short*, weighed 256 pounds when we went into the camp. When I was repatriated seven and a half months later, he was down to 156 pounds, and felt better than he had for years. He had been a tinsmith, and had his tools with him. Anybody in the camp who received a package with canned goods through the Red Cross took him the empty cans and he made pots and pans out of them, all sorts of containers. His greatest work of art was a coffee percolator, with an inverted pickle jar for the dome on top. He was the only person in camp who improved those first seven and a half months, but by the time he got out he was down to 86 pounds, and not so good.

233

We did all the work in the camp, except guard duty. We even had a police force of our own. Food preparation, cooking, sewing, gardening, boiler-room duty (for the hot water supply), and all the other jobs were assigned as far as possible to those able and willing to do them. I worked in the infirmary. We hadn't much to work with, but usually managed to send serious cases out to hospitals, under guard.

We were determined to get the first woman in camp who was about to deliver out to a hospital. We thought that if she delivered in the camp it would set a precedent and the Japanese would never let us take out another, who might be more in need.

I wrote a note to the commandant and told him this woman was in labor and we had to get her into a hospital, and that it would be a good thing to send one of the doctors with her in case she delivered while on the bus. He said I could go with her. So we rode down to the city hospital of Shanghai where the Mother Superior told us they didn't take delivery cases, and we would have to go to another hospital. I explained this to the lieutenant accompanying us, and he said, "My orders are to take her here." Then I insisted he call the camp commandant.

"But he will be very angry," said the officer.

I said, "Well, he will be angry with me, not you. We must get this order changed." Finally we got the permission, but it took a long time.

When we got the woman settled in, we had to return the bus we had borrowed from the fire department, then walk about two miles back to the camp. I was carrying a very heavy kit, and the officer wasn't much help. He suddenly said, "I help you," and put his hand on the handle and the two of us carried it along about fifty steps. Then he said, "Wait." He took off his big overcoat and hung that over the handle so that it was over both of our hands. So we were carrying his overcoat as well, and he wasn't taking much of the heft of it, either.

As we walked along a rickshaw approached and I recognized the principal of McTyeire School. I saw she recognized me, and looked the other way, as I knew it could be bad trouble for her if she got the officer's attention. And I prayed God I would forget her name. By the time I got back to camp I couldn't remember her name, and have never been able to remember it.

As we walked along the officer asked me, "You like gardening?" When I said I did, he said, "You have some." That school we lived at had been bombed and chunks of its walls were imbedded in the grass roots. We were sent out to work to get them out. The trouble with that was that we were within a short distance of the fence and people would watch to see if they recognized a Chinese friend on the outside. But that meant trouble. One girl recognized a friend and waved. The friend didn't know any better and waved back. For that she was tortured. Some of the people walking by were concerned about me because the McTyeire principal saw how the officer and I were walking and thought we were handcuffed and spread the word. I never looked up.

We had religious services, Catholic and Protestant, and plenty of clergymen to conduct them. We had music and other entertainments. Every Saturday night we got together everybody who could play an instrument and gave a concert. The leader was a black trumpeter who had come to Shanghai to play in nightclubs, and was a marvelous jazz musician. He made it up as he went along, and the rest of us—a small organ, a large accordion, two violins and a mandolin—tried to add harmony, a bit difficult as we never knew in which direction his music would jump next. Anyway, we had great fun, and under the spell of it we all forgot we were behind barbed wire and that many of us didn't know whether our families were dead or alive; we forgot we were hungry and would be for months to come.

One time the commandant invited the men of our internee committee to go to a bangup, big Japanese feast in a restaurant. The idea turned out to be to get our men drunk on saki and then get military secrets out of them. Our men drank some saki and pretended to be drunk while the Japanese got sozzled and began to roar Japanese songs and appeared to be really enjoying themselves.

Then they stopped and said, "Now YOU sing American

songs." So our men sang, "God Bless America!" The Japanese said, "Good song! You teach us, we sing!" So our men taught them, and the commandant and all his men lustily sang, "God Bless America!". Along about midnight they all got back to the camp and our men waked everybody to tell us the story and got the whole camp laughing, which did us a lot of good.

We organized a school, nursery through the grammar grades. Teachers had brought along blank diplomas, and we had a June graduation ceremony for the children.

Adults who wanted to study some subject, joined or taught a class in it. If you knew anything, you taught it. Another woman and I taught astronomy, of a sort, as I'd had only a beginners course many years before. Bob Johnson joined our class and at one point asked me, when no one could hear, "Can you name the four stars in the great square of Pegasus?" I said, "Certainly not! Can you?" Those stars are not of the first magnitude and weren't named on most star charts. He could name them. I already knew he was not what he seemed, and he knew I knew and said, "For the purpose of this camp, all the astronomy I know I learned in your class." Then he helped me out. When we came to the erratic movement of Venus among the stars, he expounded it to me so that I could remember it long enough to explain it to the class. The benefit for Bob was that if he absentmindedly said something about the stars that made people wonder, he could now say, "Oh yes, I've joined Dr. Watters' astronomy class."

In October 1943, after months of bickering over categories between the Japanese government and our own, about 1500 people were selected from the various camps for repatriation on the Swedish liner *Gripsholm*.

When the ones selected from our camp went out, we left everything we owned behind for the people who had to stay. And the day we actually walked out that gate, what was left of the camp orchestra stood where we boarded the busses and played, "Over there . . . Send the word over there, that the Yanks are coming, the Yanks are coming . . ." It was a tremendously happy day for us, but not for those we left behind without much hope for future prisoner exchanges.

We went first on the *Tia Maru*, of unholy memory that was no fun, to Portuguese Goa, praying all the way that Portugal wouldn't get into the war. In Goa we were exchanged for Japanese who had been interned in America, and continued on the *Gripsholm*.

At the pier in Goa, I suddenly heard a voice calling up to the ship, "Is Hyla Watters on board?"

"Yes! I'm here!" I shouted back. It was Lee Henry, a chaplain and friend of my brother Philip. "I saw your brother two weeks ago, alive and well!" he shouted back. That was the first word I had had from my family in two years.

At Goa, before we went aboard the *Gripsholm*, we had a chance to go on the wharf and talk with some of the Japanese with whom we were being exchanged. I asked one lady what the food had been like in her camp in America. She looked very scornful and said, "Sometimes the ice cream was soft."

"Ice cream!" I almost shouted at her. "Did you say ice cream? What is that!" and I shouted to a group of others from the *Tia Maru*, "Hey! Come over here! Come talk to this girl from the internment camp in America! They had ice cream!" And the word went up and down the wharf with a shout: "Ice cream—in an internment camp!"

There was one man who had come out of the Hong Kong camp, and I don't know how he managed to get out, but he knew that when he was out he shouldn't eat too much and was careful. But it was so much more than he had had in the camp that it killed him. All of us doctors on the *Tia Maru* were worried that when we got to the *Gripsholm* everybody would eat like fools and have a terrible time.

The next morning, when we boarded the *Gripsholm* they marched us past a table where everybody got one stick of chocolate about as thick as your finger. In spite of all I knew, I said to myself, "I'm going to eat that whole thing, right now!" and started in. I ate one square, and managed a second one. But that was plenty. Everywhere we went after that we carried our chocolate and never laid it down. At intervals we'd stop and chew a little more. As a result our terrible hunger was satisfied without getting too much. A close watch was kept on us. For days after we carried that chocolate, and finally when we ate it all we were given another.

For our first meal we couldn't go to the dining room because it was being overhauled. So we ate on deck. We moved in a line to pick up our trays, then found some place to sit down and eat. By the time I got my tray all the seats on deck had been filled. I looked around and thought, "I'd like to sit down right here on the deck. But this is such a grand ship, maybe they don't allow it." So I asked one of the officers, "Please, would it be permitted to sit down here on the deck to eat?"

I thought he was going to cry. He said, "You sit down anywhere you want to."

I'm quite sure there have been few ships in the history of the world more dearly beloved by so many people as the *Gripsholm*. She gave us a marvelous trip with so many extra kindnesses that the crew must have sat up nights to think of them all. Red Cross representatives had clothing and shoes for us, and vitamin pills. Because of the war in Europe, we sailed down to Port Elizabeth, around the Cape of Good Hope and across to Rio de Janeiro, given a great welcome everywhere we docked. When we reached New York we anchored for the night near Lady Liberty, and were so excited we could hardly sleep. Next day we were all lined up for something and Bob Johnson stood with me near the end of the line. I asked him if he were going to give his right name now, but he waited until the F.B.I. came on board. When he told them who he was they took him off to debrief him.

As for the rest of us, they said, "Your families are over in the city at your denominational offices; there's not room enough for everybody on the wharf." But they didn't know my family. Philip and his wife, Grace, saw the *Gripsholm* come up the harbor and went down to the Battery and got on a tugboat, and Grace got the captain to swing around the *Gripsholm*.. I didn't know that, but I knew they would be somewhere near. I climbed up on a big pile of luggage on the wharf and gave our family whistle, the whistle of the white-throated sparrow. Above all the commotion on the wharf, I heard a white-throated sparrow answer.

Yangtze at I-chi-shan landing

239

Boarding and disembarking Yangtze steamer *(Helen W. Hayes)*

Yangtze launch at Wuhu *(Paul G. Hayes)*

Over The Edge of The World

1944-1945

S even thousand of us, in helmeted lines, marched up the gangways to that huge U.S. Army troop ship, the *Admiral William S. Benson,* in 1944. Only four of us could say to each other, "Aren't *we* the lucky ones!"

The Methodist Board had found a way to get me back to unoccupied China, Free China. At the embarkation camp I had learned to use my gas mask in real gas, and how to abandon ship by swarming over high obstacles on rope nets, wearing my G.I. helmet. When we marched down to the train to take us to the pier, all our gear hanging on us, I could see how worried the young fellows were. Most had not been far from home before. And this was war. So I asked the officer in charge if I could unload "Mandy," and soon the men were calling for one song after another. Suddenly the officer leaned toward me and said, "Let me call you sweetheart," and I thought, "Well, my goodness, that's fast work . . ."

We four lucky ones were three women (two doctors and a nurse) and a Belgian priest. I bunked with a group of Red Cross girls, our bunks three deep, and liked them better and better as the trip went on. We had lots of drills, for no one knew when we might be torpedoed, and I thought for the rest of my life if somebody were to say, while I was sound asleep, "Up all hands! Up all bunks!" I'd jump up and get busy. We wore our life jackets all day long. At night they hung by our bunks and when we went for showers hung on the edge of the cubicle.

From Los Angeles we went around Australia and up the west coast of India to Bombay; then, still under Army orders, across India first class, since we ranked as officers. Missionaries always traveled third class, because there was no fourth, so first class was an amazing experience for me.

In Calcutta we waited to fly over the Himalayas, "The Hump," to Kunming, and finally the woman eye surgeon who had come along on the troop ship and I got passage. It was cloudy and we bumped up and down; sometimes through a clear spot we could see a rocky peak. I said to the man in the next seat, "I hope the fellow up forward steering us can see more than we can."

And he told me, "He's got a new method. Nobody knows how it works, but they can see through the fog."

We came down on the La So side, then stayed with Brownie who was running an inn in Kunming. Next day we flew up to Chengtu where we were told to wait at the airport until some vehicle went into the city. Finally we were told one vehicle was going in, but maybe we wouldn't want to take it. I said we wanted to take anything they had. The man laughed, "It's a garbage wagon." We took it, the garbage cans making music the whole way as they bumped into each other.

Chengtu was the provincial capital of Szechuan, an old city that still had its ancient wall. Outside the south wall of Chengtu ran a river like a moat, called "the big river" to distinguish it from the small streams and canals that made up its great irrigation system, two thousand years old and still functioning efficiently, that made the plain rich and green. At the city it was narrow and about knee-deep, supporting a small fleet of sampans, but downstream it deepened for the junks. I liked to think that this water joined the Yangtze and flowed down past Chungking and through the gorges and on down past villages and under my window at Wuhu.

North of the river was the city, south of it the campus, formerly of West China Union University, which during the war housed also Nanking University, Ginling, Cheeloo University and Peking University Medical College. Yenching University was within the city.

I lived with the Fisher family, who had escaped the Nazis in

Vienna. Fritz Fisher was an internist, specializing in tuberculosis, and among other duties cared for a small sanitorium in an orchard nearby. Among the students, chiefly refugees and undernourished, there was a fourteen percent incidence of tuberculosis.

I was assigned part-time to the hospital at Four Spirits Temple (part of the system of allied hospitals of the university but formerly the Canadian Methodist Hospital), part-time to Yenching hospital. But there were so many medical people evacuated to Chengtu that there wasn't much for me to do.

In August 1945, Dr. Allie Gale, a physician of our mission, came up from Tzechung and eight of us, four foreign and four Chinese, started off for Mt. Omei, the most sacred and famous mountain of the region. We took off downriver in a salt boat chartered for the two-day trip to Chiating. Something like a barge, the salt boat was square-ended with narrow bow and stern, the mid-section covered by matting on an arched frame with just enough room for me to stand almost straight in the center. Its chief function was to haul grey blocks of salt from Chiating. Beneath the deck was cargo space. Since we had chartered the boat there wasn't supposed to be any, but there were two huge bales of Chengtu red peppers, their owner riding with us. Two rowers stood on the forward deck facing forward, each pushing an oar; aft the helmsman held a long helm. But our chief motive force was the swift stream.

At first the green countryside was flat and we looked up to the edge of irrigated fields, the rice-heads beginning to bend over with heavy grain. Then we came into hilly country cultivated to the tops of rounded hills, chiefly with kaoliang grown for making alcohol and whisky, and corn interspersed with graceful clumps of bamboo-like great ostrich plumes.

At intervals we could hear singing, a phrase from the leader answered by a chorus, and soon a group of a dozen or so trackers would approach, some bent way over, swaying forward to the slow rhythm like some Greek choral dance, pulling, each with a wide webbing loop over one shoulder, the long split-bamboo rope towing a boat like ours upstream loaded with salt or silk or firewood. Our mast was stowed under the matting, but those towed upstream had their masts stepped, the tow rope leading from halfway up it rather than the masthead as with our downriver junks.

We passed villages on the river banks, the house walls built up about six feet with big blocks of local red sandstone; above that a framework of beams with plastering between, like many old English houses. Roofs were gray tiles with upturned corners and ridgepoles.

There were frequent rapids, where the river ran over an oblique low dam leading down at one side to a flume turning a wooden paddle-wheel, eighteen or twenty feet in diameter, each paddle carrying an obliquely-placed bamboo tube to dip up water from the river and pour it into a high trough for irrigation. Every time we went over one of these rapids the crew had to do some careful seamanship to keep bow-on and hit the channel. One time an upward-bound boat occupied the passage we needed, and it was exciting. It rained at intervals all day, making the world soft gray-green and beautiful. I gave thanks that planes flying over weren't Japanese bombers.

Sometimes we passed large up-bound boats, anchored by a big stake let down through a socket through the forward deck and jammed into the river bed. Sometimes we passed water buffaloes grazing, watched by a herder in a yard-wide bamboo hat and palm bark rain-cape. Several times we passed red sandstone cliffs with Buddhas carved on them. Gutzon Borglum didn't tackle anything new when he took on Mt. Rushmore. By one dam a row of children, all in wide rain hats, fished with bamboo poles. Further downstream another child practiced for his life work with a small edition of the circular fishnets weighted at the circumference, thrown twirling so that they spread open to fall full circle.

The river grew wider and wider, the country hillier, although we passed through one narrow gorge beautiful enough to rate fame but not as dangerous as the Yangtze gorges, and before noon of the third day drew up at the foot of wide stone steps among other boats at Chiating. Famous for silk, Chiating was on a point where our river and another met to form the Min, which flowed down to the Yangtze. There we stayed with my friend Helen Hui Kui of medical school days. Her husband, a Wuhan University professor, was in America, and she and her five children had refugeed westward with the school. They gave us a sightseeing tour by sampan, and we were presently swept downstream in a trough of rough water to the broader Min and along it, under red cliffs, past the great seated Mi-lo Buddha, 300 feet high, carved out of the cliff. He had sat there nearly two thousand years, and trees and vines made a great cloak about him as he looked placidly across the river to the hills beyond.

Landing by red sandstone steps, we followed a beautiful walk up a steep hillside, past caves of T'ang dynasty tombs, and climbed past several temples. Most interesting was the Temple of Five Hundred Buddhas, with five hundred life-sized and life-like statues of Buddhist saints, all individual and obviously citizens of a number of different countries. They were a cheery lot, who did not gaze placidly ahead but apparently enjoyed chatting together in groups.

Returning to Chiating, we were drenched by rain. The two boys poling us upstream couldn't manage against the current, and most of the way I stood on deck and poled with them. We were all so wet that the sight of us greatly amused the Chiating populace as we walked up from the dock; all good-natured and friendly laughter in which we joined.

Next day we set out on an all-day rickshaw ride across the great plain, across one river by ferry where a bridge had been destroyed, up hills where the runners objected to our getting out to spare them, and down hills where with no brakes the runners leaned their elbows on the shafts and nearly flew. So we reached Protect the Country Temple, where our company divided. The others began their 11,000 foot ascent of Mt. Omei, while Allie Gale and I went to a summer settlement for a few days.

It could be reached by dark provided we rode in *hua-kar*, a hammock of transverse slats strung between two poles, with a bar below for one's feet. It looked awful but was comfortable, and the men carrying us went much faster than we could have gone.

We took a beautiful winding trail up past bamboos and pines, wild honeysuckle and ferns and the wild grandmother of all hydrangeas, along ledges that seemed appallingly narrow and slippery, where we looked down through mists into deep valleys. A genial Scottish missionary from Chengtu University Middle School welcomed us to a comfortable wooden house on a grassy terrace on a steep hillside.

While we rested on our five-thousand-foot perch a farmer came up all excited, saying, "Something important has happened. Down on the plains they are shooting off firecrackers and we have sent a man down to find out what it is all about." When he returned he told us that America had dropped a terrible bomb on Japan and the war was over. We couldn't believe it at first, and perhaps most affected was Allie, who had not heard from her husband since he had been interned in the Shanghai Putong camp four years before.

We wanted to get back downriver, but knew we couldn't get passes right away and decided to go on with our climb. Allie Gale, sixty-seven and greatly underweight, wisely decided to ride the whole way up, while I felt recovered enough from a recent illness to hike. I took a *hua-kar* along, though, and was glad of it.

The evening before we started we took a steep trail around the far shoulder of our mountain. There, on a narrow path cut out of the hillside, we looked down into the green valley below filling with shadows, and up at the pass beyond. Sunshine slanted through the pass lighting the rim of trees along the hilltops and lay in broad shafts of golden light across the bluer hills beyond. Above the pass, at a steeper angle than one would think possible, stood the sheer top of Omei, deep blue against the sky. Chin Ting, they called it, "Golden Summit."

That evening it was the sky beyond that was golden, and those great shafts of light. As we watched, the blues deepened, the light faded, the gold died and evening mists rose. A farmer with three gaunt cows came along the path and we squeezed back against the rock and ferns to let them pass. Then with one last look upwards, we made our way back along the darkening hillside to prepare for an early start.

In the gray of early morning our way led downhill through a pass into the main valley. It was lovely and cool as we picked our way down, knowing we'd have to climb back all that altitude. Frequently we walked through steep hillside cornfields, and learned it was planted up to nine thousand feet. Having grown up believing corn had been developed by American Indians from wild grasses, I inquired about the introduction of corn to this region, and of tobacco, but their origins seemed to have been lost in the dim past, "before and before and ever so long before."*

On sunny parts of the trail we caught glimpses of light sparkling on the ground, and stooped to pick up clear quartz crystals. The mountain was famous for them and pilgrims prized them as souvenirs. Before we had gone far, I saw a track that stopped me short. Squarish, but something like a cat's, about four inches each way. "Tiger," the carriers said, and we remembered that one of the farmers had lost a dog to a tiger a couple of nights before. This may have been a panther or young tiger, as adult tiger tracks were a good six inches across. But there were real tigers on that mountain, and people kept their children, and themselves, indoors at night.

Still down we went until we came to Protect the Country Temple where we left part of our gear to pick up on the down-trip. From there the real climb began, very steep, through beautiful woods. I walked most of the way, but, when I wanted to stop and rest, the carriers, who had definite ideas about stopping anywhere but the temples where they regularly stopped, insisted, "No, you get into the *hua-kar* to rest." They would keep on going until I was ready to walk again, and began to ask me to ride when they started out fresh, so that I'd be ready to walk when they were tired.

Many gods in the Mt. Omei temples were different from the ones down in the Yangtze Valley, but we also found old friends like O-Mi- To-Fu and Ta-mo. We felt the Indian influence strongly and in a number of the temples I saw pictures of the Shwe Dagon

---

* Corn was introduced to China via the Spanish in the late-Ming era, the sixteenth century.

Pagoda in Rangoon, one of the most sacred places of Buddhism, and stacked much rank with the priests for having been there. One temple was built with a dome and a lot of small Indian arches, with a little Buddha in each. Many images sat on elephants and frequently an elephant and a tiger were placed so as to balance each other. One elephant, cast in bronze, was life-size; how they got it up that mountain was a marvel. When told it looked like a real elephant, the priests asked doubtfully whether elephants could really be that large. Strangely, some elephants had two or three tusks on each side. Never was the elephant a god, always the throne for a god, or part of the decorative background.

In general, animals in China were not gods, but there was an interesting exception on that very mountain where in front of practically every temple was a nearly life-size figure of a tiger in a shed. Beside him sat a human figure brandishing at him a businesslike sword.

Pu-hsien, one of the four great *p'u-sa* universally worshipped in China, was said to have ridden a white elephant from India to Mt. Omei in the second or third century B.C. Pu-hsien and his elephant were represented in a number of the temples, and one claimed it was there Pu-hsien stopped to bathe the elephant when it got hot.

The trail up Omei consisted largely of red sandstone steps cut on long steep flights built on the shoulders of hills instead of in the folds as the Lushan steps were. We had the impression of walking up the edge of the world, with often a precipice of real depth on each side. Our carriers called such places, "two sides empty." Ridges like that appear in many Chinese landscape paintings, and in a particular kind of allegorical picture represent the difficult path to heaven, with people tumbling off both sides. On Omei one had to walk the straight and narrow way with care. The weather was misty and foggy on our up-trip, rainy going down, which enhanced the effect.

On the long steep flights (one, called Climbing Heaven Stairway, had more than 1300 steep steps in one section), I plodded up with a pilgrim's staff bought at one of the temples. The carriers puffed too, but not as badly as I did. It was in such places that I was amazed to have them ask me to do my resting in the *hua-kar* instead of sitting by the wayside a few minutes. They must have had a high hemoglobin in their blood, as the Alpine guides do. I wished I had some way to test it.

I counted up to twenty-five different ferns along that trail, and then lost count. It was a joy to see fireweed and Saint-John's-wort, and there was what appeared to be corydalis but in pale blue and deep lemon and a marvelous indigo that shaded into purple. There were lovely white anemones on long stems, everlastings and edelweiss. Jewelweed appeared with blossoms twice as large as the ones that doused us on wet mornings in Tupper camp woods, and in pale yellow and orange and even a pink. The carriers had never noticed the touch-me-not fruit of it, and laughed when I handed it to them to have it explode in their fingers.

They kept talking about *p'u-erh* and looking for it and asking whether we liked it. That was a mystery until they suddenly leaped into bushes and came back with a handful of sprays loaded with black caps. From then on we picked them as we went, without slowing the expedition, and they were refreshing and juicy. Another kind of berry resembled a raspberry with a delicious flavor.

And so we came by late afternoon to the temple on Flowery Crag Summit, where we stopped in the temple hostel. Our room was one of several in a row that opened on a piazza with a view down over the edge of the crag and way out over the hills. From the end of the piazza we saw the sun set, red beside the sheer Golden Summit, still high above us. While the priests prepared supper, we looked at the images that obviously represented the visible results of an earnest search after God. The benign figure of Buddha, seated on the lotus that means ascent of the soul from darkness to light, often with hand raised in blessing or down in the Oriental beckoning position leading the soul toward greater enlightenment, was certainly a long step beyond the crude pre-Buddhist gods. A lot of the worshippers missed the symbolism and prayed to the image itself, earnest worship directed to the highest being they knew.

While waiting for supper we went into the great hall of the images, where one priest was beating a great drum and a wooden gong and a metallic one, while the selection from the great book was read, incense burned in an old bronze burner, and over all the golden faces of the images looked placidly down.

Later in the evening I heard the drum again and returned to the hall where a priest read the Buddhist scripture by a flaring candle, one hand beating rhythmically on the wooden gong. Most of the room was dark, the face and book of the priest candle-lit, red points of incense glowing, and a few points of the gilded images catching the candlelight. At intervals through the night we heard the drum, for prayers were said every few hours just as at St. Lioba in Wuhu where the angelus every six hours reminded us to stop whatever we were doing and pray.

Early next morning we were off for the second day's climb. It was cool, the valleys full of mist, when we stepped out under the high trees. This climb was steeper, harder because of the higher altitude, and even more beautiful than the first. Bamboos gave way to pines and spruces and balsam, and the birds were different, too, one lovely gray one smaller than a bluebird, with a bright coral beak and coral epaulette. The fireweed and Saint-John's-wort grew thicker, and I came on my old friend, closed gentian, stunted by altitude and weather, and hailed it with such a whoop of joy that the carriers were disappointed to find only a little blue flower the cause of all the excitement. Openings in the mist showed steeper and deeper valleys below us, and the "two sides empty" places gave us a feeling of unlimited depth. There were fewer tile roofs on the temples, more bark roofs overgrown with ferns, bushes and trees, until they looked like part of the mountainside and in some cases had accumulated so much weight they had caved in.

The cold grew more noticeable as we climbed, so that at each resting place the carriers crowded around charcoal braziers, and the priests wore thicker and thicker gowns at successive temples. Clouds swirled past us, and sometimes we heard waterfalls off in the clouds. At last we went across a slanting field to a couple of temples perched on the dizzy edge of a sheer drop, and we were at Chin Ting, the Golden Summit.

As temples those two were hardly inspiring, badly battered by the weather, their images crowded together during repairs. But the temple where we stayed was called Glory Appears, and it lived up to that. We stood on its rickety little piazza hanging over the edge of the world and looked out into masses of clouds, which now and then separated to show us isolated peaks far below, sometimes hillsides and valleys.

I looked at our temple and gave thanks there was not much wind blowing, and wondered how it had managed to cling to that giddy summit through real storms. From our second storey room we looked straight down over the brink and out to a far mountain view.

There were three things that pilgrims who climbed Omei hoped to see. One was the snow mountains to the west, and toward evening the clouds parted to reveal ranges stretching far off into Tibet. We missed, for lack of clear sky and sun, the light effect called Buddha's Glory. But we had seen that at Kuling: with clouds or mists below and the sun at one's back, there sometimes appeared a strange halo effect with one's own shadow at the center.

Buddha's lanterns we saw from our windows after dark. When the clouds parted enough to see, far down in the valley a dim point of yellow light appeared, brightening until it was like a lantern. But it was not a lantern, for it moved along as a bit of mist drifts in the wind. The light would last for a few seconds or a minute, then fade out. Sometimes there were none to be seen, sometimes two or three at once. They tended to appear in certain places, which may have been swampy, and were probably will-o'-the-wisp, but on Omei it seemed like spoiling a poem to try to find a rational explanation.

The night was cold, really cold. Other guests had "fire pans" lighted in their rooms. But remembering fatalities we had heard of from carbon monoxide from those charcoal braziers, we didn't let ours be lighted, but put on all the clothes we had, kept the window open to let out fumes from other rooms, and climbed into sleeping bags.

251

At intervals through the night I woke up and heard the tapping on the wooden fish gong in the temple and knew that someone read and prayed. While I slept, I dreamed. And in my dream we were all in the worship room of this temple, and God came to us in a great radiance and someone said, "Tell us thy name that we may know what to call thee." I waited and wondered, "What will He say? Yahweh? Allah? Jehovah?" Then there came a great voice: "I am O-Mi-To-Fu. This is the name they know to call me here."

We had planned to spend a day at the summit, but there was nothing but fog and it was too cold to stay with no view. Our shivering carriers were overjoyed when we announced we would start down immediately, and agreed to pay them extra to do the whole down-trip in one day. About ten minutes onto the trail the rain began softly and continued crescendo. I tried to walk as I had on the way up, but the cold had developed a fine Charley horse in the calves of both legs. Massage hadn't helped, and when I tried to walk down, it was like a person with two wooden legs. The carriers said, "Yes, we knew that would happen. You are too new and we can't wait for you, so you must get into the *hua-kar* and ride." So I sat in the *hua-kar* while the carriers romped down that mountain in the rain, the cliffs dropping off in unlimited space to each side. The steps were wet and slippery, but our men wore straw sandals with their firm grip. Sometimes a long flight of steps below us would end in nothing but mist, and one would have to take a firm hold on reason and remember that there must be steps below.

By the time we reached Protect the Country Temple the rain had stopped and we were ready to hang up our bedding and other gear on ropes strung about the courtyard to dry in the sunshine. A good night there, an all-day rickshaw ride the forty miles to Chiating, a ride in a weapons carrier with some G.I.s, and we were back in Chengtu.

Fifteen Hundred Miles to Wuhu

1945

"Stand not upon the order of your going." read a message waiting from our bishop. Next morning I was enroute to Wuhu. To reach Chungking on the first lap, there was a six day trip on a large sampan with an arch of matting over the middle of it. On the forward deck three men stood and rowed, facing forward. Astern the captain steered, or sometimes didn't, with a bent wood helm. Our crew were farmers, not boatmen, not very boatwise, and we had some interesting times.

The swift water carried us along the 120 miles to Chiating much faster than on our earlier trip, and below Chiating, where we began to encounter bigger whirlpools than above, our boatmen caught the downstream side of each whirlpool for an extra push. That is, they usually did. When they missed, and went around, it was alright with them. The water on that stretch of river seethes and swirls, either from rocks below the surface or, as our crew claimed, from deep springs, so that we heard a loud continuous hissing. Often there were rapids. Once our men risked a just-off-a-shelving rocky point and found it was more than they could hurdle. We pitched wildly, shipped waves fore and aft, and sprang several seams. But the bump I expected from a submerged rock, that would have opened the boat like a flower, didn't happen. Everyone fell to and caulked seams and I spoke some winged words to the crew and they became a bit more cautious.

We moored each night along some village waterfront, along with similar boats and friendly neighbors. But one boat, crowded

253

with restless and unhappy pigs on their way to market, we were glad to leave behind at dawn. Each evening we explored the town and its temples. In Hsi Ch'ing, Clear Mud, we found a temple with a forlorn and crippled lot of idols gathered from surrounding temples and left to collect dust and spiderwebs. Wang-I, the pre-Buddhist local water god worshipped by the boatmen, had some incense sticks. His paired inscription read, "Originally he was a wanderer among the four seas and the clouds; so he has become the patron of the rivers, streams and rolling waves." In another town we watched men pouring iron in an iron-foundry that had refugeed from central China ahead of the Japanese. We marveled to find them there, for to have reached that village it was as though workers of an iron-foundry in America had carried their heavy equipment and walked from Delaware to Kansas.

Our crew had the same idea that many of our boatmen downriver had, that if they could cross close in front of a larger ship, its prow would scrape off any devils that might be following them. A lot of small boats got plowed under doing that, and I had words with our crew on that subject. They didn't much care which end of the boat went forward, which added to the interest but dismayed my seamanship.

Three hundred miles downriver from Chengtu, at I-p'ing, we came into the Yangtze, rushing along between hills, and three hundred miles beyond I-p'ing, we looked up at the rocky promontory of Chungking, with a record high-water mark painted about a hundred feet above us. The boatmen said we would land at the American airbase. We flew an American flag, which the crew thought might protect us from bandits along the way, and when I realized we were headed for the base stern first, I refused to risk embarrassment, seized the stern sweep and turned us around.

Presently I was dickering with coolies to carry my bicycle and seabag up a dirty, slippery path to the sorry-looking city that had been heavily bombed and hastily rebuilt, mostly with shacks. Chungking was jammed with downriver people all homesick and trying strenuously to get back. I spent my time chasing about government offices, filling out documents, pulling all the wires I could find. It took weeks to get away; then only because the National Health Administration recommended me to U.N.R.R.A., The United Nations Relief and Rehabilitation Administration, and C.N.R.R.A., The Chinese National Relief and Rehabilitation Administration, who gave me a letter to the American Embassy. They gave me one to the Department of Foreign Affairs who got me a visa for Wuhu. Then the Police Department cleared me, and the National Health Administration gave me a huge letter, very impressive, with a big red seal, which virtually made me a Chinese official with authorization to take back and reopen the Wuhu hospital, and therefore eligible for passage on one of the steamers chartered to carry Chinese officials back to reestablish the government on the east coast.

After several weeks of devious and complicated efforts, numerous false hopes, suddenly the word came, "If you will come IMMEDIATELY we can get you on board a ship for downriver." There was no chance to pick up the medical supplies the National Health Administration and International Relief had ready for me, but they said they would send them down later and to go ahead. So I jammed a few things into my seabag and tried to get a ticket. I couldn't seem to get one in the regular way, so John Yü, the son of Episcopal Bishop Yü and nephew of one of my friends at Wuhu hospital, and I finally got tickets by way of a black market rascal who didn't have an office in any definite place but met us on a street corner. We made for the steamer, with some misgivings as to whether our papers were complete, but they passed inspection and the ship sailed. A couple of days downriver we got a radio message to return, that the ship was too large for the next part of the river. A compromise was made by anchoring off Chungchow to wait for a launch from Chungking. Another inspection of papers declared ours incomplete; there was talk of putting us ashore, but they took us on to Wanhsien.

At Wanhsien an inspector looked at our papers. "Get off the ship. These are no good," he said. I showed him my precious document from the National Health Administration, and he was not impressed. So off we got, bag and baggage, and walked about the town and inquired about getting a small boat, but the gorges were ahead with their deadly swirls, and no one would chance it. We asked if there were a foreign mission in town, and were told two Americans had returned the day before. So we plodded up a hill and found two young Americans and told them our tale of woe.

They said they would go along to the shipping office to plead for us, but meantime sit down and have some lunch. Now I like preserved eggs, which was all we had had for a couple of days, but there are limits, and we were glad to share their lunch. When we went back to the shipping office we hoped for a different inspector, but there sat the same man who had thrown us off the steamer. One of the young Americans said, "We have come to speak for Dr. Watters," but that same inspector said, "You don't have to speak for Dr. Watters. She operated on me ten years ago in Wuhu. Take your friend, Dr. Watters, and go back on the ship." He had figured out that I was the same doctor. Of course I looked different without my white uniform.

That trip was the first time I had been on the Yangtze above Kiukiang, and the one hundred fifty miles through the gorges lived up to the fearsome stories told about them. Sheer cliffs formed a gateway to the first and shortest, Ch'ü-t'ang Gorge, which was only 350 feet wide and five miles long, but it had the fastest current and the sheerest cliffs, with towpaths, for trackers hauling huge junks upstream, cut into the face of the sheer rock. Then there was a breather of calmer water before we hit the Wu-hsia Gorge, twenty-five miles of the worst whirlpools and spectacular cliffs rising a thousand feet to sharp peaks. A second breather of wide river and gentle landscape ushered in Hsi-ling Gorge, the most dangerous and feared gorge, not as spectacular as the other two, but thirty miles of terrible rapids formed by landslides of shale and great rocks that stood in the channel.

We made it safely through the rushing water and whirlpools to I-ch'ang, the westernmost port that had been occupied by the Japanese. I-ch'ang was dead, deserted and ghastly, with pieces of walls and chimneys sticking up out of the wreckage. Some Chinese troops were there, and a few shopkeepers in shacks to sell food to them and to us.

The spirit aboard our steamer was great. We were all on our way home. Even children born in Szechuan, talked about "home" to Shanghai. People slept on the deck and ate what they could and drank water if they could get it, and got wet when the deck above us leaked in the rain.

The usual comment was, "It doesn't matter; we're going home!" But it did matter, for a lot of people, particularly the children, got sick. Of the Chinese troops on board, many were sick, and two came down with cholera. I hadn't any intravenous saline for those, and hardly anything else. With my continuous spinal outfit we gave the sicker cholera patient intra muscular saline of river water (cleared with alum) and salt boiled up in a kettle, stopping short of the muddy sediment. It was horrible stuff, but apparently saved his life. We finally got both of them to a small hospital. One had developed severe bronchial asthma, and we had nothing for that, although we got a *huang*, the plant from which ephedrine was developed, in a Chinese village drug shop, and that helped. Two Chinese doctors on board and I wrote prescriptions and sent relatives ashore to buy medicines as we went along.

And so we came to Hankow, where several things happened. Our ship could not get coal, and there was also some disagreement between the company running it and some transportation bureau that wanted it to turn around and go back upriver to fetch troops to take surrender of the Japanese in Peking. There were Japanese troops aplenty in Hankow, but they had already surrendered.

So the ship sat and sat and we went ashore for meals and something happened that really frightened me. Some wild duck seemed a bit high but, not wanting to be finicky, I went ahead and ate it. That night I got called out for a patient, and found myself worse off than the patient. What appalled me was to find I was blind in one eye, so that a flashlight turned directly on it showed only a very dim dark blue, I supposed from a toxic optic neuritic as part of the food poisoning. And who could tell when the other eye might follow suit? After some hours vision gradually returned, but I was limp with fever.

In the midst of that along came another ship, minus some parts from bombing but supplied with coal, and our captain advised us to transfer. There was difficulty about our papers, but a letter from our old captain got us a place on deck and we bought a supply of bread and preserved eggs.

Jampacked with people, the new ship had hardly enough deck space to lie down, but we managed. There was a dining room where it was possible to order food, but if you put your head in the door you went no further. It reeked of stale food and swarmed with flies and cockroaches. So when we tied up nights to avoid the mines we went ashore for supper and bought more preserved eggs for breakfasts and lunches.

At Kiukiang one of the doctors there went with us to the Perkins' home and other residences, and to the Water of Life Hospital. All were occupied by Chinese military officers, their headquarters in the hospital, all considerably the worse for Japanese occupation.

Next day there was much speculating whether we would reach Wuhu by nightfall. When I asked the captain he said, "We have a moon tonight, and I am going to make it by eight-thirty, especially for you." With what excitement I watched for the lights of Wuhu. John Yü asked where I planned to stay. We learned that the Japanese had not yet surrendered at Wuhu, and that soldiers still occupied I-chi-shan, so I thought maybe with Pastor Wang in the city, or the Spanish Sisters. "Or maybe someone will be over at St. Lioba's, the Episcopal convent."

"That isn't good enough," said John Yü, and he went off the steamer with me. We found no one at Wang's, so went to the St. Lioba convent and I banged loudly on their gate. We heard a great scurrying inside. Finally the gate swung open, and there, to my horror, stood Japanese troops in phalanx formation with rifles and fixed bayonets at the ready. "You fool," I thought, "you got out of their hands once just to walk back in."

I had had a few lessons in Japanese in Manila, so tried to ask them, "Is there any American here?" To my amazement they said yes, and I thought, "Oh my, they must have some wounded flyer," and asked them where. They beckoned me in, closed and bolted the gate behind me. At every step across the campus I liked it less.

When we reached the convent itself, the man leading me pointed at the door and said, "Here." So I went up the steps and pounded. No reply. I banged harder and shouted, "Is there any American here?" Then I heard, "Woops!" and some shouting upstairs and a clatter of footsteps. The door opened, and there stood Sister Constance and Dr. Morgan. They had arrived the day before.

We had last seen each other in 1942 when our Wuhu crowd was taken down to Shanghai and Dr. Morgan stayed behind with Sister Constance who was down with a bad heart. Later they were taken to a different internment camp in Shanghai, and Sister Constance was repatriated. But Dr. Morgan, suffering from a bad heart himself, had spent the whole four years as a prisoner, and had barely come out alive. He was so concerned about Wuhu hospital, though, that when he was offered a place in the first hospital ship returning to America, he had chosen to stay at the internment camp in a tiny shack set in a swamp, in the hope he could get back to Wuhu. At the camp many people claimed that Dr. Morgan was the best-loved man among the 450 internees, and that without him it was doubtful whether a large number would have survived. The Japanese food ration was insufficient to support life, sometimes one beet or one turnip per day per person; food sent to Dr. Morgan from America he had divided among those who needed it in his usual generous way. Dr. Morgan gave medical attention to everyone in need, and set up a dental clinic with improvised equipment. He was seventy years old, remarkably strong, but no longer equal to the strains upon his vitality. After we reclaimed Wuhu Hospital he went home—under coercion. He wasn't sure he would live to get back, but he made it.

Laura Clark and B.W. Lanphear had also returned to Wuhu. What a joyful reunion! By virtue of my document from the National Health Administration, we got permission to move to I-chi-shan on 27 October. Dr. Morgan and our old cook, Lin Shih-fu, went to the Brown's home; Liu Hsing-ching, Pastor Liu's oldest daughter who had trained as a nurse at our hospital, and I went to my old home. It was filthy. The walls were black from cooking smoke, the whole inside of both houses black like the inside of a camera. Our front door had been unhooked from its hinges and thrown out on the hillside. The back door, too. No window frames, no sashes or glass. The Japanese had wanted to be able to get out in a hurry if the bombers came.

When the Chinese Army arrived at the bottom of our hill to accept the surrender of the Japanese Army at the top, we were sandwiched between. Luckily, both armies considered themselves our protectors. So many of the city officials had been killed by the Japanese that once they surrendered there was no order. The Chinese begged the Japanese to take over again until they could get organized, which the Japanese did.

The Japanese military medical people on I-chi-shan welcomed us most civilly and even sent a truck and a car to help move our things. On the day of our move we stopped at the Spanish Sisters' to pile our table and chairs and beds in the big Japanese truck, and on the very top the red neon cross. At our I-chi-shan gate we stopped and had the cross unloaded first. A group of our hospital employees had turned up, and some Japanese soldiers. Together the Chinese and Japanese carried that cross back up the hill.

We couldn't install it immediately, as the axis it turned on was among our many things missing. But our engineer, Chang Shih-fu, was still there, although he had lost a foot. He thought of a method, and soon the cross was in place and we were glad to hear its machinery working again as it turned. At first we ran it only an hour or so, because we didn't have much money. But we got a request from city officials: would we please run that cross all night, because people sailing up and down the river needed it as a beacon. So we turned it on for all hours of darkness.

I-chi-shan was a mess. Bomb shelters had been dug everywhere. All the gardens had been dug up, the rose bushes thrown out. All the trees had been cut for fuel. The hospital was beyond belief. All the windows were broken. It was filthy, and smelled as I have never smelled anything before or since. The first thing the Japanese had done when we turned it over to them for a military hospital was to put tea leaves down all the drains. Every drain in the place was plugged. The second thing they did was to throw all the steam radiators out the windows. Then they banged two holes in the floor of each of our two sunporches, put pipes down and made toilets of them. When we got to work on the hospital, one of the things I was gladdest about was getting those toilets out. With great joy I took a sledge hammer and took the first whack.

The Japanese Army doctor in charge had studied in America and was very helpful. I asked about our surgical instruments, that I had heard had all been thrown out on the hillside. He said, "Unfortunately, yes, that is true. When I got here I went out and picked up all I could find. Some were complete, some in pieces. I sanded them to get the rust off and scrubbed them and greased them and put them in a zinc-lined box in the operating room with a lot of things piled on top."

I said I had heard that all our medical books had been thrown out. He said, "Yes, that's true too. I collected those books and washed the mud off them, they were soaking wet anyway; I got them as clean as I could and stood them all up on end in the sunshine to dry. Fortunately you had labeled the shelves in the library, and I put them back on the shelves as much in the same order you had them as I could." We learned that he had also tried to put a stop to cruelty that he saw others inflicting on the Chinese.

He was worried about what his friends in America would think of him after reading the press stories about the Japanese in China. I told him they would think the better of him as they knew what kind of person he was.

A flock of ducks being taken down the river to market.

Rebuilding

1945-1948

S evere malignant malaria was upon us, and we had no screens.
The Japanese had driven our pump to death and we had no
water. Food was short, ghastly expensive and prices kept going up.
Our rice house was empty—no rice, no machinery. There were
beds, but no linens.

We recommended that a Chinese who was not a medical
person tackle the restoration of the hospital so that the medical
work could go forward, and Colonel Gilbert Nee approached
Bishop Ward at about that time to offer his services. Gilbert had
studied in America and returned to China in 1941 as liaison officer
in the Chinese army. His last assignment was to supervise the
disarming of 20,000 Japanese troops near Shanghai.

A New York City church sent us a generous gift which we put
toward a dependable food supply for patients and crew. By the
time the gift got through the red tape of international exchange it
was rice harvest time, the best time of year to buy rice, and we filled
the rice house which was one of the first buildings repaired. It
would have been impossible to keep the hospital open the following winter without the rice, and it carried us through to the next
harvest.

U.N.R.R.A. sent us eight people, a corking group. Gilbert
found screening and bought it with U.N.R.R.A. funds. An U.N.R.R.A.
engineer put in full time with Chang on our pump and brought it
back to life. It could work only during the limited hours the city
could furnish electricity, but we had the promise of the loan of a

generator until we could rehabilitate ours. Liu Hsing-ching and I bought cotton cloth on the street to be made into bed linens.

Gradually the problems were tackled and as we got supplies and personnel we opened one floor at a time. By May 1946 three floors of the west wing were open and full. The new east wing was still to be equipped, and children we tucked in wherever there was an empty bed. For women we had ten beds on the medical and surgical floors.

Paul Sommerfreund was back to head the medical side, while Stella stayed in Shanghai to run one of our mission hostels. Tommy Yü, my right-hand man before the breakup, was back as associate in surgery, where we also had three young doctors. Two of them gave up remunerative positions with lots of responsibility to come to us to learn surgery. Liu Hsing-ching got the school of nursing going again, with nine upperclass students transferred from other schools, and twenty-nine probationers who wandered around wide-eyed. Culley was back, but down with fever for some weeks.

A New Zealand orthopedist who worked in a big government hospital in Nanking, came up to run a clinic for a couple of days and got stalled with us by the number of cases to be done and difficulties in transportation. He did outstanding work, and we worked him like a buffalo. We also needed an eye specialist, but none was in sight.

One day during a lull in hospital activities, somebody raised the cry, "L.S.T.!" We all ran out and read a signal from the ship, "Sorry we are not stopping." The head of our U.N.R.R.A. group had asked us to try to get one of their men onto an upriver L.S.T. for Kiukiang, so I flagged back that request, and they agreed to pick him up. To our surprise, the ship that was in such a hurry then asked,"Can we come over for tea?" They anchored off the hill and presently a landing craft came over with a dozen men aboard, a fine lot, the kind we liked to have represent America abroad.

Midsummer 1946 I had a week's trip with U.N.R.R.A. and C.N.R.R.A. people to study conditions to the north of us. We started out in a staff car aboard a barge pulled by a small tug, which took us past I-chi-shan and diagonally across the river about eight miles to

Yu-chi'-kao, which had been the end of the railroad going north to Hefei and on to Peking.

After considerable maneuvering got the car ashore, we rode a trackless railroad bed northwest to a gap in the range of mountains we could see from Wuhu. A few miles beyond was the old city of Ch'ao-hsien, where we visited what was once a small mission hospital. Practically empty, it was much the worse for war. The two doctors graciously showed us about, and then we started for Hefei.

But that road got slipperier by the minute, and about a mile out was completely blocked by a skidded truck; another truck beyond that had gone off the roadbed and turned over. With difficulty we turned around and got back to Ch'ao-hsien, where Dr. Chang of the hospital appeared and insisted on our going to his home, where they graciously readjusted their household to take in us three women, and put the men up at the hospital.

We waited three days for the road to dry enough to be navigable, attended a meeting of the local doctors, few of them graduates of anything, and were entertained at a grand dinner at the hillside home of the local magistrate. He was a young man who made a valiant effort to conduct an honest administration. His residence, without anything in it that Americans consider essential, was most impressive, a series of open-front buildings connected by steep stone steps, with lots of armed bodyguards who saluted with loud shouts as we passed.

From the hillside back of his residence we could see the broad expanse of Ch'ao Lake, covering the old site of Ch'ao-hsien city. He told us the story that there had once been a prophecy that the city would be flooded, and then an earthquake shook it down some hundreds of years ago and the water swept over it.

There were three dispensaries in Ch'ao-hsien. One was run in what was left of the hospital by our hosts, two doctors doing a lot of good work without benefit of diplomas. The second was run by a very thin, very gracious bearded Spanish Jesuit Father, the third by the priest at the one remaining Buddhist temple, who was also an old-style Chinese doctor. He ran an active clinic and was repairing his temple on the proceeds. We had an interesting visit with him and I wished I had some way to know how his medical results compared with the others. There were effective medications among the old Chinese herbs, and we made heavy use of them when we opened our clinic.

At Hefei we found the mission hospital a worse mess than ours had been. The provincial hospital was also open, with two doctors formerly at Wuhu in charge and a former nurse of ours in charge of the nursing. There were several other places we had planned to visit, but more rain had set in, bridges were out and in several cases it was apparently the goodness of God and no known law of physics that kept up the bridges there were, and us on them, so we headed back to Wuhu.

Soon added to my diversions was that of shooting paddy birds, the white herons so beautiful in flight but horribly unsanitary. The rice fields were paddies where these birds caught frogs and small fish, then dropped pieces from their nests that attracted swarms of flies. With cholera nearby, anything that invited flies had to go. One loses one's original dread of leprosy, but never of cholera. So several of us took turns shooting them, and they fortunately tasted rather like wild duck and were put to good use.

Early August 1946 warmed up after a relatively cool July, and promised to warm up in other ways, too, as war planes flew overhead and we heard heavy firing nearly every day between Nationalists and Communists. In spite of that, we opened another ward and capped our practitioners and staged a brush-up course in cooperation with U.N.R.R.A. for doctors in the area, and prepared to take in another class of probationer nurses. That brush-up course looked to be one of the most useful things we ever did. Doctors and semi-doctors of the region had been cut off from new ideas and methods for several years of war, and in medicine, as in many other things, those who don't advance go backwards.

When we reopened our clinic I started to keep lists of names and addresses of patients I wanted to see specialists, one page for neurological cases, another for eye problems, and so on, and did what we could meantime.

Then we set to work to get the specialists. The orthopedist, who was with the National Health Administration, agreed to return on a once-a-month schedule. He gave our staff splendid training, and saw that our equipment was improved to a new level. A Viennese neurologist and psychiatrist, who was at the National Medical School recently returned from Chengtu, came by for a fortnight, and U.N.R.R.A. specialists in opthamology, obstetrics and gynecology, and tuberculosis returned at intervals.

In September I heard that Georgie Perkins was dangerously ill, so I hopped the next plane for Kiukiang where I found her in a bad way with a combination of malignant malaria, phlebitis, and with typhoid which she should not have had as she had kept up with her inoculations. The typhoid was waning by the time I reached her, and she had had enough treatment to sink any malaria, but she was in danger from the phlebitis.

A go of dengue fever in Kiukiang at the same time just about floored the hospital. Such a large majority of their crew were down with it that they had to stop admitting patients and scheduling all but critical operations. Cases that should have been in hospital had to be handled as outpatients, and I was needed.

Toward the end of the month I came down with dengue myself. It is an unusually uncomfortable sort of disease, much more so than I had realized as we had very little of it in the Yangtze Valley before the war. It had apparently come over The Hump from India and spread downriver. The good things about it are that it rarely lasts more than seven days and people rarely die of it or have bad sequelae. You get this disease through the bites of mites and ticks and have a high fever for five to seven days with lots of muscular pain. Then comes a day worse than the others and it is over.

On that last day the palms of my hands burned as though on fire, like taking hold of a steam pipe. I looked around for some sort of relief and found a lot of empty saki bottles left by the Japanese. So I filled four of them with cold water, held one in each hand until they warmed up and exchanged them for the other two.

That night I sat up all night holding cold saki bottles, and by morning my hands were normal. I was better, but still couldn't eat.

The wife of one of our pastors brought me a bowl filled with bits of Chinese food and urged me to "just take your chopsticks and poke at it. If you see any bits that look good, try them and poke again." So I poked, and in the end ate the whole bowlful, and it was good.

When I had finished, the lady's husband suddenly appeared and said, "I've come to take you to call on an old lady who is sick," and urged me into a rickshaw. I asked him who the old lady was and he said, "She is the grandmother of all the family who make the finest porcelain of China, over at Ching-te-chen, the people who made that set of porcelain the government of China recently sent to England as a wedding gift to the princess."

A very worried son of the old lady welcomed us, worried because he believed his mother had gone crazy. But she said, "I'm sick, very sick, but not crazy! My hands feel as though they are burning and I keep calling for cold things to hold and they think that means I am crazy, because my hands aren't burning!"

I said, "Lady, if you are crazy, so am I. All last night I sat up holding cold saki bottles because my hands were burning. That's the way the sickness works. Now it is day and they don't burn any more. Your sickness is finished, and you won't have any more of it." She was so delighted that she gave me a stack of the most beautiful bowls, one the same pattern that was sent to the princess.

When I recovered from dengue, Mollie Townshend, who was acting head of the Nanchang Hospital, and I went up Lushan to stay with an elderly Swiss lady who, as a neutral, had been there all through the war. The mountains were cold and to keep warm we did a lot of hiking. Some of it was in the course of investigating damage to our mission property, although our valley got off better than most parts of Kuling. One house burned early in the occupation, two others were beyond repair and those that might have been restored were so wrecked by pilfering that little was left. Unfortunately a lot of trees had been cut down as well. At my favorite Buddhist Yellow Dragon Temple we learned that the scholarly old abbot, who had been so gracious to us on other visits, had died during the war.

When Mollie had to head for a visit to Nanchang and then

back to Kiukiang, there was no point in my staying on in the cold without a hiking companion, so I went along. We caught a ride to Nanchang on a weapons carrier at the foot of the mountain. The trip was spectacular, dominated by the Lushan range to our right, Poyang Lake to our left, and the Western Mountains ahead.

We had ten orphans with us who were going to a new orphanage run by the government with C.N.R.R.A. help. At Nanchang we found some buildings on the edge of town with 370 orphans looking very orphanish, and didn't blame those traveling with us for looking down-in-the-mouth about staying there. They were all too homesick to eat the supper prepared for them, and in the morning had disappeared. The older ones, who had some money, had rounded up the younger ones and taken off. The lady in charge found and scolded them, but I thought that showed independent thinking and originality, savoir faire and generosity on the part of the older ones, and was glad to learn later that they settled in well.

Nanchang is a provincial capital and a big city, with much more of a big-shop business section than either Wuhu or Kiukiang. We stayed at the Methodist mission by the bank of the Kan River, where it was about a mile wide, and went out to visit the provincial medical school outside town, where two of our I-chi-shan boys were studying. The school was being rebuilt and already had its chemistry labs and dissecting room in place, and was hard at work trying to find enough medical books. There were so few reference books that several students had to study out of one at the same time, and it was nearly impossible to get textbooks.

The president told me that during the war the school had hiked over a lot of southwest China, carrying books and equipment. They had stayed at eight different places as they dodged the war, for periods ranging from one month to three years. That meant establishing practice-clinics and in several places hospitals, then dismantling and carrying along equipment each time they had to move on. I asked whether they had lost students at each move, and they said no, the school had grown larger and larger.

On our way back to Kiukiang, Mollie and I hopped off the

weapons carrier near White Deer Grotto, which we had often looked down on from Lushan. By some considered to have been the oldest university in the world, in the time of Abraham it was a literary gathering place and school. By imperial decree it was later rated a university. Its site is a beautiful piney glen with a musical brook nearby and sheer, jagged cliffs towering three thousand feet above grassy slopes of perhaps another thousand. The Japanese took the grotto for a guerilla hideout and wrecked it all, buildings, images and even many of the priceless stone tablets given by ancient poets and emperors.

We picked up a farmer to guide us up a short path that led to Hai Huai Szu, Sea-Meeting Temple, named from Confucius's saying, "All streams meet in the sea." His short path, though shorter than the road, was a strenuous scramble, but the temple just the place for a few days of quiet rest. On a hillside near the foot of Lion's Leap with those towering cliffs behind and Poyang Lake with its islands spread out before, it was high enough for mountain breezes. There were ruins nearby, which had been an army officers' training school before the Japanese wrecked it. The provincial government planned to rebuild it as a university.

The chief priest was a scholarly man, as was his assistant. They gave us comfortable rooms and let us explore the numerous temple halls and courts at will. They talked to me about a brook nearby, along whose course the people had deserted their farms because everybody got a sickness; in some of the villages all the men had died. New families had come in, but they too got the sickness. The priests brought one of the sick men to the temple so that I could examine him, and as I suspected, he had schistosomiasis from a parasite in the water.

For more than an hour we discussed the disease. I drew pictures of the parasite and said people living in the area must grow dry crops instead of rice, which involved working in the water. The people also needed intravenous injections or they would die, and sanitation measures should be taken to keep further infection from being washed into the stream. When I got back to Wuhu later, we tried to get the new and struggling local beginnings of public health service, helped by C.N.R.R.A., to tackle the problem. Of course the epidemic was more widespread, but those villages were a good place to start.

At Hai Huai Szu Mollie came down with dengue and malignant malaria, so I wangled a car to get us back to Kiukiang. There we found supplies had arrived from Shanghai for the Water of Life Hospital, and with a borrowed truck got beds and mattresses and intravenous glucose, big bags of clothing and a lot of powdered milk to the hospital.

We had a lot of serious operating the winter of 1946-1947, a number of difficult abdominal cases of the sort that made us wish we had "taken that job in the bank," but there were also a lot of results that cheered us. Selma Mueller, the U.N.R.R.A. ob-gyn expert temporarily with us, took out an ovarian cyst that made my sixty-four and a half pound cyst look small. And there was a lady with her upper jaw so disorganized by a bullet that we had to hang portions of it by rubber bands from a plaster of Paris crown around her head. She went home with a mouth that felt and looked human.

The government put us on the spot by ruling that all doctors and nurses, to qualify for required licenses, put in at least one year in government institutions. I was thankful to have gotten my license among the first, but that meant almost all of our doctors and nurses would have to leave us. With a civil war on, of course the government institutions had to be staffed, but we could see that the next couple of years would be a hard test for mission hospitals. Our nursing school, long registered under the Nurses' Association of China, had to be reregistered under the government, and so had the hospital. That was right to do, but the process was so complicated that it was extremely difficult and time-consuming.

Our British U.N.R.R.A. engineer, who helped Chang Lao-pan rehabilitate the engine room equipment, then acquired for us a still for distilled water for intravenous solutions. It was a big Navy model, so large we hoped to supply other hospitals as well.

That winter a second snowstorm turned our hill into a thing of beauty, but with fuel short, our operating room stood at 52° for major surgery before we got in a stove that improved it somewhat. Our boilers for central heating were not usable for another year, and a lot of window glass was still missing. We did the best we could and didn't listen to chests more than necessary.

We hadn't enough of an x-ray outfit left to take films, but the fluoroscope was usable and with tuberculosis rampant, as it was among returned refugees, was in constant use. A pair of Navy adaptation goggles was a great aid.

It was good to see the Dragon Festival again that spring, when boats decorated to look like dragons raced up and down the river, each paddled by about twenty men with more sitting between the two rows of paddlers beating drums. And with spring we were getting fresh vegetables and were able to buy up some Army surplus in Shanghai and fell heir to food as gifts from the U.S. Navy and others.

We took in quite a number of new doctors, including a dozen or so interns. Four who arrived by the end of June 1947 had studied in a medical school that had had to move its location thirteen times in eight years, all hands helping to carry books and instruments. Of textbooks they sometimes had enough for eight students to share one. We knew we would have to teach them a lot the school hadn't been able to, but believed they rated a chance on the basis of perseverance alone. Three girls and one man formed the group and they were wide awake, bright and likeable young people.

We also started something that had been a dream of mine ever since I first arrived in China, a Department of Public Health with an experienced Chinese chief to take the job. He had charge of staff health, the health of all I-chi-shan students, of contracts, clinics including country clinics, health work in city schools, and general public health education. It was a big job with no end of opportunity for important work, and he was an able and enthusiastic man. We still hoped to set up a separate ob-gyn department as we had to include all that work under general surgery.

Rebuilding

For Christmas 1947 the hospital looked more festive than usual, and after our annual candle-march, singing through the wards, we filed out onto the front lawn and there made a large circle and sang more carols, the white and blue uniforms and candles shining beneath the winter stars. Above were the gaily-lighted hospital windows, so long dark, and above those our big neon cross on the roof slowly alternating its red glow with a brilliant star that had been hung on its back. Looking at that scene and thinking of the contrast between it and the condition of the hospital at the end of the war, it was hard to realize it was less than two and a half years since we took our hill back from the Japanese Army. From the mess of those days had evolved a hospital. There were still a lot of problems to be worked out: we couldn't yet use our boilers for lack of fuel, which meant no steam in our pipes, no hot water except as our crew carried it from a primitive hot water shop. Our elevator was still immobilized. Except for one wood stove in the operating room suite, there was no heat. We wore padded clothing to keep warm and feared most post-operative pneumonia. But most of our wards were open, and we hoped to have enough personnel to open soon the last section.

There certainly was no monotony in our work. One of our patients was a man with a strangulated hernia of several days' standing who had emergency operation three hours long that involved resection of forty-seven inches of gangrenous large and small gut under most difficult conditions, in an operating room 42° F when we started and about 52° when we finished. According to the textbooks he should have died of post-operative pneumonia, but he made an uneventful recovery and went happily home.

There was a fantastic currency inflation, with all our money in paper banknotes, the latest and largest denomination worth about fifteen cents in our money. We had to carry huge bundles of money around, and took to paying some of our people mostly in rice. We now had about 115 *mou*, or twenty acres, of our own rice fields. A merchant who sold us rice was robbed, and through no fault of his own defaulted on the last quarter of what he owed. He offered us instead the ownership of a part of his ancestral rice-bearing land, which was better for it meant a yearly yield of rice. Our fields were about nine kilometers from I-chi-shan, on the road south of us: fine, fertile rice land within easy foot-pumping distance of river level, very important for irrigation.

In August 1948, our last ward unit opened and was alive and active again. We didn't have quite all the parts of the hospital in action, as the boilers were still out for lack of fuel, and therefore the steam laundry and elevator were inoperable. We hadn't let the wards fill to full capacity, as we put our emphasis on building up standards and techniques first, but we had something over 160 patients. When the Japanese Army pushed us out we had 230; but then we were jammed with beds along the corridors and in every open space.

We decided to keep on three of our interns for a second year, which we required before we would let them be assistants. One very nice, quiet, hard-working girl whom we all liked, nearly wept with joy when invited. She hadn't heard from any of her family and didn't know whether they were alive, and had come to feel that I-chi-shan was the only home left to her.

In most Chinese hospitals interns could be assistant residents after one year, even full residents or heads of departments in many places, so those we invited to stay with us were not only those of whose work we approved, but those wise enough to appreciate that a good foundation of experience was more important than face. We had planned on twelve new interns the first and second year, but so far had had only five as several failed to make their grades or got appointments in larger cities. Several of our Chinese upper staff doctors left for America, and on the medical side Paul Sommerfreund and his family went to Canada to take out Canadian citizenship. They had been with the hospital ten years, and we missed them.

The railroad between Nanking and Wuhu was being reconstructed, with a construction gang of 500 men. We kept a medical team there, two weeks at a shift, to look after them. Aside from the actual satisfaction of overcoming our isolation, it gave our young doctors a great sense of doing real service for the country. They lived in a boxcar at the end of the line, and worked at the front all day, moving as the track advanced, then being pulled back to the nearest town to spend the night. Our young doctors and medical students worked day and night to push the work forward, and came back to us brown and vigorous and full of enthusiasm. One shift, an assistant resident and two interns, were girls. The head of the railroad was very pleased when he heard they wanted to go, and had the company fix up the boxcar especially nicely for them and supplied an amah to take care of them. It was a fine example of the new spirit among the young people, to be willing and eager to live in a baking-hot boxcar for two weeks to further reconstruction of the country.

We had heavy and continuous rains early in the summer of 1948, but most of the dykes held around Wuhu. Several times in the night we heard the gongs and with the gong the cry, "The dyke is going to break!" Then the answering shouts of people arriving in the dark with lanterns to fight the river.

It was our good luck to escape what was a very bad flood elsewhere, and one personal piece of good luck was that none of us developed rabies after a fight with a mad rabies patient. For that we were thankful to God and to Louis Pasteur and to the good men, French and Chinese, who carried on his good work in Shanghai.

During my vacation in 1948, unaware it would be my last visit to Lushan, we took all our old favorite hikes, to the Cave of the Immortals, Emerald Pool and the Three Graces, and paid our respects to P'i-lo, the special dark green bronze Buddha head at Yellow Dragon Temple by the Three Trees, and made a new excursion to find the Temple in The Clouds.

Our last trip was to see the full moon rise from Nankang Pass. Lots of us went, and there were groups singing all along the narrow ridge looking straight down about four thousand feet to the plains and Poyang Lake. Then that great yellow moon rose and cast its reflection on the big lake and its light into the deep purple shadows between the long sweeping mountain folds and on the high rocky peaks.

Back down on the plains we heard that the Communists were

approaching Wuhu and would take over our hospital. We had evidence they were, because for some time the queerest things had been happening. Some of the young people working with us had evidently been infiltrated by the Communists and were working for them.

They would call a meeting, for example, of the dietetics department or the kitchen crew and ask them: "Has anybody done any kind of thing that has ever offended you? What about the nurses? Have they always been polite to you? Have they ever criticized you? Yes, yes. Now, what did they do?" This is what they called accusation meetings.

Meantime another group of the Communists had called a meeting with some other group and got everybody stirred up against everybody else. They did that with all our departments. I tried to break it up. I said to these young men, "If you wouldn't hold these meetings the nurses could care for the patients and the patients could get something to eat. But when you turn everybody away from their work and against each other, who can take care of the patients?"

"That isn't our problem," they said, and continued to stir up anger and dissension and set one group against another just as they did all over China.

They divided, and they conquered.

At the end of December 1948, when the Communist armies were across the river from us, our Chinese friends begged us to leave. "This time it is different," they said. "If they come and find us working with Americans, it will mean our lives. Don't try to stay to help us, for you could not. A lot of people in the North have already been killed for working with Americans."

I took that to Pastor Liu, who was very level-headed and never stampeded. "It's true," he said. "The kindest thing you can do for us is to get on the first train you can and don't come back. Trust us, pray for us, but don't even write to us. A letter from America might mean our lives."

With great regret, and instantly, Culley and I got that first train.

Under Heaven One Family

1980

When China reopened her doors to Americans, I spent a fruitless year trying to get a visa. Finally I wrote to Tommy Yü, who had been my right-hand man and to whom I turned over my surgery when I left Wuhu. He was a doctor at Hefei, the capital of Anhwei province. He sent me a document about three feet long with a big red seal at the bottom, which was an official invitation from the local branch of the Provincial Medical Association to lecture Chinese students in Hefei and Wuhu on current trends in Western medicine. I sent a copy of it to the Chinese Embassy in Washington, and a visa application blank came in the return mail with permission for one companion to accompany me.

We met our Faithful Shadow in Kuang-chou (Canton), the young lady from China Travel Service who accompanied us on to Nanking, Wuhu, Hefei, Peking and Tientsin, and toured as was expected, but enjoyed most talking with people wherever we went and meeting old friends.

When we reached Wuhu we were first taken to a factory where they make iron pictures. Our old friend who hand-forged them years ago was the last member of his family who knew the secret of how they were made, a craft that had been handed down in his family for generations. He finally took on an apprentice, but didn't show him all the secrets. The apprentice, however, was quite a lad. He climbed up on the roof and bored a hole through the ceiling so that he could see what the master craftsman did, and the secrets were preserved.

At first the present regime had no use for such arts but when they discovered that things made for beauty could also be useful by bringing in money, the apprentice was called on to start making iron pictures once more. Now a lot of young people work together on an assembly line.

In the front hall of the factory was a huge Welcoming Pine made of iron. The original tree grew on Huang Shan, the beautiful mountain in southern Anhwei. The first large iron Welcoming Pine was made for the Great Hall of the People in Peking, where it represents Anhwei Province. As it is the logo of China Travel Service, you find pictures of it in hotels and restaurants.

We were taken to a ballbearing factory, and I thought we'd see it in action with all the wheels going and a terrible noise, but it was shut down for the day. The Chinese always had months and years in their calendars, but not weeks, which was an idea introduced to China by missionaries. They found out that people do much better work when they have a regular day off, so now every factory closes one day a week, usually on Sundays, not for religious reasons but so that better work will be done.

So we didn't see any wheels going around, but we did see some old friends, among them a pastor I had known as a young man. He was no longer young and he worked in the ballbearing factory, but he had recently been appointed by the government to be pastor of the old church which was being reconditioned. We talked of old times and new times, and as we talked I kept thinking of that verse, "These are they that had come up out of great tribulation . . ."

We went to the lake which gives Wuhu her name. It had been enlarged and beautified, with a large exhibit building built where our Iron House dispensary once stood. Two little girls led us through an exhibit of imported plants in bloom. It was a wonderful exhibit and it was fun to have the little girls as guides. They said they would come to visit us in America, and maybe they will.

When we had been sufficiently instructed in factories in Wuhu, where they also made thermos bottles and embroidered and feather pictures, we went over to the hospital. We didn't take the road we used to take, but a big wide road around to a new entrance at the back of the hill. Big apartment buildings filled the fields where the mustard once spread its cloth of gold.

When we reached the hospital I looked with great interest to see whether the two bronze plaques were still there. They were. One reads, "Not to be ministered unto but to minister," and the other, "Who is my neighbor?" Those sentiments fit right in with what they believe in China now. Then I looked for *my* window, or "porthole" as they called it, and found a red star in it.

The hospital was the biggest building by far in the city of Wuhu when I was there. Now there was a new building alongside it that made the hospital look small. As we entered, there were so many memories, so many people who had worked with me there to greet us. But I had to be told who they were, because I remembered young people, and these were all middle-aged. And I was old. I was fifty-six when I left Wuhu, and now I was eighty-seven.

Among those who stepped up to me and asked, "Dr. Watters, do you remember me?" was John Ting.

"Yes, indeed," I said, "I remember John Ting was one of our interns that everybody liked."

Then he asked, "Do you remember when you said to me, 'John, you are very good in art, and if you are wise you will forget about being a doctor. It's much better to be a first rate artist than a third rate doctor.'?" Yes, I remembered, for he needed a good kick to get down to work, and he did. He is now professor of ear, nose and throat at the medical school.

Another asked if I remembered him, Julian T'an. "Do you remember the day," he asked, "during the Japanese occupation, when you started for home on your bicycle after clinic was finished downtown, and the sentry stopped you and asked to see your pass and you had forgotten to take it with you?" Indeed I did remember. The sentry was very stern and was going to turn me over to the authorities when he went off duty. Then along came our dresser boy on his bicycle, Julian T'an, who found out what had happened and brought Dr. Morgan to take my pass down to me. Julian T'an was now professor of chest surgery.

After my lecture I asked if I could see an operation done with acupuncture anaesthesia, and it was arranged for our old operating room. There we saw the removal of most of a thyroid from a woman's throat. She had two acupuncture needles in her hand, no novocain, ether or gas, and was conscious and comfortable through the operation. The anaesthetist kept track of her blood pressure with a cuff on her right arm, while the left hand had a very fine wire from the upper end of each needle to a current interrupter on the other side of the table. Five times a second she got 1/600th of a volt which made her fingers contract. The anaesthetist kept careful records throughout surgery.

The medical school director asked if I wouldn't like to ask the patient some questions. I said I certainly would, and went around in front of her and asked if she were comfortable, had any problems. She said no, no problems.

When the nodule was out, I asked a stupid question. I said that when we did these operations we sent the nodules to the labs at two medical schools. "Where do you send them?" I got a reproving look, "Doctor, this *is* a medical school."

During the operation one of the doctors fed a cookie to the patient, which pleased her. She wanted another, so they gave it to her and then cut up an apple and fed it to her. Meantime they went ahead operating. At the end she sat up, a bandage around her throat, to have her picture taken.

We went up to the hospital roof to look up and down the Yangtze and across the city of Wuhu. There was very little traffic on the river, no steamers, no gunboats and the great junks were gone. But there were three ferry crossings, one for people, one for automobiles and one for the train down where the Standard Oil installation had been. Cars from the Shanghai-Nanking-Wuhu train were loaded onto a ferry this side and connected to an engine north of the river to go on to Hefei and Peking.

We took the train to Hefei where I lectured to the medical students, then went on to Peking, which looked so changed, with wide streets where they once were so narrow. There we went over to see the lake where the Empress Dowager had her Summer Palace. A lot of young people were out on the lake in rowboats, so we rented a boat too, and when we got out on the lake we found that a lot of them didn't know that when you are rowing you must look over your shoulder occasionally to see where you are going. At intervals I called out, "Collision course! Pull to your right!"

We did all the expected touring and enjoyed most sitting down to watch and talk with the people. There were little snack bars at special places where we could get our lunches, peanut brittle and sesame candy and little packages of ice cream that we would take outside to eat. Wherever we sat down someone would offer to share his lunch with us and we could talk. People were like that everywhere.

We attended a service in one of the newly reopened churches in Peking. After many years, when people had to go quietly and secretly to homes to hold services, often in the dark with just a bit of candle and in whispers, our preacher shouted his sermon, and when the people sang they sang with might and main.

When the service was over and a number of us stood around talking, one nice looking teenager kept looking at my hat. She'd look at it from one side then walk around and look at it from the other side. She held out her hand and said, "Please, may I look at your hat?" So I handed her my very battered old black beret that I'd worn for a good many years. She turned it over and looked at it inside and out and said, "Why, I always thought they made these out of two circles sewed together, but this is all in one piece."

She kept looking at it and another young lady who was a little older kept motioning her to give back the hat. Finally she spoke up and said, "Give the lady back her hat."

The young girl said, "Oh yes, surely," and with one hand went through the polite motions of giving me back the hat, while with the other she kept hold of it.

After she had struggled a few moments I said, "You keep the hat, I have another and don't need this one." She was so pleased she put the hat on and cocked it up on one side, and it was much better looking on her than it had ever been on me. The older lady was very displeased. She said, "No! This is not good. This is not good at all! You are old and your head will be cold, and for an old person's head to be cold is not good." She had a beautiful silk scarf over her own head, with a knot under the chin. She took it off and tied it under my chin and said, "Now your head will not be cold." From the girl who loved my hat I have had several letters that all begin, "Dear Black Hat Friend . . ."

The Chinese friend with whom I had attended the service suggested we go to a restaurant for lunch, so we turned off the fine broad street into a small *hu-t'ung*, and as we walked along asked people we met if there were a restaurant nearby. They told us to keep on to the end of the *hu-t'ung*, and finally, sure enough, there were two restaurants. My friend asked the next person who came along which was the better and he said, "Oh, take this one, it is famous for *chiao-tzu* (dumplings)."

Now I like *chiao-tzu*. You take a small meatball, roll it up in thin dough, pinch it together along the edges and then boil it. You can fry it after that if you like.

So we went in and found the restaurant crowded with men and walked between the tables looking for a place to sit down. My friend went off and found some chairs that she set down at an empty space. The man on my left was giving an order. He said, "Don't put any pork in mine. No pig meat. I don't eat it."

So I said to him, "The fact that you don't eat pig meat has to do with your faith, doesn't it?" And he said yes, it did. So I added, "and perhaps before you eat you say *Basmalah: al-Rahman al-Rahim*, which is the Muslim blessing that I learned from our lab technician in Ganta, Liberia, the blessing they say before they eat or start a journey or anything of importance, "in the name of God, most compassionate, most merciful."

He looked surprised and said, "We do. We worship one God, the only God, and there isn't any other. We call him Allah."

I said, "You are right. I agree with you absolutely. We also worship one God, the only God, and there isn't any other. We don't call him Allah, we call him Shang-ti,* but it's the same God."

He thought about that. You could see him wrestling with it, but finally he said, "Well, that's right. But the Jewish people don't believe in Shang-ti."

"Somebody has misinformed you," I said. "The Jews do believe in Shang-ti, very firmly and very devoutly. They don't call him Allah, they don't call him Shang-ti, they call him Jehovah, but he is the same God with a different name."

My friend came back and we ordered our *chiao-tzu*, but before they came the young man offered me some of his. I thanked him very much and took some of his no-pig-meat *chiao-tzu*, and we continued talking. He asked, "Have you any relatives in China?" And I said, "Oh yes, lots of them." He looked surprised, so I added, "You know, you have a proverb in China, *T'ien-hsia i chia*, 'under heaven one family.' In that way I have lots of relatives."

---

* Shang-ti: Protestant translation for "God."

Wuhu I-chi-shan Hospital 1980

Epilogue

1987

"Do you remember the Song of the White Seal," asked Hyla Doc, poking the fire at Birchwood. She was nearly ninety-four and in fine spirits, restored to much her old self with a pacemaker. After a winter away from Tupper with family and friends, she rejoiced to feed the birds and chipmunks, carry in armloads of firewood, search for each new wildflower as it appeared.

Slowly remembering one of the many Kipling poems she loved, Hyla Doc recited,

> *Oh! Hush thee, my baby, the night is behind us,*
> *And black are the waters that sparkled to green.*
> *The moon, o'er the combers, looks downward to find us*
> *At rest in the hollows that rustle between.*
> *Where billow meets billow, then soft be thy pillow;*
> *Ah, weary wee flippering, curl at thy ease!*
> *The storm shall not wake thee, nor shark overtake thee,*
> *Asleep in the arms of the slow-swinging seas.*

We had spent two weeks together rereading the letters she had written to her family throughout her life. She had forgotten many of the adventures of the young Hyla and was surprised and pleased to relive them, eager to correct the vision of "that young fool."

But for the moment the eagerness vanished as she sat in the

285

soft firelight and glanced around the rough-birch walls of Birch-wood. Beside the great stone fireplace hung the piece of wood lettered, "IF THEM WATTERS WILL KEEP THAR MOUT SHUT THEY AL BEE BETTER OF," near it the painting of the boathouse on the Raquette River; across the room was the piano where friends gathered every Sunday night for a hymn sing; family photos, flower books, seed for her birdfeeders, carved Buddhas and an elegant carving of a gazelle, all seemed to move nearer to her as she smiled and softly repeated, "Ah! weary wee flippering, curl at thy ease!"

Soon after, Hyla Doc had congestive heart failure. Following a few days in intensive care, a remarkable rally that got her back to Birchwood for two weeks, surrounded by family members and two of us who had known and loved her in China, Hyla Doc died 3 August 1987.

In the cemetery behind Birchwood, beneath the sheltering boughs of two towering pines she loved, she is buried, and on her stone are carved in Chinese characters the words with which she always said farewell to her friends:

I-lu p'ing-an

May you have a peaceful journey all the way.

Hyla Doc and Elsie Landstrom. *(Esther Schubert Chambers)*

Postscript

Wuhu General Hospital has seen many changes since Hyla Doc left at the end of 1949. During the Cultural Revolution the building was badly damaged and closed, doctors and nurses sent to the countryside. But today the old red-brick hospital, once the hill's crowning glory, is dwarfed by new structures.

The mustard fields, that spread their cloth of gold around I-chi-shan, are now crowded with apartment houses and factories, and the hospital has grown to meet the challenges of a Wuhu area population that increased from 200,000 to 900,000 over the past half century.

Now the proud teaching hospital for the leading medical school of Anhwei Province (Wannan Medical College), I-chi-shan Hospital as she is now known, recently increased her bed capacity to 700 with the opening of a new surgical building. There are nearly a thousand medical staff, including some 300 doctors and nursing heads, 21 clinical departments, 19 medical technology departments and 15 teaching-research stations. There is an impressive array of technical equipment, active research and publishing, participation in a foreign-aid program to Yemen.

On 1 October 1989, Wuhu I-chi-shan Hospital celebrated her centennial. Two hundred representatives from other Chinese hospitals and medical schools attended, as well as ten of us who stood in for those who established the hospital and served through her first sixty years.

It was a joyous and interesting occasion that began with firecrackers, expanded into an impressive plenary session, and carried on through two days of forums, tours of the facilities and banquets. Carrel Morgan, son of Loren and Ruth Morgan, spoke fittingly at the plenary session. Patrick Hu, taken into Hyla Doc's home after the 1931 flood, gave an eloquent tribute to her and the work of the hospital. Other speeches were made by provincial, municipal, medical school and hospital officials.

At the forum for us non-medical people, Elizabeth Stuntz Allen, Hyla Doc's niece, presented a check to I-chi-shan Hospital for $13,700, along with a list of the 250 people who had contributed to this memorial fund, a framed photograph of Hyla Doc (featured on the cover of this book), and a copper plaque which read:

A GIFT OF LOVE
TO THE PEOPLE OF WUHU
FROM FRIENDS AROUND THE WORLD
IN MEMORY OF
DR. HYLA S. WATTERS
ON THE OCCASION OF THE CENTENNIAL OF
IJISHAN HOSPITAL
1889–1989.

A hard-bound history of the hospital's first sixty years, which had been requested by officials for the hospital library, was my contribution, with copies for each Centennial Committee member.

Wuhu I-chi-shan Hospital today would gladden the hearts of George Stuart, Edgerton Hart, Robert Brown, Loren and Ruth Morgan, Hyla Doc and all the others who poured their lives into serving the Chinese people through Wuhu General Hospital. Those of us present at the October festivities were thankful to be there to represent the hospital's pioneering founders and to express our friendship for and support of the Chinese people by our presence.